Fast Track

MCSE

Windows® 98

Emmett Dulaney

R. Andrew Brice

Dale Holmes

New
Riders

201 West 103rd Street, Indianapolis, Indiana 46290

MCSE Fast Track: Windows® 98

International Standard Book Number: 0-7357-0016-8

Library of Congress Catalog Card Number: 98-87721

Printed in the United States of America

First Printing: December, 1998

00 99 98   4 3 2 1

TRADEMARKS

WARNING AND DISCLAIMER

Executive Editor
Mary Foote

Acquisitions Editor
Nancy Maragioglio

Development Editor
Nancy Warner

Managing Editor
Sarah Kearns

Project Editor
Jennifer Chisholm

Copy Editor
Gayle Johnson

Indexer
Sandra Henselmeier

Technical Editor
Andrew Brice

Proofreading
Jeanne Clark

Layout Technician
Cheryl Lynch

Contents at a Glance

TABLE OF CONTENTS

ABOUT THE AUTHORS

Emmett Dulaney, MCP+I, MCSE, is a consultant for D S Technical Solutions and an instructor for a national training company. He has been teaching certification courses for the continuing education department of Indiana University/Purdue University at Fort Wayne for over four years, and is the "Certification Corner" columnist for *NT Systems Magazine*. In addition, Emmett is the author or co-author of over a dozen computer books, including *CNE Short Course, Teach Yourself MCSE Windows NT Workstation in 14 Days*, and *MCSE TestPrep: TCP/IP*. He has also written over 100 magazine articles on computing for several publications.

R. Andrew Brice currently works as a Senior Instructor for ProsoftTraining.com. His certifications include Novell's CNA and CNE in both 3.x and 4.x, as well as Microsoft Certified Professional, Microsoft Certified Trainer, and Microsoft Certified Systems Engineer in Windows NT 3.51 and 4.0. He has currently been certified as a Certified Internet Webmaster (CIW) in Security, Administration, and TCP/IP. Since 1991, he has consulted in network design and implementation to small and large organizations, including Fortune 1000. Over the last four years, he has included training on both Microsoft and Novell curriculum. He has co-authored and been a technical editor for more than 10 books, published by Macmillan, some of which include *Windows 95 TestPrep* and *Fast Track for Windows 98*. As a speaker at trade shows like Internet World '98, he has presented daylong seminars on topics ranging from TCP/IP to Windows NT and UNIX integration. He credits his accomplishments to the love and support provided by both his wife, Susan, and daughter, Katie. He can be reached at andrewb@prosfttraining.com.

Dale Holmes is an MCSE, CNE, and holds a UNIX Systems and C programming certificate from George Washington University. He has been a network and systems consultant to Fortune 500 companies for the past five years. He has co-authored *MCSE TestPrep: Windows 95* first and second editions and *MCSE Training Guide: Windows 95*; he was also a technical editor for *MCSE Training Guide: TCP/IP*. He is currently providing consulting services in Baltimore, MD, and can often be seen walking his dog Roxanne along the sidewalks of the city. He can be reached via email at sysguru@yahoo.com.

DEDICATION

Andrew Brice   I would like to dedicate this book to my beautiful and loving wife, Susan. I love you, kitten! You make my life complete!

Dale Holmes   I'd like to dedicate this book to my beautiful baby girls, twins, who are due to be born this New Year's Eve. I'd like to thank my wife, Emma, for tolerating me while I worked on the book. I know she is glad that I finished it before the babies came. Thanks also to everyone at MCP for their help and dedication. I couldn't have done it without them.

ACKNOWLEDGMENTS

Andrew Brice   I would like to thank everyone at Macmillan, including Steve Weiss, Nancy Warner, Nancy Maragioglio, and David Dwyer, for their continued patience and guidance. A special thank you goes to Emmett Dulaney for allowing me the opportunity to participate in such a wonderful project. I would be remiss in passing up the opportunity to thank my Mom and Dad for the wonderful guidance they provided me in my youth. Lastly, I would like to thank my wife, Susan, and daughter, Katie, for their continued patience and support through the long hours I spent huddled next to my computer. Thank you, girls!

TELL US WHAT YOU THINK!

As the reader of this book, *you* are our most important critic and commentator. We value your opinion and want to know what we're doing right, what we could do better, what areas you'd like to see us publish in, and any other words of wisdom you're willing to pass our way.

As the Executive Editor for the Certification team at Macmillan Computer Publishing, I welcome your comments. You can fax, email, or write me directly to let me know what you did or didn't like about this book—as well as what we can do to make our books stronger.

Please note that I cannot help you with technical problems related to the topic of this book, and that due to the high volume of mail I receive, I might not be able to reply to every message.

When you write, please be sure to include this book's title and author, as well as your name and phone or fax number. I will carefully review your comments and share them with the authors and editors who worked on the book.

Fax: 317-581-4663

Email: certification@mcp.com

Mail: Mary Foote
Certification
Macmillan Computer Publishing
201 West 103rd Street
Indianapolis, IN 46290 USA

Introduction

The *MCSE Fast Track* series is written as a study aid for people who are preparing for Microsoft Certification Exams. The series is intended to help reinforce and clarify information you're already familiar with. This series isn't intended to be a single source of preparation, but rather a review of information and a set of practice tests to help increase your likelihood of success when taking the actual exam.

WHO SHOULD READ THIS BOOK

This book is intended specifically to help you prepare for Microsoft's Implementing and Supporting Microsoft Windows 98 (70-098) exam—one of the workstation possibilities in the MCSE program.

HOW THIS BOOK HELPS YOU

This book is designed to help you make the most of your study time by presenting concise summaries of information that you need to understand in order to succeed on the exam.

HOW TO USE THIS BOOK

When you feel like you're prepared for the exam, use this book as a test of your knowledge.

After you have taken the practice test and feel confident in the material on which you were tested, you are ready to schedule your exam. Use this book for a final quick review just before taking the test to make sure that all the important concepts are set in your mind.

WHAT THE WINDOWS 98 EXAM (70-098) COVERS

The Implementing and Supporting Microsoft Windows 98 certification exam measures your ability to implement, administer, and troubleshoot Windows 98 computer systems in small and large processing-intensive environments. It focuses on determining your skill in six major categories:

◆ Planning

◆ Installation and Configuration

◆ Configuring and Managing Resource Access

◆ Integration and Interoperability

◆ Monitoring and Optimization

◆ Troubleshooting

The Implementing and Supporting Microsoft Windows 98 certification exam uses these categories to measure your abilities. Before taking this exam, you should be proficient in the job skills discussed in the following sections.

Planning

The Planning section is designed to make sure that you understand the hardware requirements of Windows 98. The knowledge needed here also requires understanding of general networking concepts.

Objectives for Planning

◆ Develop an appropriate implementation model for specific requirements in a Microsoft environment and a mixed Microsoft and NetWare environment. Considerations include the following:

• Choosing the appropriate file system

• Planning a workgroup

◆ Develop a security strategy in a Microsoft environment and a mixed Microsoft and NetWare environment. Strategies include the following:

  • System policies

  • User profiles

  • File and printer sharing

  • Share-level access control or user-level access control

Installation and Configuration

The Installation and Configuration part of the Windows 98 exam tests you on virtually every possible component of the product.

Objectives for Installation and Configuration

◆ Install Windows 98. Installation options include the following:

  • Automated Windows setup

  • New

  • Upgrade

  • Uninstall

  • Dual-boot combination with Microsoft Windows NT

◆ Configure Windows 98 server components. Server components include the following:

  • Microsoft Personal Web Server 4.0

  • Dial-Up Networking server

◆ Install and configure the network components of Windows 98 in a Microsoft environment and a mixed Microsoft and NetWare environment. Network components include the following:

  • Client for Microsoft Networks

  • Client for NetWare Networks

  • Network adapters

- File and Printer Sharing for Microsoft Networks
- File and Printer Sharing for NetWare Networks
- Service for NetWare Directory Services (NDS)
- Asynchronous Transfer Mode (ATM)
- Virtual private networking (VPN) and PPTP
- Browse Master

◆ Install and configure network protocols in a Microsoft environment and a mixed Microsoft and NetWare environment. Protocols include the following:

- NetBEUI
- IPX/SPX-compatible protocol
- TCP/IP
- Microsoft DLC
- Fast Infrared

◆ Install and configure hardware devices in a Microsoft environment and a mixed Microsoft and NetWare environment. Hardware devices include the following:

- Modems
- Printers
- Universal Serial Bus (USB)
- Multiple Display Support
- IEEE 1394 FireWire
- Infrared Data Association (IrDA)
- Multilink
- Power management scheme

◆ Install and configure the Backup application.

Configuring and Managing Resource Access

The Configuring and Managing Resource Access component concentrates mainly on daily administrative issues.

Objectives for Configuring and Managing Resource Access

- ◆ Assign access permissions for shared folders in a Microsoft environment and a mixed Microsoft and NetWare environment. Methods include the following:

  - Passwords

  - User permissions

  - Group permissions

- ◆ Create, share, and monitor resources. Resources include the following:

  - Remote computers

  - Network printers

- ◆ Set up user environments by using user profiles and system policies.

- ◆ Back up data and the Registry and restore data and the Registry.

- ◆ Manage hard disks. Tasks include the following:

  - Disk compression

  - Partitioning

  - Enabling large disk support

  - Converting to FAT32

Integration and Interoperability

The Integration and Interoperability component of the Windows 98 certification exam concentrates on how to use the various interconnecting components of the TCP/IP protocol, RAS, and NetWare, among others.

Objectives for Integration and Interoperability

◆ Configure a Windows 98 computer as a client computer in a Windows NT network.

◆ Configure a Windows 98 computer as a client computer in a NetWare network.

◆ Configure a Windows 98 computer to access the Internet by using various methods in a Microsoft environment and a mixed Microsoft and NetWare environment. Methods include the following:

• Dial-Up Networking

• Proxy Server

Monitoring and Optimization

The Monitoring and Optimization component of the Windows 98 certification exam focuses on performance issues.

Objectives for Monitoring and Optimization

◆ Monitor system performance. Tools include the following:

• Net Watcher

• System Monitor

◆ Tune and optimize the system in a Microsoft environment and a mixed Microsoft and NetWare environment. Tasks include the following:

• Optimizing the hard disk by using Disk Defragmenter and ScanDisk

• Compressing data by using DriveSpace3 and the Compression Agent

• Updating drivers and applying service packs by using Windows Update and the Signature Verification Tool

• Automating tasks by using Maintenance Wizard

• Scheduling tasks by using Task Scheduler

- Checking for corrupt files and extracting files from the installation media by using the System File Checker

Troubleshooting

The Troubleshooting component of the certification exam has seven components, spanning the entire gamut of troubleshooting.

Objectives for Troubleshooting

- Diagnose and resolve installation failures. Tasks include the following:

  - Resolve file and driver version conflicts by using Version Conflict Manager and the Microsoft System Information Utility

- Diagnose and resolve boot process failures. Tasks include the following:

  - Editing configuration files by using the System Configuration Utility

- Diagnose and resolve connectivity problems in a Microsoft environment and a mixed Microsoft and NetWare environment. Tools include the following:

  - Winipcfg

  - Net Watcher

- Diagnose and resolve printing problems in a Microsoft environment and a mixed Microsoft and NetWare environment.

- Diagnose and resolve file system problems. Tools include the following:

  - ScanDisk

- Diagnose and resolve resource access problems in a Microsoft environment and a mixed Microsoft and NetWare environment.

- Diagnose and resolve hardware device and device driver problems. Tasks include the following:

  - Checking for corrupt Registry files by using ScanReg and ScanRegW

HARDWARE AND SOFTWARE RECOMMENDED FOR PREPARATION

The *MCSE Fast Track* series is meant to help you review concepts with which you already have training and hands-on experience. To make the most of the review, you need to have as much background and experience as possible. The best way to accomplish this is to combine studying with working on real networks using the products on which you will be tested. The following sections describe the minimum computer requirements you will need to build a solid practice environment.

Computers

In order to ensure that you can study everything you'll be tested on, the minimum computer requirements are one or more workstations running Windows 98, and one or more servers running Windows NT Server, all connected by a network.

Workstations: Windows 98

- Computer on the Microsoft Hardware Compatibility List
- 486DX 33MHz
- 16MB of RAM
- 200MB hard disk
- 3½-inch 1.44MB floppy drive
- VGA video adapter
- VGA monitor
- Mouse or equivalent pointing device
- Two-speed CD-ROM drive
- Network Interface Card (NIC)
- Presence on an existing network, or use of a hub to create a test network
- Microsoft Windows 98

Servers: Windows NT Server

- One or more computers on the Microsoft Hardware Compatibility List

- 486DX2 66MHz

- 32MB of RAM

- 340MB hard disk

- 3½-inch 1.44MB floppy drive

- VGA video adapter

- VGA monitor

- Mouse or equivalent pointing device

- Two-speed CD-ROM drive

- Network Interface Card (NIC)

- Presence on an existing network, or use of a hub to create a test network

- Microsoft Windows NT Server 4.0

WHAT'S IMPORTANT TO KNOW ABOUT EXAM 70-098

MCSE Fast Track: Windows 98 is written as a study aid for people preparing for Microsoft Certification Exam 70-098. The book is intended to help reinforce and clarify information with which the student is already familiar. This series is not intended to be a single source for exam preparation, but rather a review of information and set of practice tests to help increase the likelihood of success when taking the actual exam.

Part I of this book is designed to help you make the most of your study time by presenting concise summaries of information that you need to understand to succeed on the exam. Each chapter covers a specific exam objective area as outlined by Microsoft:

1 **Planning**

2 **Installation and Configuration**

3 **Configuring and Managing Resource Access**

4 **Integration and Interoperability**

5 **Monitoring and Optimization**

6 **Troubleshooting**

ABOUT THE EXAM

Exam Number:	70-98
Minutes:	90*
Questions:	59*
Passing Score:	709*
Single Answer Questions:	Yes
Multiple Answer with Correct Number Given	Yes
Multiple Answer without Correct Number Given	Yes
Ranking Order	No
Choices of A-D	Yes
Choices of A-E	Yes
Objective Categories	6

*Note: These exam criteria will no longer apply when this exam goes to an adaptive format.

▶ Develop an appropriate implementation model for specific requirements in a Microsoft environment and a mixed Microsoft and NetWare environment. Considerations include the following:
  · Choosing the appropriate file system
  · Planning a workgroup

▶ Develop a security strategy in a Microsoft environment and a mixed Microsoft and NetWare environment. Strategies include the following:
  · System policies
  · User profiles
  · File and Printer Sharing
  · Share-level access control or user-level access control

CHAPTER 1

Planning

COMPARING OPERATING SYSTEMS

Microsoft currently has three operating systems that it actively promotes: Windows 98, Windows NT Workstation 4.0, and Windows NT Server 4.0.

At A Glance: Minimum Hardware Requirements

Hardware	Windows 98 Workstation 4.0	Windows NT	Windows NT Server 4.0
Processor	486DX/66	486DX/33	486DX/33
RAM	16MB	12MB	16MB
Free space	120MB	120MB	130MB

> **NOTE**
> Microsoft lists a CD-ROM or DVD-ROM as a system requirement, but you can purchase 3½-inch high-density disks if necessary. For additional information, go to http://www.microsoft.com/windows98.

Windows 98 is an enhancement to Windows 95 that is designed to work with a variety of peripherals and legacy systems and provide ease of use. It offers Plug and Play features, supports preemptive multitasking, is available only for the Intel platform, and can network in a workgroup or domain-based network. Windows 98 can't be a server (performing centralized authentication and security) or make use of multiple processors. Although Windows 98 does have File and Printer Sharing and can be configured in a workgroup as a centralized resource, it still lacks the ability to authenticate users and apply security from a centralized database. Because of this limitation, a Windows 98 machine can't technically be referred to as a server, even though several small- to medium-sized business utilize it in this manner daily. We will discuss the configuration and benefits of workgroups and domains in more detail later in this book.

Windows NT Workstation 4.0 is an operating system product almost identical to the server, only tweaked for client use. It offers the same networking features as Windows 98 but doesn't utilize Plug and Play by default.

However, Windows NT does have the option of limited Plug and Play capabilities. When installed, Windows NT can utilize an abridged Plug and Play mechanism to give it limited functionality similar to Windows 95 and Windows 98. Located in the \DRVLIB\PNPISA\X86 directory on the Windows NT installation CD-ROM, the PNPISA.INF file (for the Intel platform) can be installed by right-clicking the file and selecting Install. Once installed, it will give your Windows NT system the ability to detect hardware components, prompting you for the drivers to complete the installation.

To install the Plug and Play ISA component on a Windows NT system, do the following:

1. Start your computer and choose Windows NT as the operating system.

2. Open Windows NT Explorer and select your CD-ROM.

3. Find the PNPISA.INF file for the Intel platform, located in the directory *D*:\DRVLIB\PNPISA\X86 (where *D*: is your CD-ROM).

4. Right-click PNPISA.INF and select Install.

5. Click OK to reboot.

Windows NT can be run on Intel or RISC-based machines (including MIPS, Alpha, and PowerPC) and utilizes multiprocessing and multi-tasking. It is designed for compatibility with DOS 5.0 and greater, Windows 3.x, and POSIX applications. It differs most significantly from Windows 98 in the area of security: To use files or printers, a user must be authenticated.

Windows NT Server 4.0 differs from Windows NT Workstation in that it offers services for Macintosh clients, RAID fault tolerance, domain login validation, directory replication, 256 possible remote access sessions (as opposed to one with Workstation), and an unlimited number of concurrent connections (as opposed to 10 with Workstation). It also can handle more processors, includes Internet Information Server (Workstation has Peer Web Services), and offers advanced services such as DNS, DHCP, and WINS. Table 1.1 illustrates the differences between the Windows operating systems.

TABLE 1.1

WINDOWS OPERATING SYSTEM FEATURES

Windows 98	Windows NT Workstation 4.0	Windows NT Server 4.0
486DX/66	486DX/33	486DX/33
16MB	12MB	16MB
120MB	120MB	130MB

NOTE
Although only NT Server can be an export server for directory replication, you can set up an NT Workstation to be a directory replication import-only server.

Additionally, Server is the only product that can act as a domain controller, and Workstation preloads a Virtual DOS Machine (VDM) at startup to speed the first load of an older application (Server doesn't do this to conserve memory). Additionally, Server can't participate in a workgroup unless it's configured as a standalone server.

DEVELOPING AN IMPLEMENTATION MODEL

Windows 98 was built with ease of implementation in mind. It will work in a workplace as a standalone PC or interact with a number of different networking environments. A workgroup can be created by networking a number of Windows 98 machines (or mixing in some Windows 95 and/or Windows 3.11 machines). Alternatively, it can easily be placed on a Windows NT Server network or a NetWare network. We will discuss network interoperability in more detail throughout this book.

To better understand implementation, we will look at the file systems it can operate with, as well as the workgroup model.

Planning Drive Configurations

Partitions are logical organizations of a physical disk. A disk can be sub-divided into several partitions—each formatted separately. NT will assign a different drive letter to each partition, and the user is free to interact with it as if it were a completely separate disk.

There are two types of partitions: primary and extended. There can be up to four primary partitions, and these are the only ones that can be booted. If you elect to use an extended partition (of which only one can be used per disk), the maximum number of primary partitions drops to three. The extended partition can be subdivided into up to four logical drives, but none of them are bootable.

If you install NT into an active partition, the partition remains active. If you install it into another partition, that partition becomes active. The two main partitions under NT are the system and boot partitions.

At A Glance: Drive Configurations

Drive	Contents	Partition
C:	Boot files	System partition
D:	Windows NT system files	Boot partition

Confusion can result from the counterintuitive naming of the partitions, so you must always remember that the boot partition contains the system files, while the system partition contains the boot files.

A volume set, configurable on Windows NT, is a collection of the free space on a number of physical disks gathered into one single logical drive. This makes disk growth transparent to users and simplifies their tasks. The downside, however, is that only one drive can be accessed at a time, so volume sets can slow access time. Neither the boot partition nor the system partition can be part of a volume set.

Choosing an Appropriate File System

Windows 98 can run on two types of *file systems:* FAT (also known as FAT16) and FAT32. When discussing FAT, it is important to know that the inference is to VFAT, even though that is no longer specifically spelled out.

The original FAT accompanied DOS and is available in versions through 6.22. VFAT became available with the initial release of Windows 95. FAT32 became available with Windows 95 Release B (an OEM-only release).

FAT32 is a 32-bit protected-mode file system that is available with Windows 95 OSR2 and Windows 98. Because of its design, it allows optimal access to hard disks and CD-ROM drives as well as network resources.

An additional complement to the FAT32 file system is the ability to use long filenames and directory names within Windows 98 and in any other application that supports long filenames. MS-DOS 6.22 and previous versions had an eight-character limit on file and directory names.

> **NOTE** Windows 98, just like Windows 95, continues to support filenames up to 255 characters long. For computers that aren't running Windows 95 or Windows 98, your filenames will have to conform to other standards. Some of your network servers might not support long filenames.

File system utilities are given exclusive access to disk resources in Windows 98. For example, ScanDisk is a file system utility that requires exclusive access to the hard disk and file system. If you have ever run ScanDisk and accessed a file or folder while the utility is at work, ScanDisk will begin anew, ensuring that it has exclusive access. Data corruption is the main concern with ScanDisk. One additional feature found in ScanDisk is its ability to detect if Windows 98 has been shut down properly. ScanDisk will automatically run in real mode if it detects an improper shutdown of a Windows 98 client. This feature was added to avoid hazardous errors that might occur in the File Allocation Table (FAT).

The File Allocation Table (FAT) is similar to a library's catalog cards or computerized database of books. When a person enters a library to find a book, she usually heads for the catalog card display or computer terminal. Once there, she can find the exact location of the book or resource she wants. This method of information retrieval is very similar to the use of a File Allocation Table. The computer simply checks the FAT to determine the location(s) of a file or resource for quick retrieval. Can you imagine having to locate a book by walking up and down the aisles of the library?

Although computers process information at very high speeds, it would take a tremendous amount of time to locate resources on a hard disk.

FAT16 was introduced in MS-DOS version 3.0, allowing access to drives up to 2 gigabytes in size. When accessing drives of that size, 32KB clusters are coupled with slower access time. The 32KB cluster size also lends itself to a higher amount of wasted hard disk space. For example, a 40KB file would end up using two 32KB clusters. One cluster would get filled up, and the remaining 8KB would be placed in the second cluster. In this example, 24KB of space would be wasted.

FAT32 is an improvement over FAT16 in that it has support for even larger hard drives, up to 2 terabytes in size. If we compared a 2 gigabyte drive formatted as FAT16 to a 2 gigabyte drive formatted as FAT32, one major difference would be the size of the clusters. The FAT16 cluster size would be 32KB, allowing for a higher percentage of wasted space, while the FAT32 cluster size would be 4KB. Our 40KB sample file would take up 10 clusters on the FAT32 file system with no wasted space. Although FAT32 does present some additional benefits over FAT16, the only operating systems that can view a FAT32 file system are Windows 95 and Windows 98. Another shortcoming of the FAT32 file system is the fact that it can't be compressed using the Microsoft DriveSpace 3 utility.

> **NOTE** Keep in mind that a FAT32 volume, with all its advantages, can't be recognized by Windows NT.

Table 1.2 compares the cluster sizes of FAT16 and FAT32.

TABLE 1.2

FAT16 AND FAT32 CLUSTER SIZES

Drive Size	FAT16 Cluster Size	FAT32 Cluster Size
256 to 511MB	8KB	NA
512 to 1023MB	16KB	4KB
1024MB to 2GB	32KB	4KB
2 to 8GB	NA	4KB

continues

TABLE 1.2 continued

Drive Size	FAT16 Cluster Size	FAT32 Cluster Size
8 to 16GB	NA	8KB
16 to 32GB	NA	16KB
32GB and above	NA	32KB

FAT32 is currently available only in Windows 95B and Windows 98, and it is incompatible with Windows NT Server and Workstation 4.0 for dual-booting purposes. This is extremely important when dual booting a machine with both Windows 98 and Windows NT. For example, consider a computer that has two hard disk drives, each partitioned as its own drive. If you installed Windows 98 on drive C running FAT and installed Windows NT on drive D running FAT, each operating system could see both drives. However, if you converted drive D (Windows NT) to NTFS, Windows 98 would no longer be able to view the contents of drive D. The same would hold true if you were to use the Windows 98 Drive Converter to convert drive C to FAT32. Windows NT would no longer be able to view the contents of drive C. However, while running either FAT or FAT32 on the client machine, Windows 98 can interact across a network and share files with Windows NT servers running NTFS. Mixing file formats is an issue only if it's done on the same machine. In most NT networks, the file system on the Windows NT server is NTFS, while the clients use either FAT or FAT32.

The following are features of the different file systems:

Feature	FAT	VFAT	FAT32	NTFS
Filename length	8.3	255	255	255
8.3 compatibility?	N/A	Yes	Yes	Yes
Maximum files in root directory	512	512	No limit	No limit
Maximum files in non-root directory	65,535	No limit	No limit	No limit
Partition size	2GB	4GB	2TB	16EB
Local security?	No	No	No	Yes

Feature	FAT	VFAT	FAT32	NTFS
Transaction tracking?	No	No	No	Yes
Hot fixing?	No	No	No	Yes
Overhead	1MB	Minimal	Minimal	>2MB (average 4.5 to 10)
Required for dual booting?	Yes	Yes	No	No
Required for RISC-based?	Yes	Yes	No	No
Accessible from DOS?	Yes	Yes	No	No
Accessible from OS/2?	Yes	Yes	No	No
Case-sensitive?	No	No	No	POSIX only
Case preservation?	No	Yes	Yes	Yes
Compression?	No	No	No	Yes
Efficiency	<200MB to 400MB	<200 to >400MB>	<400MB	
Convertible?	To NTFS only	To FAT32 or NTFS only	No	No
Fragmentation level	High	High	High	Low
Extensible attributes?	No	No	No	Yes

On machines where is the file Windows 98 has been preinstalled, in almost all instances FAT32 is the file system that was chosen by the vendor. During an installation (or any formatting operation), you are asked whether you want to enable the partition for large drive support. If you choose Yes, FAT32 is installed. If you choose No, (V)FAT/FAT16 is used.

NOTE

One key thing to know for the exam is that DriveSpace3, the compression utility, can't be used on a FAT32 volume.

While planning the implementation of Windows 98, you can begin with the FAT16 file system to ensure compatibility with legacy applications. While your network evolves and applications are upgraded, you can consider changing to the FAT32 file system. The FAT32 Drive Converter utility, shown in Figure 1.1, can be used at any time to convert a FAT16 partition into a FAT32 partition without losing any data. It simply converts the file system to the new selection and requires you to reboot. After you reboot, you are operating under FAT32.

To convert a FAT16 partition to FAT32, complete the following steps:

1. In Windows 98, select Start | Programs | Accessories | System Tools | Drive Converter (FAT32).

2. The Drive Converter Wizard will begin and will guide you through the steps. Click Next to continue.

3. Select the partition you would like to convert, and click Next to continue.

4. You might be warned that conversion would eliminate access by any operating system other than Windows 95/98 on the same machine.

FIGURE 1.1
The Windows 98 Drive Converter (FAT32) utility.

5. Click Yes to continue the conversion.

6. Reboot your computer.

It's important to know that there is no utility for converting from FAT32 to FAT16. The conversion from FAT16 to FAT32 is a *one-way* process, similar to using the Convert utility in Windows NT to convert a FAT partition to NTFS.

If you need to convert back to FAT16, you must back up all the data on the drive to removable media (usually tape), reformat the hard drive with FAT16, and restore the backup.

NOTE   For the exam, it's good to know that the only way to convert from FAT32 to FAT32FAT16 is to create a backup, reformat with FAT16, and then restore the backup to your new partition.

Fault Tolerance

Fault tolerance is defined as the ability to recover from a hardware failure. It is implemented and supported in NT through the endorsement of RAID (Redundant Array of Inexpensive Disks). As a client, Windows 98 can access, across a network, a Windows NT server with RAID implementation. As a server, Windows 98 currently doesn't support RAID. Windows NT supports RAID levels 1 and 5.

At A Glance: Fault Tolerance

RAID level	Implementation
0	Disk striping
1	Disk mirroring
5	Disk striping with parity

Disk mirroring is the replication of data between two physical disks. When data comes in, it is written to both disks virtually simultaneously.

If one disk fails, the system can stay up and running since both disks contain identical information. Only two actions can be performed: establishing the mirror and breaking the mirror in the event of a hard drive failure. Both of these actions are performed in the Disk Administrator utility. With mirroring, one disk controller controls two drives. Fifty percent of the available disk space, or one complete hard disk drive, can't be used, because it is set aside for replication.

Disk duplexing is a hardware enhancement over mirroring that doesn't involve any additional software interaction. In duplexing, two controllers are used instead of one. If one controller fails, the system can still stay up and running. This is still considered RAID 1 and is implemented as mirroring in Disk Administrator. With both mirroring and duplexing, read operations are performed more quickly, because whichever disk isn't busy at the moment can process the request. Write requests are minimally slower because data must be written twice rather than once.

> **N O T E**   Disk Administrator is used to create all fault tolerance in Windows NT.

Disk striping with parity is RAID 5. With RAID 5, a minimum of three drives must be used, and a maximum of 32 can be used. An amount of free space on each drive is set aside as a portion of the set. When data comes in, it is written across all but one of the drives. The last drive is used for a parity check on the data, which is written there. If any of the drives fails, the others can compute the missing data and re-create it. Disk Administrator is used to implement disk striping with parity through the command Create Stripe Set with Parity. If a drive fails and is replaced, the Regenerate command is used to place on the new drive the data that existed on the old.

Disk striping with parity slows down system performance on both read and write requests, because multiple disks must always be accessed and parity always computed. Disk striping with parity can't be used on the system or boot partitions—they can be mirrored only.

Disk striping without parity doesn't offer any fault tolerance whatsoever and is thus classified as RAID 0. In this scenario, data is written across a number of drives. It offers the highest level of read and write performance of any disk management system. Disk striping without parity requires only two disks.

The following are examples of fault-tolerant implementations:

- Mirroring. Data comes from the controller and is written to two hard drives. In the event of drive failure, the system can continue running because the same information is duplicated on each disk.

- Disk striping with parity. Data comes from the controller and is written to multiple hard drives, with parity computed and added on the remaining hard drive. In the event of drive failure, its value can be obtained by the parity check computation.

Planning a Workgroup

A workgroup is a number of computers networked for the purpose of sharing resources. No single machine constitutes a server, and the resources shared are located on the peer machines. Security is based on what you are sharing, and is thus known as *share-level security.*

You should take some care in choosing a workgroup name for Windows 98. If the name is different from the workgroup names used by any servers on your network, you won't be able to browse network resources without knowing the names of the servers you want to visit. The term *server* in a workgroup environment can refer to any computer on your network that shares resources, so it encompasses Windows for Workgroups, Windows 95, Windows 98, and Windows NT. If you decide to make your workgroup name the same as your domain name, your computer will appear to have joined the domain in the Network Neighborhood. The benefit of this is that you can see the domain servers as soon as you open the Network Neighborhood, which makes navigating your server's unmapped drives much easier.

NOTE

Windows 98 can only be a part of a workgroup on a network. Windows NT is the only operating system that can create and have a computer account in a Windows NT domain. However, if you give your Windows 98 workgroup the same name as the Windows NT domain name currently in use, both computers will share a list of resources. The Windows 98 computers will also appear listed in Windows NT administration tools, such as Server Manager. This appearance is an illusion of sorts, because Windows 98 computers can't have computer accounts in the domain.

To increase the response in displaying the available resources inside Network Neighborhood, you should select a name for the workgroup that differs from the domain. Your list of available resources will be shorter, and the response in displaying the browse list will be quicker. The drawback, however, is the increased effort required to locate an available resource by working your way through the list in Network Neighborhood.

If you choose to manage your workgroups under different names, you must configure at least one computer, a Windows 98 machine, with File and Printer Sharing. When you install File and Printer Sharing, the computer will maintain a list of servers in the workgroup, as well as a list of other workgroups or domains that exist on the network. If you don't have this list, you will receive an `Unable to browse the network` error message when you try to access the Entire Network icon in the Network Neighborhood. Later in this book we will discuss the steps required to configure a Windows 98 client machine to always maintain a browse list.

The opposite scenario of this is a domain. A domain has at least one server—a machine dedicated to authenticating users and governing the resources they are allowed to share. With a domain, you have *user-level security,* meaning that all resource access is based on the user who authenticated himself during the logon. In the absence of a domain (the presence of a workgroup), you have *share-level security,* meaning that security is based on what is shared.

Here are the key differences between the models:

- In a Windows 98 workgroup, each workstation that shares resources must offer share-level security only, with no user account authentication for resource access—just share-level passwords.

- In a domain, access to resources is assigned to local groups, and then global groups are added to local groups in the domain.

> **NOTE**
>
> Microsoft pushes the AGLP rule of user management. Accounts are placed into global groups, global groups are placed into local groups, and local groups are assigned permissions to a resource.

The concept of workgroups will be revisited many times in this book in the different objective categories.

SECURITY STRATEGIES

A solid security strategy consists of combining a number of different items into a cohesive structure. Security can be measured in many ways, beginning with physical security and ending with encryption. Windows 98 gives an administrator some selected security that falls somewhere in between. This section discusses these elements and how they compare to things we find in the real world. Let's first take a look at categories that are covered when discussing security:

- File and Printer Sharing
- Access control (share-level or user-level)
- User profiles
- System policies

Each of these topics is examined in the following sections.

File and Printer Sharing

Chapter 2, "Installation and Configuration," explores the installation of File and Printer Sharing, which allows you to share resources on your computer with others. After it's installed, you can choose to enable either file or printer sharing or both. A key distinction to be aware of is that even though the name includes file sharing, it is really folder sharing. Windows 98 (as opposed to Windows NT running NTFS) doesn't let you assign sharing on a file-by-file basis; it must be managed on a folder-by-folder basis. Although you can set file permissions under NTFS, which controls access to a file, you can't actually create a share to a single file on a Windows NT machine.

File and Printer Sharing services can represent a major security problem on any network. From a security standpoint, this is something you must consider before conducting your upgrades and installations.

Just the thought of personal file and printer sharing makes most network administrators cringe. This is because it takes control away from the central security authority (usually the administrator) and delegates it to less-qualified people. This section elaborates on the purpose and use of File and Printer Sharing services, as well as the differences in sharing methods between the two services that Microsoft supplies.

Files are kept safe, and information is kept hidden most effectively, if the files reside on a central server where a central security authority can control access to them. With the files in this central location, administrators can control who is on the list of users who have access and the level of access they have. On the point of safe files, most sites have implemented procedures to regularly back up the servers' contents daily.

When files are kept on local hard drives, security is compromised. By ignoring the network login dialog box, you will gain access to all local files with total control, unless some type of local security has been implemented. Local files usually aren't part of a regular and systematic backup procedure. If the issues of security and safety don't convince you to keep files on a central server, allowing users to share local files with others increases the risk to the files.

When network users have access to, or are allowed to share files with, other network users, they usually accomplish sharing through File and Printer Sharing for Microsoft Networks. It is also usually implemented with the default system security—share-level access control. With share-level access control, users are asked for a Read-Only password, a Full Access password, or both. Either password can be left blank, which might leave the shared folder open to Full Access with no check in place. This security breach is impossible to control if each user is responsible for his or her own file sharing.

If you haven't had the opportunity to dine at a nice restaurant, I highly recommend doing so. Not only does someone else do the cooking, but there aren't any dirty dishes in the sink, waiting for you to wash them. Couple that with wonderful food, and you can see why people like to dine out.

So what does a restaurant have to do with File and Printer Sharing? Well, like File and Printer Sharing, a restaurant must be open. It must be in business in order for you to go there and eat. File and Printer Sharing must be installed before anyone can access the resources controlled by your Windows 98 client machine. File and Printer Sharing isn't installed by default. As I mentioned earlier, Chapter 2 explores the installation of this service.

Access Control

Once you have decided to share resources (create a network), the next decision is whether the network will be one of multiple peers (a workgroup) or will include a server (a domain).

In our example, a single owned or franchised restaurant has the ability to make decisions much like a peer-to-peer workgroup. Each restaurant would make its own decisions regarding management, accounting, hours of operation, and so on. On the other hand, a chain of restaurants would answer to the "home office" or the corporate "domain." The corporate domain would centrally define policies and security.

Peer-to-Peer

In a peer-to-peer network, you simply take the machines currently in existence, install networking cards in them, and connect them through some type of cabling. Each machine is known as a *peer* and can participate in the sharing of files or resources. No server is required, so there is no additional cost for a dedicated machine, but there is no real security either. Peer-to-peer networks require an operating system (or add-on) that can understand networking and function in this way. Microsoft's Windows 95, Windows 98, Windows NT Server, and Windows NT Workstation can all function in a peer-to-peer environment.

If File and Printer Sharing has been enabled on a Windows 98 system, for example, you may create a share by selecting a folder and choosing to share it. By default, no password is associated with it, but you can choose to assign one that a user must give to access the resource. Figure 1.2 shows that access permissions can be Read-Only, Full, or Depends on Password. This is known as *share-level security,* wherein the security is passed when a user supplies the correct password to access the share.

Any computer in a peer-to-peer workgroup running File and Printer Sharing services can share with and connect to other clients running a compatible File and Printer Sharing service. These clients can connect to shared resources such as folders, printers, and even CD-ROM devices.

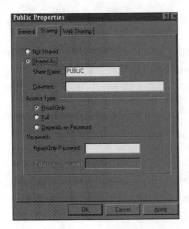

FIGURE 1.2
Sharing a resource using share-level permissions.

Windows 98 clients configured as peer "servers" in a small- to medium-sized company give that company the advantage of resource sharing using a secure, inexpensive method. Because it is run on the 32-bit Windows 98 protected-mode platform, all the advantages of high performance are available. In addition to increased performance, utilities and tools can be added at the company's request. System policies, for example, can restrict a user's ability to access the peer server, based on username, computer name, or simply being a member of a group. A step up in security would be to implement user-level security, which is an additional enhancement built into the peer server capabilities of Windows 98.

When you're planning secure access to resources throughout a network, it's good to consider the following:

- ◆ Select a File and Printer Sharing service that meets the needs of the general public. If the majority of the users are running NetWare clients from a 3.x or 4.x environment, install File and Printer Sharing for NetWare Networks.

- ◆ If the majority of users are running Windows for Workgroups, Windows 95, Windows 98, or Windows NT, the best choice would be to install File and Printer Sharing for Microsoft Networks.

In your evaluation of network security and needs, it is prudent to plan based on common denominators—the users' requirements, not necessarily their desires.

Share-level security is equivalent to a peer-to-peer security implementation. Windows 98, like Windows 95, provides support for share-level security. In configuring share-level access control, a password is the layer of security provided by Windows 98.

The Universal Naming Convention allows a computer name and share name (typically limited to 15 characters or less) to be used to identify a resource without tying up a drive letter assignment. Here's the syntax:

\\computername\sharename\ path\ file

If mapping is used, a redirector maps network names used by an application to a physical network device name.

Peer-to-peer networking works in small environments. If you grow beyond approximately 10 machines, the administrative overhead of establishing the shares, coupled with the lack of tight security, creates a nightmare.

Have you ever gone to a restaurant that allows you to seat yourself? You can sit almost anywhere you like. The restaurant is open, much like having File and Printer Sharing installed, and access to the dining room has been granted, similar to sharing folders on your client machine. In this example, the restaurant has shared the dining room resource with the default setting (no password), giving everyone the authority to decide what table they would like to access. From a security perspective, the dining room is somewhat vulnerable, but you haven't been granted access to the kitchen or the manager's office.

Server-Based

In the presence of a server, whether NetWare or NT, you can implement *user-level* security on your network. Keep in mind that the default access control method is *share-level,* so to utilize *user-level* security, you must configure your Windows 98 client through the Access Control tab, found on the Network properties sheet (see Figure 1.3).

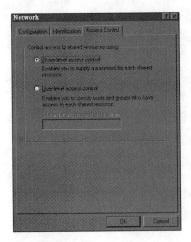

FIGURE 1.3
The Access Control tab on the Network properties sheet.

To configure the access control, complete the following steps:

1. In Windows 98, select Start | Settings | Control Panel.

2. Click the Network icon.

3. The Network properties dialog box appears. Select the Access Control tab.

4. From here you can select either Share-Level or User-Level access control.

5. Click OK and reboot when prompted.

When you configure user-level security, you are actually setting up your Windows 98 clients as a workgroup "server" that can access a centrally administered account database located on a NetWare server or Windows NT domain controller. By gaining access to the account database, pass-through user authentication takes place to validate the user's access to the resource. The benefits include increased security, based on additional levels of assigned access. Although it's true that the downside is the requirement of a user account on the Windows NT domain controller or the NetWare server, most network administrators believe that to be an acceptable trade-off.

When authentication of a user occurs, the 32-bit protected-mode client cooperates with the 32-bit protected-mode service to access and pass user-level security requests through shared connection information.

Whether it is File and Printer Sharing for Microsoft Networks or File and Printer Sharing for NetWare Networks, an authentication server must be provided to completely enable user-level security. This server must contain the user accounts with the valid permissions to access the shared resource.

With user-level security, permissions are based on how the user logged on and was authenticated by the server. This server could be a Windows NT domain controller or a NetWare server. It is important to understand that every user has an *account*. In this environment, you can assign permissions to shares based on user permissions or group permissions.

In Windows NT, there are only two ways a user gets rights and permissions to resources:

+ He is explicitly assigned a right or permission through his account.

+ He is a member of a group that has a right or permission.

Windows NT user accounts, with their unique identifiers, allow a user to log on to the Windows NT network. Thus, his account/password combination is his access ticket to all resources on the NT network.

Windows NT user accounts are created in User Manager for Domains. To create a new account, the user running User Manager for Domains must be a member of either the Administrators local group or the Account Operators local group.

User Properties

Each user has several property pages. When you're creating a new user, the first screen allows for individual settings.

This User properties dialog box displays such items as the user's name, password, and how to handle the changing of that password. Specifically, each setting is set as follows:

+ Username. This is the name that each user will use to log into the network. This name must be unique in the domain. The name must have no more than 20 characters and can't contain the following characters: " / \ [ ] : ; | = , + * ? < > The goal of enterprise networking is for each user in the enterprise to have only *one* user account.

◆ Full name. This allows for the display of the user's full name. You can use this as a sort setting by selecting View | Sort by Full Name.

◆ Description. This setting is copied from account to account if used as a template. It is used to further describe a user.

◆ Password/Confirm password. The password for the user can be up to 14 characters long. If the user is working at an NT-class system, the password is also case-sensitive. If the user is at a Windows 98 or lower system, the password is not case-sensitive.

Of the five properties at the top of the dialog box, only the description will be copied from account to account. All other settings must be re-entered for a copied user.

The lower settings in the User properties dialog box relate to how passwords will be handled:

◆ User must change password at next logon. This approach forces the user to change his password when he next logs on to the network.

◆ User cannot change password. This selection is used in higher-security networks where users are assigned passwords for their accounts.

◆ Password never expires. This setting overrides the account policy of password expiration. It should be used only for service accounts in Windows NT.

◆ Account disabled. This setting prevents the user from using this account.

◆ Account locked out. This setting is active only if a user's account has been locked out by the operating system for failing the Account Lockout settings. To reactivate an account, just clear the check box for this setting.

Group Properties Tab

The Group Properties tab is used to assign the user whose account you are modifying to various groups.

This tab only allows the assignment of users to global and local groups in the same domain as the user (generally, users are assigned to global groups). To assign a user to a group in a different domain, you must use that domain's local group properties.

The Primary group option at the bottom of the dialog box is used by Services for Macintosh. You can designate a primary global group for the account.

User Environment Profiles Page

The User Environment Profiles page is one of the main configuration pages used in an enterprise network.

The User Environment Profile dialog box allows the administrator to configure the following as centrally located:

+ User profile path

+ Login script

+ Home directory

The main reason to centrally locate these items is so that you can have all of them stored on a central server. Having the users store their profiles and home directories centrally makes the process of backing up their data more manageable.

User Profile Path

The user profile path designates a specific location on a specified server where the user's profile will be stored. As the directory structure reveals, the profile path contains the user portion of the Registry in the file NTUSER.DAT. The directory structure itself also contains a user's Start menu, desktop layout, and recently used file listing. By using this profile path, the user can have his desktop and personal configuration settings follow him to whichever NT computer he uses.

The most common path that is entered for the user profile path is \\SERVER\PROFILESHARE\%USERNAME%. It should be noted that this location is server-specific. Consideration should be given to locating the user's profile on a server in the same subnet as the client to limit WAN traffic.

Login Script

The login script lets the administrator configure common drive mappings, run central batch files, and configure the system. When configuring a login script, simply use the name of the *.BAT or *.CMD file that you want to execute. The logon scripts are stored by default in this directory:

\%*systemroot*%\system32\repl\import\scripts

This directory is shared as the netlogon share. The main purpose of the logon script is to present a common network layout to all clients on the network.

Home Directory

The home directory setting for the user's profile creates a personal directory where the user can store his data on a network server. The most common entry used to create home directories is a share called USERS. Assuming that this share has been created, you would enter the path for each home directory as \\COMPUTER\USERS\%*USERNAME*%.

Logon Hours Properties

The Logon Hours Properties tab allows the administrator to set what hours the user account is given access to the network.

If the user attempts to log on to the network during non-allowed hours, he will see a dialog box stating that he isn't allowed to log on during these hours.

If the user is currently logged on and his logon hours restriction goes into effect, he won't be able to connect to any further net shares. Likewise, he won't be able to use any of his current shares. If the user actually logs out, he won't be allowed to log on to the network until the next block of time when he is allowed to log in.

Logon to Properties

The Logon to Properties page is used to restrict users to working at specific workstations.

You can specify up to eight computer names. They are entered as the computer name, not UNC format. For example, you would type **PORTLAND**, not **\\PORTLAND**.

Account Properties

An administrator uses the Account Properties page to define one of two things:

- Setting an account expiration date. This is used for any term employees for whom the administrator would know when the account should stop being accessible.

- Setting whether the account is global or local. Global is the default.

Dial-In Properties

The Dial-In Properties page allows the administrator to determine which users are granted dial-in access to the network and whether call-back security is to be implemented.

If No call back is selected, the user will immediately be able to use network resources. This is commonly used in low-security networks and for users working out of hotel rooms.

If Set by user is selected, the user will be prompted to enter the phone number where he is presently located, and the Remote Access Server will call him back at that number. If Preset to is configured, the user dials in to the office network. Upon connecting, the line is dropped, and the user is called back at a predefined phone number.

Each user or group is defined on the server and referenced by the client sharing the resource when *user-level access* is invoked. In Figure 1.4, the Windows 98 client is assigning permissions to users and groups found on the Windows NT domain. In short, you must have a server on the network to have user-level security, but you can have share-level security with or without a server.

> **NOTE** For the exam, it's important to know that *only* user-level security can be used when you're utilizing a NetWare server as the authentication server. File and Printer Sharing for NetWare Networks must also be the selected service to complete the security procedure.

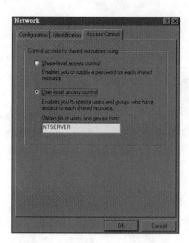

FIGURE 1.4
User-level access control.

Also known as *client/server* networking, server-based networking's downside is that it requires a dedicated machine (the server). The upside is that you gain centralized administration and authentication. With centralized administration, you can add all users in one location, control logon scripts and backups, and so on. With centralized authentication, you can identify a user to your entire network based on his logon name and password, not based on each share he attempts to access.

This is similar to a restaurant that only accepts reservations. If there is no open seating, and no reservation exists for you or your party, you probably won't gain access to the restaurant. If a reservation does exist for you or your party, you are given access, but only to the table you are assigned. In other words, you can't seat yourself, as you could with share-level access.

Peer-to-peer networks can exist comfortably within server-based networks. In many businesses, combinations of the two models are used. A server-based network is used to provide email and other resources to all users, while peer-to-peer networks are established within divisions to share resources among select users.

Microsoft also calls peer-to-peer networks *workgroups,* and server-based networks *domains.* The respective terms are used interchangeably in almost all Microsoft documentation.

User Profiles

User profiles hold information about individual users, such as their desktop, wallpaper, background, shortcuts, and so on. You can enable them for individual users (instead of using the same one for all users) by selecting the Passwords applet in Control Panel and going to the User Profiles tab (shown in Figure 1.5). From there, check the box that says Users can customize their preferences and desktop settings.

In our example of dining out, some people go to nice restaurants quite often. During each visit, they may request a certain bottle of wine or a specific table. These are special arrangements customized for that particular client, much like Windows 98 user profiles.

At any given time, two files comprise what is called the Registry: SYSTEM.DAT and USER.DAT. SYSTEM.DAT holds information pertinent to the computer itself, and USER.DAT is the user's profile (the user portion of the Registry).

When a user logs on, the following steps occur:

1. The SYSTEM.DAT file is loaded into memory, along with settings from the default user's USER.DAT.

2. The user identifies himself and successfully logs on—either locally or to the network.

3. The user profile is read locally or from the network.

4. The setting for the current user overwrites those for the default user.

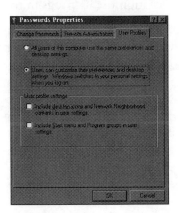

FIGURE 1.5
The User Profiles tab in the Passwords Properties dialog box.

User profiles can be implemented as either *local profiles* or *roaming profiles*. A roaming profile allows a user to have the user portion of his configuration follow him to whatever machine he logs in to on the network.

Local Profiles Versus Roaming Profiles

Whenever a user logs in to a system, he creates a local profile on that system. The local profile is implemented as a set of directory structures. This directory structure includes the desktop folder and the Start Menu folder. The user portion of the Registry is stored in the file USER.DAT.

> NOTE
>
> For the exam, it is important to know that the Windows 98 client incorporates the USER.DAT file, while Windows NT uses the NTUSER.DAT file to store the user portion of the Registry.

The problem with local profiles is that every workstation you log in to will have its own version of the local profile. User configuration settings will have to be set at each workstation that the user logs in to.

To overcome this problem, you must implement roaming profiles. Roaming profiles have the user portion of the Registry download from a designated system to the system that the user is currently logged on to. Any changes to the user's settings will be stored in the central location so that they can be retrieved at the next workstation the user logs in to.

In Windows 98, whenever a user logs on, the hardware portion of the Registry, mainly HKEY_LOCAL_MACHINE\Software\Microsoft\Windows\ CurrentVersion\Profile List, is checked to see if the user has a profile of his own locally. It also checks the home directory of the server, if configured to do so from User Manager for Domains, to see if there is one there (roaming). If there is one on the server and it is newer than the one on this workstation (or there is none on this workstation), Windows 98 copies the server version and uses it for the session. If a newer version is on the workstation, a dialog box informs you of the situation and allows you to choose which profile you would like to use.

NOTE For the exam, it'sexam good to know that user profiles are stored in the user's defined directory, configured in User Manager for Domains in a Windows NT domain. In a NetWare environment, user profiles are stored in the user's *mail* directory. This is often confused with system policy files, which are stored in the Netlogon share of the Windows NT domain controller or the Public directory in a NetWare environment.

Configuring Roaming Profiles in Windows NT

If you want to configure a user account to use a roaming profile, the first thing to do is set the profile path in the User Manager for Domains for that account. If you are configuring a block of users, the best method to use is to do a group property change by first selecting all users you want to have roaming profiles and then selecting User | Properties.

The most common setting to perform is to have a directory shared with a share name such as profiles. It should give the local group USERS the permission of Full Control. With this share, you can now set the user's profile path to be *server\share\%username%*. The next time the user logs on, his profile information can be saved to this central profile directory.

Windows 98 users can also have roaming profiles configured so that their user-based configurations can follow them from workstation to workstation. Implementing roaming profiles in Windows 98 differs from Windows NT in the following ways:

- Separate user profiles are not implemented automatically in Windows 98, as they are in Windows NT.

- The user portion of the Registry is saved in the file USER.DAT in Windows 98, while it is stored in NTUSER.DAT in Windows NT.

- The user profile path setting in the user's properties has no effect on Windows 98 clients. Their roaming profile information is stored in their Windows NT Home directory.

System Policies

System policies help the network administrator restrict what configuration changes the user can perform to his profile. By combining roaming profiles and system policies, the administrator can not only give the user a consistent desktop, but can also control what the user can do to that desktop. Likewise, the administrator can be assured that the user can't modify certain settings.

When you frequent your favorite restaurant, you must observe certain policies. For example, there might be a dinner menu as opposed to a lunch menu, or a jacket might be required. More commonly, there might be a nonsmoking section or certain hours of operation. All of these define the restaurant's system policies. They help the restaurant managers or owners administer and restrict the client's ability to access the facility.

System policies work very much like a merge operation. You can think of system policies as a copy of your Registry. When you log in to the network and the CONFIG.POL file exists on the domain controller, it merges its settings into your Registry, changing your Registry settings as indicated in the system policy. Keep in mind that the CONFIG.POL file is used by both Windows 95 and Windows 98 clients, while Windows NT clients use NTCONFIG.POL.

> **NOTE** For the exam, it's good to know that system policy files are stored in the Netlogon share of the Windows NT domain controller or in the Public directory in a NetWare environment.

You implement system policies using the System Policy Editor, shown in Figure 1.6. You can configure them to do the following:

- ◆ Implement defaults for hardware configuration for a specific machine or for all computers using the profile.

- ◆ Restrict the changing of specific parameters that affect the hardware configuration of the participating system.

- ◆ Set defaults for all users in the areas of their personal settings that they can configure.

- Restrict the user from changing specific areas of his configuration to prevent tampering with the system. An example would be disabling all Registry editing tools for a specific user.

- Apply all defaults and restrictions on a group level rather than just a user level.

The System Policy Editor can also be used to change settings in the Registry of the system that System Policy Editor is being executed on. Many times, it's easier to use the System Policy Editor, because it has a better interface for finding common restrictions you might want to place on a Windows 98 machine.

Implementing System Policies

To create computer, user, and group policies, you must use the System Policy Editor. The System Policy Editor is installed through the following steps:

1. Select Add/Remove Programs from the Control Panel.

2. Choose the Windows Setup tab, shown in Figure 1.7, and click Have Disk.

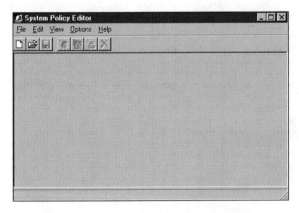

FIGURE 1.6
The System Policy Editor.

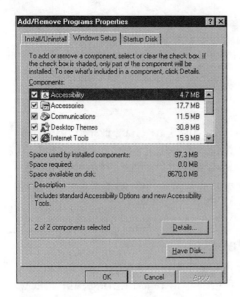

FIGURE 1.7
The Windows Setup tab allows you to install the System Policy Editor.

3. Click Browse, and look on the Windows 98 disk in the Tools\Reskit\NetAdmin\Poledit directory, as shown in Figure 1.8.

4. Select both Group Policies and System Policy Editor. Click OK for all the installation questions.

5. Once it's installed, you can run System Policy Editor by selecting Start | Run and typing **POLEDIT.EXE**. Alternatively, you can select Start | Programs | Accessories | System Tools | System Policy Editor.

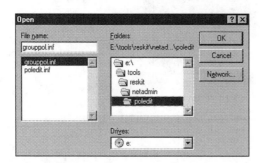

FIGURE 1.8
Select the appropriate INF file to install the System Policy Editor.

When you choose to create a new policy file by selecting File | New Policy, you will see two default icons within the policy, as shown in Figure 1.9:

- Default Computer is used to configure all machine-specific settings. All property changes within this section will affect the HKEY_LOCAL_MACHINE subtree of the Registry. The default computer item will be used for any client that uses the policy and that doesn't have a specific machine entry created for itself in the policy file.

- Default User is used to specify default policy settings for all users who will be using the policy. The default user setting will affect the HKEY_CURRENT_USER subtree of the Registry. If the user is configured to use a roaming profile, this information will be stored in his centralized version of USER.DAT in his profile directory.

Configuring Computer Policies

Computer policies can be configured to lock down common machine settings that will affect all users of a Windows NT system. This is very similar to the Windows 98 configuration settings. One subtle difference is that Windows NT clients look for an NTCONFIG.POL file, while Windows 98 clients look for a CONFIG.POL file. Here are some common settings that are configured:

- Programs that run automatically at startup. These can include virus scans. Opening the System/Run option in the Default Computer properties sets this.

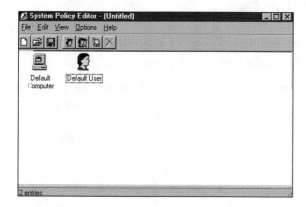

FIGURE 1.9
The two starting icons for a new system policy.

♦ Ensuring that all Windows NT clients will have the administrative shares automatically created on startup of these systems. This enhances the administrator's ability to centrally manage the network. Opening the Windows NT Network/Sharing option in the Default Computer properties sets this.

♦ Implementing customized shared folders. These include the desktop folder, Start Menu folder, Startup folder, and Programs folder. These can be set to point to an actual network share location so that multiple machines can have common desktops or Start menus. Opening the Windows NT Shell/Custom shared folders option in the Default Computer properties sets this.

♦ Presenting a customized dialog box called the Logon Banner that can be used to inform users of upcoming maintenance to the network or for other network information. Opening the Windows NT System/Logon option in the Default Computer properties sets this.

♦ Removing the last logged-on user from the Authentication dialog box. Because many users have poor passwords, knowing a user's login name can help someone guess that person's password. This is also set in the Windows NT System/Logon option in the Default Computer properties.

Computer policies can also be implemented on a computer-by-computer basis. Selecting Edit | Add Computer does this. This will add a new icon to the policy with that computer's name.

Configuring User Policies

User policies can also be implemented through the system policy editor. These policies will affect the HKEY_CURRENT_USER Registry subtree. Each user will be affected individually by these settings.

User policies can also be implemented on a user-by-user basis. To create an individual user policy, select Edit | Add User. When a user logs on to the network on a Windows NT client, NTCONFIG.POL will be checked to see if there is a policy for the specific user. Unlike a user's logging on to the network on a Windows 98 client, CONFIG.POL will be checked to see if there is a policy for the specific user. If there is not, the default user policy will be used for the login process.

Implementing Group Policies

If you need to have user settings affect multiple users, you can implement group policies. Group policies add another level of complexity to the processing of the policies. Here are some of the additional considerations:

- The System Policy Editor uses global groups for group membership. Appropriate trust relationships must be implemented to see the necessary global groups.

- Because a user can belong to multiple global groups, the order in which the groups are processed is very important. One group's settings could be the opposite of another group's. You set the group order by selecting Options | Group Priority.

Processing Order for System Policies

When a user logs on to a network where system policies have been implemented, the following steps will occur:

1. The user successfully logs in to the network.

2. The user profile is read from the NETLOGON share of the authenticating domain controller.

3. If a predefined policy exists for a user, that policy is merged into the HKEY_CURRENT_USER Registry subtree. The processing then moves to step 6.

4. If no predefined user policy exists, the default user policy is processed.

5. The group priority list is examined. If the user is a member of any of the global groups for which a policy exists, he is processed according to the group priority order. The priority is ordered from bottom to top of the group priority list. Each of the group policies is applied to the HKEY_CURRENT_USER Registry subtree.

6. Once the user and group policies have been processed, the machine policies are determined. If there is a predefined machine policy, that policy is merged with the HKEY_LOCAL_MACHINE Registry subtree. If there is not a predefined machine policy for the system that the user is logging in from, the default machine policy is merged with the HKEY_LOCAL_MACHINE subtree.

On a Windows NT network, Windows 98 will search for the CONFIG.POL file in the NETLOGON share by default. On a NetWare network, it will look for the file in the Public folder. There can be only one file by that name on the network, but there can be as many individual users, groups, or computers in that file as you want to specify.

Each user will be affected individually if a policy exists that has his name. (Otherwise, the settings for Default User are active for him.) User policies can also be implemented on a user-by-user basis. To create an individual user policy, select Edit | Add User. When a user logs in, CONFIG.POL will be checked to see if there is a policy for the specific user. If there isn't, the default user policy will be used for the login process.

Here are some common implementations of user profiles:

- Locking down display properties to prevent users from changing their monitors' resolution. Display properties can be locked down as a whole or on each individual property page of display properties. To adjust this setting, go to the Control Panel and select Display. Go to the Restrict Display option of the Default User properties sheet.

- Setting a default color scheme or wallpaper. This can be set in the Desktop option of the Default User properties sheet.

- If you want to restrict access to portions of the Start menu or desktop, you can do this via the Shell/Restrictions option of the Default User properties sheet.

- If you need to limit what applications can be run at a workstation, you can do so in the System/Restrictions option of the Default User properties sheet. This option can also be used to prevent the user from modifying the Registry.

- You can prevent users from mapping or disconnecting network drives by setting the options in the Windows NT Shell/Restrictions option of the Default User properties sheet.

NOTE

You can better prepare yourself for the exam by becoming familiar with the policy options available when using the System Policy Editor.

Microsoft's Zero Administration Initiative for Windows (ZAIW) is aimed at reducing the amount of time an administrator spends administering a system. This is accomplished through a strict set of system policies: By reducing what a user can do to a bare minimum, you are also reducing what you need to administer.

By reducing the amount of time administration takes, you in essence reduce your Total Cost of Ownership (TCO) for the network. This idea has gained enormous popularity in the past year, and other vendors are coming up with similar approaches—most notably, Novell with its Zero Effort NetWare (ZEN).

Establishing a System Policy

The simplest policy to implement is one using only the two icons that first appear—Default Computer and Default User. The choices they offer you are based on the *templates* they are using. Templates give the System Policy Editor its menus to present as selections. Without templates, you can't choose anything. The more templates you add, the more choices you have.

The templates are ASCII text files that have an ADM extension. Looking on the Windows 98 CD in the Tools\Reskit\NetAdmin\Poledit directory, you will find a large number of them. The two loaded by default are WINDOWS.ADM and COMMON.ADM. We will examine them here.

When you open the Default User Properties dialog box, you see two main categories, as shown in Figure 1.10.

Each of these categories opens into subcategories, and the subcategories into choices. Figure 1.11 illustrates a policy that disables the Registry editing tools (Regedit.exe) for the users.

There are three possible choices for the check boxes in a system policy:

- Checked. The action takes place.

- Unchecked. The action is reversed.

- Grayed. The action is ignored.

In Figure 1.11, Disable Registry editing tools is checked, so that action will take place (Regedit.exe will be prevented from running). Compare that to Figure 1.12.

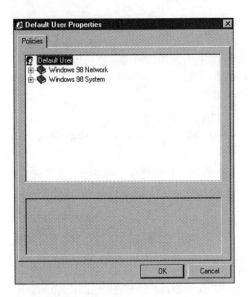

FIGURE 1.10
The two categories beneath Default User.

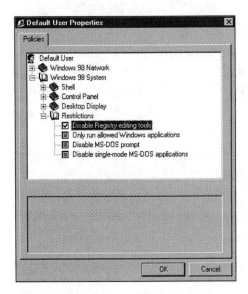

FIGURE 1.11
Disabling the Registry editing tools with a system policy.

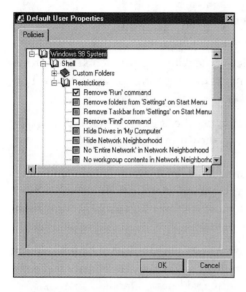

FIGURE 1.12
Three different settings are possible with the check boxes.

In Figure 1.12, Remove 'Run' command is checked, so the user won't be able to use the Run command. Remove 'Find' command is unchecked, so the user will be able to use the Find command, even if his profile had previously taken it away from him. (Think of it this way: An unchecked box gives back an option.) The other choices in Figure 1.12 are grayed. Grayed boxes ignore the action, meaning that whatever was set before (such as in the user profile) will pass through with no changes being made at the system policy.

Using Named Users

Because there is traditionally only one system policy on a network, it must be broad enough to cover all users. Whatever is configured for the default computer and default user will apply to everyone who logs on to the network. However, there must be exceptions to the rule.

For example, suppose all users on the system except the administrator should be denied the ability to use REGEDIT.EXE. Since the administrator must often troubleshoot problems, he needs access to this tool. To configure this, do the following:

1. Configure the Default User to Disable the Registry editing tools, as just discussed.

2. Add a new user to the policy by clicking the user icon on the toolbar. Give the new user the name of your administrator. Figure 1.13 shows this with the administrator being edulaney.

3. For the named user, give back the Registry editing tools by unchecking that check box, as shown in Figure 1.14.

For all users—including the named user—the defaults (user and computer) will run. After they run, the named user's profile will run. Since it is the last item to run, the settings that are set here are what the working environment for the user becomes.

You can have as many named users as you wish, all contained within the same system policy. Having too many, however, makes management difficult. Administration by groups, discussed next, simplifies matters.

Implementing Group Policies

If you need to have user settings affect multiple users, rather than using a named user policy for every user, you can implement group policies. Group policies add another level of complexity to the processing of the policies. Here are some of the additional considerations:

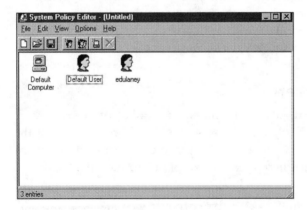

FIGURE 1.13
Adding a named user to the system policy.

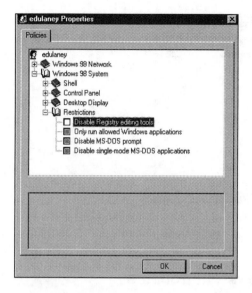

FIGURE 1.14
Giving back the Registry editing tools to the named user.

- ◆ The System Policy Editor uses global groups for group membership. Appropriate trust relationships must be implemented to see the necessary global groups.

- ◆ Because a user can belong to multiple global groups, the order in which the groups are processed is very important. One group's settings could be the opposite of another group's. You set group order by selecting Options | Group Priority.

If the policies being created apply to Windows 98 clients, you must place a copy of the GROUPPOL.DLL file in the System directory of each of the clients. In the absence of this library, group policies don't function for Windows 98 clients.

To create the group, click the group icon in the System Policy Editor (the button with more than one user) and name the group the same as what it is on the domain (or use the Browse button to access the domain and pull the name directly from there).

Figure 1.15 shows a group policy for the Sales group added into the template.

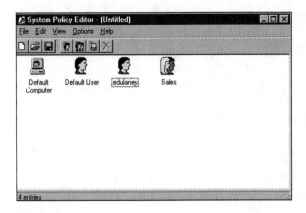

FIGURE 1.15
Adding the Sales group to the system policy.

Processing Order for System Policies

When a user logs on to a network where system policies have been implemented, these steps occur:

1. The usersuccessfully logs in to the network.

2. The user profile is read from the home directory (if configured to do so) of the authenticating NT domain controller or the user's Mail directory of the NetWare server.

3. If a predefined policy exists for a user, that policy is merged into the HKEY_CURRENT_USER Registry subtree. The processing then moves to step 6.

4. If no predefined user policy exists, the default user policy is processed.

5. The group priority list is examined. If the user is a member of any of the global groups for which a policy exists, he is processed according to the group priority order. The priority is ordered from bottom to top of the group priority list. Each of the group policies is applied to the HKEY_CURRENT_USER Registry subtree.

6. Once the user and group policies have been processed, the machine policies are determined. If there is a predefined machine policy, that policy is merged with the HKEY_LOCAL_MACHINE Registry subtree. If there is no predefined machine policy for the system that the user is logging in from, the default machine policy is merged with the HKEY_LOCAL_MACHINE subtree.

WHAT IS IMPORTANT TO KNOW

The following list summarizes the chapter and accentuates the key concepts to memorize for the exam:

- The minimum Intel-based hardware requirements for Windows 98 are a 468DX/66 processor with 16MB of RAM and at least 120MB of hard disk space.

- Windows 98 can use either FAT16 or FAT32 file systems.

- FAT16 is the old version of the File Allocation Table. It is compatible with almost every other operating system.

- FAT32 has many more features than FAT16, but it isn't compatible with Windows NT and many other operating systems. Be aware of when and how it can be used in a dual-boot situation.

- You can convert FAT16 to FAT32 without losing data, but you can't convert FAT32 to FAT16 without reformatting and possibly losing all your data if a backup hasn't been made.

- Workgroups are peer-to-peer networks that offer share-level security and that don't require a server.

- Domains are networks built around a server. They offer user-level security.

- User-level security must be used when utilizing a NetWare server for authentication.

- File and Printer Sharing allows you to share resources with other users.

- File and Printer Sharing is not installed on a Windows 98 client by default.

- File and Printer Sharing doesn't allow you to share individual files, but it does allow you to share folders.

- User profiles are stored in USER.DAT files. They hold the configuration information for each user.

- If the ability to save settings is turned on, each user will have his own USER.DAT file.

- The USER.DAT file can be stored locally or on the server, wherein it is called a roaming profile. On a Windows NT server, the user profile is stored in the home directory (if configured to do so). On a NetWare server, it is stored in the user's Mail directory.

- System policies are restrictions held within a CONFIG.POL file that prevent users from being able to perform certain actions.

- By default, there should be only one system policy on the network for all users, but it can contain as many computers, users, or groups as you want to include.

- The group portion of a system policy doesn't work for Windows 98 users unless the grouppol.dll file has been installed on the machine.

- The System Policy Editor needs templates in order to have choices to present to you. Templates are ASCII text files that have an .ADM extension.

- The two templates loaded into the System Policy Editor by default are COMMON.ADM and WINDOWS.ADM. This differs from Windows 95, where it was ADMIN.ADM.

- By default, system policies should be stored on the Windows NT Netlogon share. On a NetWare server, they should be stored in the Public directory.

▶ Install Windows 98. Installation options include the following:
- Automated Windows setup
- New
- Upgrade
- Uninstall
- Dual-boot combination with Microsoft Windows NT 4.0

▶ Configure Windows 98 server components. Server components include the following:
- Microsoft Personal Web Server 4.0
- Dial-Up Networking server

▶ Install and configure the network components of Windows 98 in a Microsoft environment or a mixed Microsoft and NetWare environment. Network components include the following:
- Client for Microsoft Networks
- Client for NetWare Networks
- Network adapters
- File and Printer Sharing for Microsoft Networks
- File and Printer Sharing for NetWare Networks
- Service for NetWare Directory Services (NDS)
- Asynchronous Transfer Mode (ATM)
- Virtual Private Networking (VPN) and PPTP
- Browse Master

▶ continues...

CHAPTER *2*

Installation and Configuration

OBJECTIVES continued

▶ Install and configure network protocols in a Microsoft environment or a mixed Microsoft and NetWare environment. Protocols include the following:
- NetBEUI
- IPX/SPX-compatible
- TCP/IP
- Microsoft DLC
- Fast Infrared

▶ Install and configure hardware devices in a Microsoft environment and a mixed Microsoft and NetWare environment. Hardware devices include the following:
- Modems
- Printers
- Universal Serial Bus (USB)
- Multiple display support
- IEEE 1394 FireWire
- Infrared Data Association (IrDA)
- Multilink
- Power management scheme

▶ Install and configure the Backup application.

INSTALLING WINDOWS 98

For the exam, you should concentrate on five key areas of (un)installation:

- Upgrade

- New

- Automated Windows setup

- Dual-boot combination with Microsoft Windows NT

- Uninstall

Each of these five areas is addressed in the following sections.

Upgrades

You can upgrade to Windows 98 in one of two ways:

- Upgrade from Windows 95

- Upgrade from Windows 3.x

Notice that you can't upgrade from Windows NT. You can migrate from it, but since Windows 98 is considered a lesser operating system than Windows NT, you can't *upgrade* from it. For example, Windows NT by default installs into the WINNT directory. Windows 98, however, installs into the WINDOWS directory by default. You can modify or change the default directory of your Windows 98 installation to reflect Windows NT. By pursuing this approach, your installation of Windows 98 will overwrite the files necessary for Windows NT to execute. It *will not* perform an *upgrade*. Instead, you will lose the ability to boot up Windows NT completely. The programs that were accessible through Windows NT will not automatically be accessible through the new installation of Windows 98.

The process of *migrating* from Windows NT to Windows 98 is the same as was the case with migrating from Windows NT to Windows 95. You must first install Windows 98 into a directory other than Windows NT. Once the operating system is installed, you can proceed by installing all your programs again through Windows 98. The term *migrating* is a little less than forthright in its meaning. In reality, you are performing a new installation of Windows 98, coupled with reinstalling all your software. This is also the first stage in creating a system that dual boots both Windows 98 and Windows NT. We will explore dual-booting issues later in this chapter.

NOTE

For the exam, keep in mind that an upgrade from Windows NT to Windows 98 is *not* possible. You are required to install Windows 98 in its own directory and then reinstall all your programs through your new installation of Windows 98.

Windows 95

At A Glance: Setup Screens

Order	Screen
1	Windows 98 Setup
2	License Agreement
3	Checking Your System
4	Internet Channels
5	Emergency Startup Disk
6	Start Copying Files
7	Restart

The simplest installation of all is an upgrade from Windows 95 to Windows 98. In so doing, Windows 98 replaces the operating system components of Windows 95, where applicable, and reuses the configuration information about the applets and installed programs. Most of the information about user name, registered organization, and so on is used, thus keeping the amount of information you must supply to a minimum.

You will be asked if you want to create a backup copy of Windows 95 in case you need to revert to it. If you choose Yes, an uninstallation file named WINUNDO.DAT is created. It consumes approximately 50MB of hard drive space.

NOTE

For the exam, it is important to note that if you select Yes and create a backup of Windows 95, you will have an option inside Control Panel, Add/Remove Programs, to uninstall Windows 98. However, if you select No, the option to uninstall Windows 98 will not be available.

The following steps make up the Windows 98 upgrade installation procedure:

1. Choose Start | Run and type *drive:* **setup**, where *drive* is the letter of the upgrade medium's drive.

> **NOTE**
>
> To upgrade your Windows 95 client and retain your computer's configuration settings, it is recommended that you run SETUP.EXE from the Windows 95 user interface. However, if you want to upgrade Windows 98 on a Windows 95 client machine but want to change the current settings, you must run SETUP.EXE from a DOS prompt. This doesn't include an MS-DOS window from within Windows 95.

2. The Windows 98 setup screen appears. Click Continue.

> **NOTE**
>
> In order to speed up the upgrade/installation process, Windows 98 skips the steps that were performed during the installation of Windows 95. These steps include performing full hardware detection, allowing you to choose the setup option (Custom, Typical, Portable, or Compact), and configuring the hardware.

3. Windows 98 performs five steps during the upgrade/installation procedure:

Step 1 consists of preparing to run Windows 98 Setup.

Step 2 is collecting information about your computer.

Step 3 is copying Windows 98 files to your computer.

Step 4 is restarting your computer.

Step 5 is setting up hardware and finalizing settings.

4. Click Continue to begin Step 1. During the first step, your system is checked, and the Setup Wizard is prepared. While your system is checked, a SETUPLOG.TXT file is created in the root of the boot partition (usually drive C:). It then checks for anti-virus software. If anti-virus software is detected, there is an increased chance that the setup process might stop or fail altogether. Setup then records the process in the SETUPLOG.TXT file. If the setup process stops or fails, SUWARN.BAT is executed the next time the system reboots, and a message is displayed, explaining a possible reason why.

5. The setup process starts the Windows 98 Setup Wizard to help guide you through the additional installation procedures. Click Continue. This will create a temporary directory named \WININST0.400 and copy the MINI.CAB file into the directory. The MINI.CAB file contains all the Windows 98 miniprogram files. It then extracts all the files found inside PRECOPY1.CAB and PRECOPY2.CAB and copies them to the newly created \WININST0.400 temporary directory.

6. Click Continue to begin Step 2. During the second step, the Windows 98 installation procedure begins collecting information about your computer. This step also prompts the user for input.

7. The End User License Agreement appears. To continue, click the radio button next to I agree and click Next.

8. You are prompted for your CD-Key, located on the back of your Windows 98 CD cover. Type in your CD-Key and click Next to continue.

9. ScanDisk is run.

10. The Setup program checks the Registry to make sure it hasn't been corrupted.

11. You are prompted for a Windows directory. To upgrade, you must install Windows 98 in the same directory in which Windows 95 was installed. Click Next to continue. You are informed that the Windows 98 Setup program is preparing your Windows directory.

12. During an upgrade, you are given the option of saving your previous version of Windows 95, just in case you need to uninstall Windows 98. It is recommended that you select Yes to save the files. This will require approximately 50MB of additional hard disk space. If you select Yes, two files, WINUNDO.DAT and WINUNDO.INI, are created.

13. The Region Settings dialog box appears, allowing you to select your region and time zone. Click Next to continue.

14. Setup prompts you to create a startup disk. This disk is very useful in troubleshooting any startup issues you might come across. The disk itself is a bootable system disk that contains real-mode Windows 98 commands and utilities, allowing you to restart your computer in time of need. To create the startup disk, place a 1.2 or 1.44 floppy disk into drive A: and click Next to continue. Click OK to create the disk.

15. Upon completion of the startup disk, Setup prompts you to click Next to begin the copying of files.

16. Step 3 begins. No user input is required during this phase. In fact, it might take a little while, so Windows 98 suggests that you sit back and relax.

17. Step 4 begins with a prompt to restart your computer once the Windows 98 files have finished copying to your system. Click the Restart Now button to immediately restart your system. Fifteen seconds will pass before the system will automatically reboot. As soon as the system reboots, you see the message `Getting ready to start Windows 98 for the first time`. While this message appears, Setup is modifying the WIN.INI, SYSTEM.INI, and Registry files to include configuration settings for Windows 98. The AUTOEXEC.BAT and CONFIG.SYS files are examined to eliminate any incompatible device drivers and/or TSR programs.

18. Step 5 begins after your computer starts under Windows 98 for the first time. It begins with the Hardware Detection phase and continues with the configuration of Control Panel, programs on the Start menu, the Windows 98 Help option, all MS-DOS program settings, tuning up application start, time zone, and the system itself.

19. After this phase, Windows 98 displays the Welcome to Windows 98 dialog box.

Before you start the upgrade, close all other applications to prevent the possibility of a conflict. Insert the medium containing Windows 98 into the system. If it is a CD, AutoRun should bring up the initial screen. If it doesn't, you can use Explorer to find the SETUP.EXE file and start it.

After the initial screen, the license agreement appears. You must agree to it. Once you do so, a Checking Your System screen appears. At this point, the existing Registry is read to identify all the installed components. The Setup routine won't give you the choice of installing additional components (or choosing not to install or reinstall the ones you already have). It assumes that you want the same components installed in Windows 98 that you had in Windows 95. If this is not the case, you can make changes after the upgrade using the Add/Remove Programs applet in the Control Panel.

The Setup routine next checks the amount of free space you have and the directory in which Windows 95 is installed (into which it will write). The Internet Channels screen appears to let you download information to your desktop. Next, a screen prompting you to make an Emergency Startup Disk appears.

The Emergency Startup Disk must be a floppy, as opposed to a ZIP or something else. It becomes your lifesaver in the event of a system failure. It contains the basic utilities needed to boot the system and troubleshoot problems related to boot failures.

After the Emergency Startup Disk is made, the next screen to appear is Start Copying Files. This is the longest part of the process (up to an hour), during which files are copied from the medium to the hard drive.

As a last step, you must restart the system. During the boot process, the configuration files are updated.

Windows 3.x

When you upgrade from Windows 3.x to Windows 98, settings in PROTOCOL.INI, SYSTEM.INI, and WIN.INI are used to create the Windows 98 Registry. Items in Program Manager become the folders in Windows 98, and migration is the default action. (If you don't want to migrate, but would rather dual boot, you must reinstall all your applications under Windows 98.) The process of dual booting Windows 3.x to Windows 98 is almost the same as with Windows NT. You must first install Windows 98 into a directory other than Windows 3.x. Once the operating system is installed, you can proceed by installing all your programs again through Windows 98.

To perform the migration, follow these steps:

1. In Program Manager, choose File | Run. Type *drive*:\setup, where *drive* is the letter of the upgrade medium's drive. Although you can exit Windows and run Setup from a DOS prompt (see the section "Installing Over DOS"), you can't run the Setup program from a DOS window.

2. The migration asks you to specify an installation type: Typical, Custom, Portable, or Compact.

3. The migration steps continue as outlined in the upgrade from Windows 95 to Windows 98 (see the preceding section).

> **N O T E**
>
> For the exam, keep in mind that in *any* dual-boot scenario, you are required to install Windows 98 in its own directory and then reinstall all your programs through your new installation of Windows 98.

Performing a New Installation

A new installation of Windows 98 implies that you are placing it on an empty partition (a freshly formatted hard drive), or over an operating system that can't (or shouldn't) be upgraded. You can do the following:

- Install over DOS
- Migrate from Windows NT
- Install over OS/2

The Windows 98 CD contains an AUTORUN.INF file that allows the Setup routine to begin once the CD is inserted into the system if the system currently recognizes AutoRun.

Installing Over DOS

The slowest installation of all, you can install over DOS if you don't currently have a graphical operating system on your machine. The primary reason why this is so slow is that an extra step is added: Windows 98 installs a miniature Windows environment on your system (16-bit) that it can use to perform the installation.

Access the Setup program from the medium (CD-ROM), and the Installation Wizard will begin. You must first choose the installation type (Typical, Custom, Portable, or Compact). The next steps are as follows:

Order	Screen
1	Windows 98 Setup
2	License Agreement
3	Registration Key
4	Installation Directory
5	Setup Options
6	User Information
7	Windows Components
8	Computer Name/Workgroup
9	Emergency Startup Disk
10	Start Copying Files
11	Restart
12	Setting Up Hardware and Finalizing Settings
13	Time Zone

NOTE

To install Windows 98 on a *new* hard drive (freshly formatted), create a DOS boot disk with the SYS, FDISK, and FORMAT utilities. Include the drivers necessary to access the CD-ROM. Boot under the boot disk, partition the hard drive, format it as bootable (FORMAT /S), and then continue with the installation as you would from a DOS machine.

As you just saw, installing over DOS results in quite a few more setup screens prompting user input. Later we will discuss the procedures, tools, and files necessary to automate the installation of Windows 98.

> **NOTE** For the exam, you must know that Batch 98 is the utility used to automate the installation of Windows 98. We will discuss Batch 98 in more detail in the section "Automated Setup."

Migrating from Windows NT

With Windows NT installed on a machine, you have two choices:

- Migrate from it
- Dual boot Windows 98 with it

As I mentioned earlier, you can't choose to upgrade to Windows 98 because Windows NT is considered a superior operating system.

If you elect to dual boot, you must be running FAT16 as the file system, not NTFS, because Windows 98 doesn't understand NTFS. Conversely, if you have Windows 98 on a machine and then decide to add Windows NT, you must be running FAT16 and not FAT32, because Windows NT 4.0 doesn't understand FAT32. The common file system that both operating systems share—and must use—is FAT16.

Remember our example from Chapter 1, "Planning"? We started with one computer that has two hard disk drives and partitioned each as its own drive. If we installed Windows 98 on drive C running FAT16 and installed Windows NT on drive D running FAT16, each operating system could see both drives. However, if we converted drive D (Windows NT) to NTFS, Windows 98 would no longer be able to view the contents of drive D. The same would hold true if we were to use the Windows 98 Drive Converter to convert drive C to FAT32. Windows NT would no longer be able to view the contents of drive C.

> **NOTE** FDISK can be used to create different partitions. Once established, they can be formatted independently. In a dual-boot environment, partitions formatted with NTFS would be visible only when Windows NT was the operating system running. Partitions formatted with FAT32 would be visible only when Windows 98 was running. Partitions formatted with FAT16 would be visible by both operating systems.

To install Windows 98 over an existing Windows NT installation, boot into DOS (to disable the boot option) and run the Windows 98 Setup executable file. If you want to create a dual-boot environment, simply execute the Setup program from within Windows NT. As I mentioned, there is no such *upgrade* for Windows NT. The process of migrating from Windows NT to Windows 98 is the same as migrating from Windows NT to Windows 95. You must first install Windows 98 into a directory other than Windows NT. Once the operating system is installed, you can proceed by you installing all your programs again through Windows 98. After you have reinstalled all your software in the new Windows 98 environment, you can delete Windows NT to complete your migration.

Regardless of which action you perform, you must reinstall all applications, because each operating system's Registry is incompatible with the other.

Dual booting is discussed more later.

Installing Over OS/2

To install over OS/2, boot the machine to a DOS prompt (an option on the Boot Manager if you're running FAT, or from OS/2 Disk 1 if you're running HPFS). Run the Setup executable file from the Windows 98 medium.

If you were using Boot Manager, Windows 98 disables it after its installation. To bring it back, you must follow these steps in Windows 98:

1. Select Start | Run and type **FDISK**.

2. Choose Set Active Partition (option 2).

3. Select No MS-DOS partition (always 1MB in size).

4. Exit FDISK and restart the computer.

Automated Setup

At A Glance: Batch 98 Options

Configuration Option	*Description*
Product ID [Setup] ProductKey="*MyProductID*"	This is the CD-Key found on the back of the Windows 98 CD-ROM Cover.

Configuration Option	*Description*
Installation Directory [Setup] InstallDir="*MyWin98Dir*"	This is the directory designated for the installation of Windows 98. If you are performing an upgrade of Windows 3.x or Windows 95, the default directory is the current Windows installation directory.
Do not show installation directory warning [Setup] NoDirWarn=1 (check box selected)	By selecting this setting, you can effectively hide the installation directory warning dialog box.
NoDirWarn=0 (check box cleared)	This is a popular option when upgrading from a Windows 3.x or Windows 95 platform. By clearing the check box, you will cause the installation procedure to display the installation directory warning dialog box.
Do not create uninstall information [Setup] Uninstall=0	This option will require the installation procedure to bypass the creation of the backup files when upgrading to Windows 98. This will eliminate the option to uninstall Windows 98 in the future.
Automatically create uninstall information [Setup] Uninstall=1	This option will require the installation procedure to automatically create backup files when upgrading to Windows 98. This will ensure the option to uninstall Windows 98 in the future.

Many network administrators have faced the challenge of upgrading multiple machines in a very short period of time. Automating the installation of Windows 98 eliminates the need for user interaction and helps standardize the configuration of Windows 98 across the entire network. By automating, you also reduce the amount of time and hours spent installing or upgrading Windows 98 on multiple machines.

The first step in automating the Windows 98 installation process is deciding whether to execute a *push* installation or a *pull* installation. A push installation gives the administrator a bit more control. It is accomplished using a network management software program such as Microsoft Systems Management Server (SMS). Designing a push installation is outside the scope of this book.

Let's examine the process of a pull installation. To begin with, the user performs the upgrade. To control user input, an administrator must complete three steps:

1. Create an automated setup script using the configuration settings appropriate for the network.

2. Copy the Windows 98 source files to a centrally accessible share.

3. Activate the installation through a logon script, or create a system policy that is configured to run the setup script.

The NETSETUP.EXE utility, which was included with Windows 95 for installing over the network, is not included with Windows 98. Replacing it is Batch 98—a batch file program that helps you install across a network.

Batch 98 can be used to create an INF file on one machine to transfer that installation to another. The Registry of the first machine is used to create the INF file. It collects data such as the time zone, installed printers, installed components, security, current machine, location of the operating system, and so on. This is the same data you're prompted for during a new installation of Windows 98.

To view the different option settings in Batch 98, you must first install Batch 98. Batch 98 is part of the Windows 98 Resource Kit Tools Sampler included on the Windows 98 installation CD. To begin the installation, do the following:

1. Select Start | Run.

2. Locate your CD-ROM, go to the Tools\Reskit folder, and run SETUP.EXE.

3. This will begin the installation of the Windows 98 Resource Kit Tools Sampler. Select a directory to continue, as shown in Figure 2.1.

4. Click the Install button.

5. After it's installed, you can access Batch 98 by selecting Start | Programs | Windows 98 Resource Kit | Tools Management Console. This will open the Microsoft Management Console, as shown in Figure 2.2.

FIGURE 2.1
The Windows 98 Resource Kit Tools Sampler.

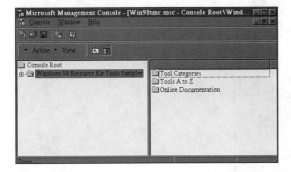

FIGURE 2.2
Microsoft Management Console.

You can customize the INF file using Batch 98 with a unique product ID number, registered owner, organization, IP address, subnet mask, and so on. Figure 2.3 shows the different elements you can configure using Batch 98.

Several components defined inside Batch 98 help you roll out the installation of Windows 98 in large and small organizations. The first step in creating an INF file is to click the Gather now button.

This will gather the information found in the Registry of the system that is running Batch 98. Next, click the General Setup Options button. As shown in Figure 2.4, this is where you can define components and information such as the installation directory or the available desktop icons. You can even define what setup prompts should be executed for user input.

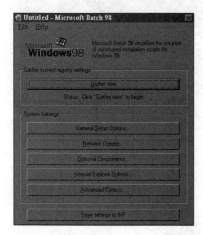

FIGURE 2.3
Microsoft Batch 98.

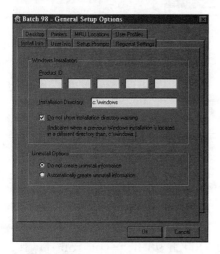

FIGURE 2.4
General setup options.

The next button on the list is Network Options. As shown in Figure 2.5, you can modify protocols, services, clients, access control, and additional clients such as Novell and Banyan VINES.

Three additional buttons let you configure programs such as Internet Explorer and Personal Web Server. All of these features make Batch 98 quite a powerful tool for implementing Windows 98 throughout a LAN/WAN environment. When you have configured the file as you want it, click the Save settings to INF button. The default name for the INF file is MSBATCH.INF.

To create a custom script with the Batch 98 utility, follow these steps:

1. Select a standard computer from within your network and install Windows 98. (See the earlier section "Windows 95" for installation instructions.) You should use a company standard configuration to set up your script.

2. Start the Batch 98 utility by selecting Start | Programs | Windows 98 Resource Kit | Tools Management Console.

3. This will activate the Microsoft Management Console (MMC). Look up the Batch 98 utility, located in the Bs, and click it to activate the Batch 98 utility.

4. The Microsoft Batch 98 utility appears with several options. Click Gather now. This will retrieve the Registry information from the current system.

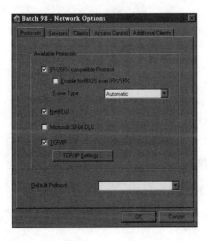

FIGURE 2.5
Network options.

5. Customize your script by selecting the variable components.

6. After you have modified all the configuration settings, click the Save settings to INF button to save your settings (the default file-name is MSBATCH.INF).

7. Once the script file is complete, save it to the network share containing the Windows 98 source files. Create or modify the logon scripts to execute the Windows 98 SETUP.EXE program, and reference the newly created script file. If all options for user input have been configured in the script file, no additional user input is necessary to complete the Windows 98 installation.

Using this tool is a wonderful advantage for administrators who are continually challenged with administrative tasks. Microsoft's Zero Administration Initiative for Windows (ZAIW) includes tools such as Batch 98 to help administrators become as efficient as possible.

ZAIW is being)developed by Microsoft to establish a management infrastructure for the Microsoft Windows environment. ZAIW is currently in development with some technology, like Batch 98, already available. Many other components are part of the ongoing evolution of ZAIW—including Windows Management Instrumentation (WMI), Web-based Enterprise Management (WBEM), and management tools such as Systems Management Server and Microsoft Management Console.

Additional information can be found on Microsoft's Web site at `http://www.microsoft.com/management`.

The final step is to use the newly configured INF file. To do so, you must invoke the SETUP command:

```
SETUP drive:\name of inf file
```

Here's an example:

```
SETUP Z:\MSBATCH.INF
```

> **NOTE**
>
> For the exam, you must be comfortable with the concept and configuration of options provided by Batch 98.

Dual Booting with Windows NT

Dual booting between Windows 98 and Windows NT is possible whenever the operating systems are installed in different directories. For example, the default operating system directory for Windows 98 is C:\WINDOWS. If you install Windows NT in that directory, you will overwrite key files that Windows 98 needs and will have only one usable operating system (Windows NT). If you install Windows NT in its default directory (C:\Winnt), you will have two usable operating systems and can choose which one you want to boot into at the beginning of each session.

> **NOTE**   For the exam, it's good to know that the only way to dual boot Windows 98 with Windows NT is to format the boot drive as FAT16, coupled with installing both operating systems in their own directories.

When Windows NT is installed in its own directory on a machine that already contains Windows 98, it creates a dual-boot machine by default. It does this by creating a file, BOOT.INI, in the root directory that lets the user choose which operating system he wants to use.

On Intel-based computers, you can install Windows NT over Windows 98, Windows 95, or MS-DOS. The boot loader screen offers the user a choice of Windows NT Server/Workstation 4, Microsoft Windows, or MS-DOS. If the user chooses a non–Windows NT operating system, a file called BOOTSECT.DOS is loaded and executed. BOOTSECT.DOS is a hidden, system, read-only file in the root of the system partition. It contains the information that was present in the boot sector before Windows NT was installed. If a user chooses Windows 95 from the boot menu, for example, BOOTSECT.DOS loads IO.SYS and passes control to it.

Because not all machines use MS-DOS–style paths (such as C:\Winnt) to refer to locations on a hard drive, Windows NT uses a cross-platform standard format called Advanced RISC Computer (ARC) within BOOT.INI. An ARC-compliant path consists of four parameters:

- `scsi(x)` or `multi(x)` identifies the hardware adapter.
- `disk(y)` is the SCSI bus number. It's always `0` if `multi`.

◆ rdisk(z) is the physical drive number for multi. It's ignored for SCSI.

◆ partition(a) is the logical partition number.

The first three parameters are zero-based. In other words, the first physical IDE drive is rdisk(0), and the second is rdisk(1). The partition parameter, however, is 1-based, so the first partition on the drive is rdisk(0) partition(1).

All the parameters—even the ones that are ignored—must be present in the path. For instance, multi(0)disk(0)rdisk(0)partition(1) is a valid path even though disk(0) is essentially unnecessary. multi(0)rdisk(0) partition(1) is not valid.

The first parameter is almost always multi, even for a SCSI controller. The only time you even see SCSI in a BOOT.INI file is if the BIOS on the controller is turned off. If this is the case, don't worry. An additional hidden, system, read-only file, NTBOOTDD.SYS, is present in the root of the system partition. NTBOOTDD.SYS is a device driver necessary for accessing a SCSI controller that doesn't have an on-board BIOS or that doesn't use INT 13 to identify hard disks.

To make a long story short, if you install Windows NT on a machine that already has Windows 98, dual booting is the default, and the BOOT.INI menu lets you choose which operating system you want to use. If you install Windows 98 on a machine that has Windows NT, the BOOT.INI file is already there, and you must edit it manually, adding the entry to let Windows 98 be a menu choice.

Uninstalling

If you're dual booting Windows 98 and another operating system (such as Windows 3.x), create a startup disk for the other operating system before you uninstall Windows 98. If MS-DOS, Windows 3.x, or Windows 95 doesn't boot properly after you remove Windows 98, boot to the startup disk and type **SYS C:** to reinstall your basic operating system files onto the hard drive.

If you're dual booting with Windows NT and you uninstall Windows 98, operations won't be affected, because the NT Boot Loader will still boot first and allow the boot to continue.

During the upgrade installation of Windows 98 over Windows 95, you will be asked if you want to create a backup copy of Windows 95 in case you need to revert to it. If you choose Yes, you will have the option of uninstalling Windows 98. If you choose No, it will be a one-way installation, and you won't have the option of uninstalling Windows 98. You uninstall Windows 98 by choosing the Uninstall Windows 98 option in the Add/Remove Programs dialog box. This will take you back to the operating system you had before.

> **NOTE**
>
> For the exam, keep in mind that the only time you have the option of uninstalling Windows 98 inside Control Panel's Add/Remove Programs applet is through an upgrade. This option isn't available with a new installation or a dual-boot Windows NT installation.

CONFIGURING WINDOWS 98 SERVER COMPONENTS

A subset of Microsoft's Internet Information Server (which runs on Windows NT Server) is available for Windows 98, where it is known as Personal Web Server. Here are several factors you should be aware of:

- Personal Web Server doesn't support controlling access by IP address. This effectively prevents it from being used as an Internet server, where security is a concern.

- Personal Web Server doesn't support virtual servers. This means that it can't be used to host more than one Web site.

- Personal Web Server can't log access to an ODBC datasource. This makes it harder to get statistical numbers on utilization.

- Personal Web Server can't limit the amount of network bandwidth used.

- Personal Web Server has a 40-bit key encryption as opposed to the 40-bit or 128-bit security of IIS. 128-bit security is available only in the U.S. and Canada.

- Personal Web Server can't scale by using multiple threads across more than one CPU.

The design goal, above all else, was for PWS to be easy to set up and administer. Installing PWS is quite simple. The SETUP.EXE file can be found on the Windows 98 CD, in the pws folder located under add-ons.

After PWS is installed, you have the ability to create and develop Web sites locally. Double-clicking the PWS icon on the task bar activates the administration of your Personal Web Server. The new design lends itself to easy management coupled with varying controls, as shown in Figure 2.6.

Personal Web Manager has five main areas: Main, Publish, Web Site, Tour, and Advanced. Each option provides special maintenance and administrative abilities, ranging from creating a home page to creating a virtual directory.

NOTE

For the exam, it is important to know the varying logs and logging capabilities of PWS.

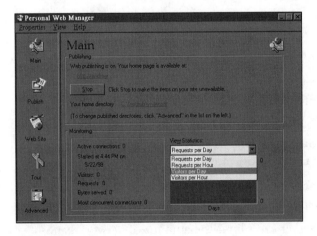

FIGURE 2.6

Personal Web Manager.

A Dial-Up Networking server is another option for a Windows 98 service. This service allows remote users to access your Windows 98 machine as if dialing into a server. They can connect to the workstation and are granted access to the files there, and on into the network if you so desire.

This feature is extremely useful for people who telecommute and need to gain access to their machines from home. If this option wasn't selected during the initial installation, you can install later using the following steps:

1. Select Start | Settings | Control Panel.

2. Select Add/Remove Programs, and click the Windows Setup tab.

3. Select the Communications option and then click the Details button. You see the dialog box shown in Figure 2.7.

4. Select Dial-Up Server.

5. Click OK twice. Point to the Windows 98 installation files if prompted.

6. Reboot.

Upon completion of Dial-Up Server, you have virtually turned your Windows 98 system into a Remote Access Server (RAS). This will allow you to contact your Windows 98 machine from another Windows machine via Dial-Up Networking.

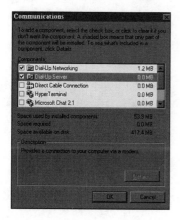

FIGURE 2.7
The Communications dialog box.

To set up Dial-Up Server, open My Computer and double-click the Dial-Up Networking icon. Select Connections | Dial-Up Server, as shown in Figure 2.8. You see the dialog box shown in Figure 2.9.

You can configure your new Dial-Up Server to not allow caller access, or you can allow caller access based on password protection.

NOTE
Dial-Up Server is covered somewhat on the exam. You should be comfortable with its components and management options.

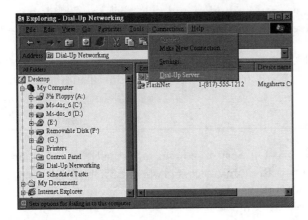

FIGURE 2.8
Dial-Up Networking's Connections menu.

FIGURE 2.9
The Dial-Up Server dialog box.

Dial-Up Networking is the same in Windows 98 as it was in Windows 95. Dial-Up Networking allows a Windows 98 machine to connect to a Windows NT RAS server, a Windows 98 client running Dial-Up Server, or the Internet.

> **NOTE** On the exam, Dial-Up Networking appears in several scenarios. You should be comfortable with the different uses of Dial-Up Networking, as well as Windows NT RAS services.

INSTALLING AND CONFIGURING NETWORK COMPONENTS

Chapter 4, "Integration and Interoperability," delves into the networking aspects of Windows 98 in a Microsoft environment and a mixed Microsoft and NetWare environment. For this portion of the exam, you should know the following:

- Networking)requires network adapters (cards) and cables.

- Client for Microsoft Networks is the service needed to communicate with Windows-based networks, or workgroups, not to exclude DOS with MS Client. If the Windows 98 machine will be sharing resources (not just accessing them), File and Printer Sharing for Microsoft Networks must be installed.

- Client for NetWare Networks is the service required for Windows 98 to be a client on a NetWare-based network. If the Windows 98 machine will be sharing resources (not just accessing them), File and Printer Sharing for NetWare Networks must be installed. Service for NetWare Directory Services (NDS) is used for NetWare 4.x and greater networks, which use NDS (the opposite of which is the Bindery, which was used by NetWare 3.x and lower).

- Changes were made in Windows 98 to NDIS (Network Driver Interface Specification) to include support for ATM (Asynchronous Transfer Mode). NDIS 5 is a vast improvement over NDIS 3.1.

It includes support for FDDI (Fiber Distributed Data Interface), power management, and WAN technology such as VPN (Virtual Private Networking) and PPTP (Point-to-Point Tunneling Protocol).

◆ Browsing and browse lists allow network resources to be compiled into a usable format and presented to users uniformly.

Universal Naming Convention (UNC)

Microsoft's Universal Naming Convention (UNC) is a standardized nomenclature for specifying a share name on a particular computer. The NetBIOS computer name is limited to 15 characters, and the share name also is usually limited to 15 characters. Share names can be given to a print queue or a shared directory of files.

The UNC uniquely specifies the path to the share name on a network. The UNC path takes the form of *computer_name**share_name* [*optional path*]. For example, the UNC path of the printer share that LaserJet created on the server called Server1 would be \\Server1\LaserJet.

NOTE A UNC name doesn't require a drive-letter assignment. Windows 98 takes full advantage of network connectivity using UNC names so that you can connect to a remote directory or printer share without having to map a drive letter to it.

The UNC can also specify the full path to a file in a subdirectory of a file share. For example, a file named DIRECTIONS.TXT located in the Sample folder on a computer named Simon is represented as \\Simon\Sample\DIRECTIONS.TXT.

All Windows 98 functions support using a UNC name, including the Run option on the Start menu and the command prompt. NetWare servers, like Windows NT servers, can be accessed through a UNC name. Instead of using a share name, substitute a volume name to access a NetWare server.

Installing Client for Microsoft Networks

These steps will guide you through installing the Client for Microsoft Networks and will let you connect to a Windows NT domain:

1. Select Start | Settings | Control Panel. Choose the Network icon to display the Network window.

2. Click the Add button. This will open the Select Network Component Type dialog box.

3. Select Client, and click the Add button.

4. In the Manufacturers list, select Microsoft. From the list of Network Clients, select Client for Microsoft Networks.

5. Click OK. Client for Microsoft Networks is added to your installed network components. When you click OK on the Network properties sheet, the system gets updated. You might be prompted for the location of required files.

6. Restart Windows 98.

Installing Client for NetWare Networks

These steps will aid you in installing the Client for NetWare Networks, allowing you to connect to a NetWare 3.x or 4.x server running Bindery emulation:

1. Select Start | Settings | Control Panel. Choose the Network icon to display the Network window.

2. Click the Add button. This will open the Select Network Component Type dialog box.

3. Select Client, and click the Add button.

4. In the Manufacturers list, select Microsoft. From the list of Network Clients, select Client for NetWare Networks.

5. Click OK. Client for NetWare Networks is added to your installed network components. When you click OK on the Network properties sheet, the system gets updated. You might be prompted for the location of required files.

6. Restart Windows 98.

Installing File and Printer Sharing for Microsoft Networks

These steps will guide you through installing File and Printer Sharing for Microsoft Networks. This service will enable the Windows 98 server service and let you share resources with Windows clients:

1. In Windows 98, select Start | Settings.

2. Click the Network icon in Control Panel.

3. The Network properties dialog box appears. Click the Add button.

4. Select Services, and click Add.

5. You see the Select Network Services dialog box. From here you can select File and Printer Sharing for Microsoft Networks.

6. Click OK twice, and reboot when prompted.

File and Printer Sharing for NetWare Networks

File and Printer Sharing for NetWare Networks allows directories and printers to be shared with other NetWare users. There are two very important points to keep in mind when considering using File and Printer Sharing for NetWare Networks:

- You can't have File and Printer Sharing for NetWare Networks and File and Printer Sharing for Microsoft Networks installed simultaneously. Only one can be configured on a particular Windows 98 workstation.

- File and Printer Sharing for NetWare Networks must use the user-level security model. The account list must be on a NetWare server Bindery or in the Bindery context of a NetWare 4.x server using Bindery emulation.

User-level security with NetWare networks is similar to user-level security for Microsoft networks. A server is queried whenever a shared resource access is attempted. The username or group membership must be on the NetWare server's account list and must have the necessary rights in order to gain access to the resource.

Windows 98 doesn't normally make a distinction between Microsoft shares and Novell volumes. Both appear as directories (also called folders) on the network to a Windows 98 computer.

You can use the net command from a DOS prompt to control connections to either type of network resource using either Microsoft networking UNC paths or NetWare *server/volume* paths. This could be useful in the creation of batch files or login scripts. At the DOS prompt, type **net /?** for a listing of net commands.

Windows 98's ability to use multiple network providers allows Windows 98 workstations to be integrated into mixed NetWare and Windows NT networks.

Installing File and Printer Sharing for NetWare Networks

These steps will guide you through installing File and Printer Sharing for NetWare Networks. This service will enable the Windows 98 server service and let you share resources with NetWare clients.

1. In Windows 98, select Start | Settings.

2. Click the Network icon in Control Panel.

3. The Network properties dialog box appears. Click the Add button.

4. Select Services, and click Add.

5. You see the Select Network Services dialog box. From here you can select File and Printer Sharing for NetWare Networks.

6. Click OK twice, and reboot when prompted.

Installing Service for NetWare Directory Services

These steps will guide you through installing the Service for NetWare Directory Services, allowing you to connect to a NetWare 4.x server utilizing NetWare Directory Services:

1. Select Start | Settings | Control Panel. Select the Network icon to display the Network dialog box.

2. Click the Add button. This will open the Select Network Component Type dialog box.

3. Select Service, and click the Add button.

4. In the Manufacturers list, select Microsoft. From the list of Network Clients, select Service for NetWare Directory Services.

5. Click OK. Service for NetWare Directory Services is added to your installed network components. When you click OK on the Network properties sheet, the system gets updated. You might be prompted for the location of required files.

6. Restart Windows 98.

The options on the sheetDirectory Services properties sheet are described in the following list:

- Preferred tree is the NDS tree where the user will want to access shared resources.

- Workstation default context is the default context where the user's NDS user object can be found.

N O T E

This service can be configured only on Windows 98 workstations that *already* have the IPX/SPX-compatible protocol and the Client for NetWare Networks installed.

Browsing Services

The Windows 98 browsing service allows reduction of network traffic by maintaining a central list of all active servers in a workgroup. This list is kept current by having all active servers send a status message to a single computer, the master browser, on a regular basis. The master browser server updates the list as servers join and leave the local network section.

In a Windows NT network, the Primary Domain Controller (PDC) serves as the domain master browser, collecting browse lists from the local master browsers. This centralized collection of browse lists allows an enterprise-wide browsable network.

If no master browser is present for a workgroup, the first workstation that attempts to access a browse list will send out an election request to the remaining servers in the workgroup. This election request will cause a comparison of all the remaining servers to determine which is most suitable to be the new master browser.

If the Browse Master parameter is set to Automatic, the default, the Windows 98 computer can participate as a master browser. If the Browse Master parameter is set to Enable, the workstation will attempt to become a master browser. This might be desirable on a little-used computer that is always left on. If the Browse Master parameter is set to Disable, the Windows 95 computer will never serve as master or backup browser. Remember that at least one computer in the workgroup must serve as master browser.

NETWORK PROTOCOLS

At A Glance: Networking Protocols

Protocol	Main Benefits	Main Drawbacks
NetBEUI	Small overhead; fast; used for compatibility with older Microsoft networks	Non-routable; uses broadcasts for address resolution
IPX/SPX-compatible	Needed for compatibility with NetWare	Used only for NetWare compatibility
TCP/IP	Routable; language of the Internet; industry standard	Management
Data Link Control (DLC)	Provides connectivity to IBM mainframes)and AS400s	Not used by many Microsoft clients
Fast Infrared	Wireless communication	Can't be used for more than two machines communicating

Transport Protocols

Windows 98 includes support for NetBEUI, IPX/SPX-compatible, TCP/IP transport protocols, Microsoft DLC, and Fast Infrared. The first four protocols interact with the network adapter driver and network adapter hardware through the Network Device Interface Specification (NDIS) interface.

Here's a look at each network protocol supported by Windows 98:

- NetBEUI is the protocol used by older Microsoft networking products—Windows for Workgroups, LAN Manager, and so on. NetBEUI is not a routable protocol, has very little overhead, and is used mostly for backward compatibility.

- IPX/SPX-compatible protocol is provided with Windows 98 to provide compatibility with NetWare. Novell created the proprietary IPX/SPX protocol and uses it in all versions of NetWare. IPX/SPX is routable and is far superior to NetBEUI in terms of network functions. This protocol is known as NWLink in Windows NT products.

- TCP/IP is the default protocol of Windows NT 4.0 and the Internet. It is a nonproprietary protocol that requires three parameters: unique IP address, subnet mask, and default gateway. These three parameters can be added by the administrator during or after installation of the operating system, or they can be provided by a DHCP (Dynamic Host Configuration Protocol) server.

- Microsoft Data Link Control (DLC) is primarily used by the SNA component of Microsoft BackOffice to communicate with IBM mainframes and AS400s. It has one additional use: Many HP network printers also use DLC, although they can be (and often are) converted to TCP/IP with the inclusion of a JetDirect card.

- Fast Infrared (also known as Microsoft Infrared 3.0) is used for communication with devices that support IrDA (Infrared Data Association) standards for Fast Infrared Devices (FIR). This technology by nature is limited to small groups communicating and is not really a *network* protocol. Typical uses include sending data to a printer or exchanging files between two machines.

Network Adapter Drivers

Normally, adapter drivers are provided by the NIC manufacturer, but Windows 98 does provide a large selection of drivers for many common NICs.

All Windows 98 network adapter drivers and protocol settings are configured using the Network Settings icon found in Control Panel rather than editing text configuration files, such as was common in Windows 3.x. Windows 98 stores these settings in the Registry.

NDIS

Microsoft networking protocols communicate with network interface card (NIC) drivers using the Network Driver Interface Specification (NDIS). The NDIS interface layer provides basic services common to all networking protocols and provides a standard interface to which NIC adapter drivers can be written. The transport protocol uses the NDIS specification to send raw data packets over a network device, and to receive notification of incoming packets received by the NIC.

Changes were made in Windows 98 to NDIS to include support for ATM (Asynchronous Transfer Mode). NDIS 5 is a vast improvement over NDIS 3.1 and also) includes support for FDDI (Fiber Distributed Data Interface), power management, and WAN technology such as VPN (Virtual Private Networking) and PPTP (Point-to-Point Tunneling Protocol).

Installing and Configuring TCP/IP

Windows 98 comes with the Microsoft 32-bit TCP/IP protocol, related utilities, and an SNMP client. The increased popularity of the Internet warrants an overview of the TCP/IP protocol in Windows 98. TCP/IP gives Windows 98 an industry-standard, routable, enterprise-level networking protocol. TCP/IP is the transport protocol of the Internet. With the included TCP/IP utilities, Windows 98 can access its rapidly growing resources.

After you install TCP/IP, the TCP/IP properties sheet will appear with these tabs:

+ IP Address

+ Gateway

+ DNS Configuration

- WINS Configuration
- Advanced
- Bindings

Choosing Manual or DHCP IP Configuration

The IP Address tab of the TCP/IP properties sheet has two radio buttons:

- Obtain an IP address automatically
- Specify an IP address

Dynamic Host Configuration Protocol (DHCP) allows automatic IP address assignment. When Windows 98 is configured as a DHCP client and then restarted, it broadcasts a message looking for a DHCP server. The DHCP server provides the client with an IP address to use for a pre-determined length of time.

A DHCP server can be configured to pass all the necessary IP address information to a DHCP client. This includes the IP address leased to the client, as well as the IP addresses of the default gateway, subnet mask, DNS servers, and WINS servers.

> **NOTE** Although this information probably isn't covered very heavily on the exam, it's useful context information for the topic.

Subnet Masking

Along with the IP address, a subnet mask is required for every TCP/IP device. A subnet mask is used to determine if a destination address is located on the local subnet or on a remote network. Subnet masks can be configured manually, along with the IP address, by network administrators. A DHCP server can also assign a subnet mask automatically. Table 2.1 lists IP address classes and their default subnet masks.

TABLE 2.1

IP ADDRESS CLASSES AND SUBNET MASKS

Class	First Octet Range	Default Subnet Mask
A	1 to 126	255.0.0.0
B	128 to 191	255.255.0.0
C	192 to 223	255.255.255.0

Configuring a Gateway

Once you have anan IP address and subnet mask, your Windows 98 computer is ready to talk to other workstations on the local network. However, it still has no way to reach a wide area network or the Internet. A default gateway provides connectivity to the rest of the networked world.

Using Name Resolution

Name resolution is the process of turning a host or computer name into an IP address. There are several ways to configure Windows 98 to attempt name resolution:

- Domain Name Service (DNS)
- Windows Internet Name Service (WINS)
- LMHosts file
- Hosts file
- Broadcasts

Configuring Windows 98 to Use DNS

DNS provides a static, centrally administrated database for resolving domain names to IP addresses. A fully qualified DNS name consists of a host name appended to an Internet or intranet domain name. Keep in mind that this is separate from a Windows NT domain name. For example, the host www would be appended to microsoft.com to give the fully qualified domain name www.microsoft.com.

You can configure Windows 98 to use DNS using the DNS Configuration tab on the TCP/IP properties sheet.

The Enable DNS fields on the DNS Configuration page allows Windows 98 to take advantage of several DNS services:

- Host is the local computer's registered DNS name.

- Domain is the organization's InterNIC registered domain name.

- DNS Server Search Order allows backup DNS servers to be configured in case the primary server fails.

- Domain Suffix Search Order tells TCP/IP utilities what domains to append and search if only a hostname is given to the utility.

Configuring Windows 98 to Use WINS

WINS allows a Windows 98 user to use a human-friendly NetBIOS name in network utilities. For instance, you could use a UNC path to access a share. Then Windows 98 can query the WINS server to resolve the NetBIOS name to an IP address, allowing TCP/IP communication to take place.

It's important to keep in mind the differences between WINS and DNS:

- WINS uses a dynamic registration system. DNS relies on static tables.

- DNS resolves fully qualified domain names into IP addresses. WINS resolves NetBIOS computer names into IP addresses.

- DNS is a hierarchical system. WINS uses the flat NetBIOS name space.

You configure Windows 98 to use a WINS server through the WINS Configuration tab of the TCP/IP properties sheet.

The three choices of WINS configuration for a Windows 98 TCP/IP client are as follows:

- Disable WINS Resolution. If WINS is disabled, an alternative form of NetBIOS name resolution, such as an LMHosts file, is necessary.

- Enable WINS Resolution. If WINS resolution is enabled, the IP address of a primary WINS server is required. A secondary WINS server can be configured to provide backup.

◆ Use DHCP for WINS resolution. If the Windows 98 client is using DHCP to configure IP numbers, you can select this option to use the WINS servers specified by the DHCP server.

INSTALLING AND CONFIGURING HARDWARE DEVICES

Windows 98 fully embraces Plug and Play technology. When a new hardware component is installed in the machine, Windows 98 should recognize it immediately, or at the next boot. If it isn't recognized because it's an older component or non–Plug and Play–compatible, you can configure most devices using the applets and wizards in Control Panel.

Here are a couple of the most common hardware components:

◆ Modems are configured through the Modems applet in Control Panel.

◆ Printers are added through the Add Printer Wizard and managed through the properties sheet that is created after the printer is added.

Windows 98 also supports the Universal Serial Bus (USB) and IEEE 1394 FireWire—two standards for connecting devices to the machine. (PCI and PC Card are two older Windows 95 methods that aren't supported by the Win32 Driver Model.)

USB is a standard for external devices such as keyboards, mice, and external hard drives. USB brings to these external devices the same level of Plug and Play that has existed for internal devices in Windows 95—allowing for automatic configuration upon attachment, without the need to reboot the machine or run the Setup program sequence. According to Microsoft, USB is supported by WDM under Windows 98.

USB TOPOLOGY

USB uses a *tiered* topology, which lets you connect up to 127 devices to the bus at the same time. Currently, USB supports up to five tiers. There is a five-meter distance restriction from the hub to each device.

The following lists the three types of USB components:

- Host. Also known as the *root,* this can be built into the mother-board or installed into the machine as a separate card. The host can both function as a hub and control the traffic on the bus.

- Hub. Provides the *point of contact* and is also responsible for detecting any new components.

- Device. This is the USB device. It can be a monitor, printer, key-board, or even a mouse.

> **NOTE** The first time you plug a device into a port, Windows 98 must go through the process of detection and enumeration for that particular device.

The specifications for USB outline standards for the connector, socket, and even the cable. This standard has been created in the hopes of reducing the amount of confusion created by current hardware devices and their connectors. FireWire is used to recognize the hot plugging of high-bandwidth devices (up to 63 of them), and it adheres to the OpenHCI standard. Digital video recorders, cameras, scanners, and videodisc players are all examples of high-bandwidth devices that can be connected per the IEEE 1394 bus topology.

> **NOTE** For the exam, you should be comfortable with the components required to connect a printer or other USB device to a Windows 98 client's USB port.

Multiple Display Support is available in Windows 98, allowing up to nine monitors to be run by a single machine. The recommended maximum number is three. Each requires a separate adapter and monitor that is a PCI or AGP device that can run in GUI mode without VGA resources.

> **NOTE** For the exam, it's good to know how to configure your Windows 98 client when installing two video cards in the same machine.

Multilink allows multiple modems to establish a connection that can be aggregated into one session. For example, four 14,400 modems can establish a connection to a Windows NT server running the Remote Access Service (RAS) to give the remote user a session running at 56K (14.4×4).

Windows 98 includes power management for laptops, allowing them to shut down when the battery gets low. This management can also be used to constantly sense the input level and read data supplied by a UPS (Uninterruptible Power Supply). In the event of a long-term power outage, Windows 98 can shut down when the UPS begins to drain.

BACKUPS

The Microsoft Backup Utility, licensed from Seagate, has been improved for Windows 98. It isn't installed by default unless you're migrating from Windows 95 and it was installed there. If it isn't installed, you can get it from the CD and install it from there.

The Backup Wizard starts first. It has three options:

- Create a new backup job
- Open an existing backup job
- Restore backed-up files

Note that it can't be used to change backup jobs—only create new ones. Without the wizard, you have full control and can configure whatever you want. QIC-40 devices are not supported by the utility. You can restore backups made under Windows 95 but not under much else (including DOS).

> **NOTE** For the exam, you should acquaint yourself with the backup strategies of Full, Incremental, and Differential.

WHAT IS IMPORTANT TO KNOW

The following list summarizes the chapter and accentuates the key concepts to memorize for the exam:

- The NETSETUP program, which existed with Windows 95 for installing over a network, is not included with Windows 98.

- When you upgrade from Windows 3.x to Windows 98, settings in PROTOCOL.INI, SYSTEM.INI, and WIN.INI are used to create the Windows 98 Registry.

- The four setup types are Typical, Custom, Portable, and Compact.

- Windows 98 and Windows NT both share the FAT16 file system, and it must be used in a dual boot for support beneath both OSs.

- Dual booting Windows 98 and Windows NT requires FAT16 on the boot drive, as well as on any partition that must be seen by both operating systems.

- When migrating from Windows NT to Windows 98, you must reinstall all applications, because the Registries of each operating system aren't compatible with each other.

- Batch 98 is used to create INF files to install Windows 98 from a server or other location.

- Batch 98 is used to create INF files used to automate several user-required responses during installation. You should be familiar with the available options.

- You uninstall Windows 98 using the Add/Remove Programs applet in Control Panel.

- You can uninstall Windows 98 from Control Panel only if your machine has been upgraded.

- A subset of Microsoft's Internet Information Server (which runs on Windows NT Server) is available for Windows 98, where it is known as Personal Web Server.

- Personal Web Server can log data based on requests per day, requests per hour, visitors per day, and visitors per hour.

- USB provides Plug and Play compatibility for external devices.

- IEEE 1394 FireWire provides for bus support of high-bandwidth external devices such as video cameras.

- Microsoft Backup utility is used to create and restore backups. It doesn't work with QIC-40 tapes.

- The Backup Wizard can create and view backup jobs but not change them.

- Backup strategies, such as Full, Incremental, and Differential, play an important role in estimating time and resources during a restoration process.

OBJECTIVES

▶ Assign access permissions for shared folders in a
   Microsoft environment or a mixed Microsoft and
   NetWare environment. Methods include the following:
   · Passwords
   · User permissions
   · Group permissions

▶ Create, share, and monitor resources. Resources
   include the following:
   · Remote computers
   · Network printers

▶ Set up user environments by using user profiles and
   system policies.

▶ Back up data and the Registry and restore data and
   the Registry.

▶ Configure hard disks. Tasks include the following:
   · Disk compression
   · Partitioning
   · Enabling large disk support
   · Converting to FAT32

▶ Create hardware profiles.

CHAPTER 3

Configuring and Managing
Resource Access

ASSIGNING ACCESS PERMISSIONS

At A Glance: Windows 98 Resource Access Control Methods

Access Control Method	Environment	Requirements
Passwords Access	Workgroup, Windows NT domain, NetWare LAN	File and Printer Sharing enabled.
User Permissions	Windows NT domain, NetWare LAN	File and Printer Sharing enabled. User-level security enabled.
Group Permissions	Windows NT domain, NetWare LAN	File and Printer Sharing enabled. User-level security enabled.

In a peer-to-peer networking environment of only Windows 98 computers or some combination of Windows 98, Windows 95, and Windows NT Workstations, Windows 98 can provide only share-level security. In this environment, when you choose to share something (a printer or folder), you can assign a password to it. The ability of users to use that resource is based on their knowing the password you assigned. Thus, it is share-level security in that the password is assigned to the share. There can be a different password for every shared resource.

Peer-to-peer networking is easy to set up and inexpensive because it doesn't require additional investment in a dedicated computer to act as a file server. It's typically used in smaller environments. Microsoft recommends it for networks of up to 15 computers. Once the network grows beyond that size, the administration required to manage all the various passwords and shared resources becomes too time-consuming to be practical. Many companies operate peer-to-peer networks of 50 or more computers. However, on the exam, if a question describes a network of more than 15 workstations, that should be a hint that the environment won't be using share-level security. Instead, it will be connected to a file server of some sort and will be using user-level security.

When a Windows 98 computer is connected to a network that uses a dedicated file server, such as Windows NT or NetWare, you can implement user-level security. The file server authenticates a user when he logs on and ascertains the rights he will have to resources throughout his session based on his identification (user name and password) and the rights and permissions the administrator has assigned to that user ID.

User-level security is more complex to implement because it requires an administrative understanding of the network operating system as well as Windows 98. However, it's easier to maintain because administration can be done centrally. All changes to users' resource access permissions can be made from the same place, rather than the Administrator having to visit each computer that shares its resources and making changes at that location.

Passwords

Under Windows 98, passwords can be assigned for access to shared resources on the network, as well as for access to the Windows 98 computer itself. If a Windows 98 computer is configured with a network client—either Client for Microsoft Networks or Client for NetWare Networks, or the new Microsoft Family Logon—users of that computer must log on before using the system by providing a user ID and an optional password. The first time a user runs a Windows 98 computer, a login prompt is displayed for each network client that is set up on the machine, as well as one for Windows 98 itself. If the password for each of these clients is the same, the Windows 98 login prompt is not displayed again, and a single login prompt will allow the user to authenticate to Windows 98 and all networks he connects to at the same time. This is known as *unified logon*.

The Passwords applet in Control Panel lets you change the password for Windows 98 and for the different networks the computer is configured to access. When you connect to a NetWare network, the *preferred server* will be the one used for authentication unless you edit the Registry or use a system policy to select Disable Automatic NetWare Login. The NetWare password can be changed with NetWare's setpass command-line utility.

To change a password for a network resource, follow these steps:

1. Choose the Passwords applet from the Control Panel.

2. Click Change Other Passwords.

3. In the Select Password dialog box, choose the password you want to change.

4. Click Change.

5. Enter the old password once and the new password twice (in both the New password and Confirm new password boxes).

6. Click OK.

To change a password for a network resource so that it is the same as the Windows 98 logon password, follow these steps:

1. Choose the Passwords applet from the Control Panel.

2. Click Change Windows Password.

3. In the Change Windows Password dialog box, choose the password you want to change.

4. Click OK.

5. Enter the old password once and the new password twice (in both the New password and Confirm new password boxes).

6. Click OK.

All passwords for network resources are cached per user in a file identified by that person's user name and a PWL extension. For example, edulaney's passwords are stored in EDULANEY.PWL. This file is created the first time the user logs on and is unlocked each time he logs on with his Windows 98 password.

You can use the Password List Editor to edit and delete entries in this file, although the actual passwords themselves never appear in this tool. When the tool is used, only the password list for the current user is displayed.

The Password List Editor is found on the Windows 98 CD in the Tools\Reskit\NetAdmin\PWLedit folder. Simply copy the two files found in that directory to your hard drive. To run the Password List Editor, run the PWLEDIT.EXE file from the directory you copied it to.

NOTE Password caching (which you can disable by editing the Registry or creating a system policy) requires the user to supply his password each time he connects to a resource. This is often done in environments where there is strong concern about password security.

User Permissions

At A Glance: Standard NT User Permissions

Permission	Description
No Access	Keeps users from accessing the directory by any means.
List	Keeps users from accessing the directory, although they may view the directory's contents list.
Read	Users can read data files and execute program files from the directory, but they can't make changes.
Add	Users can't read or even view the contents of the directory, but they may write files to the directory.
Add & Read	Users may view and read from the directory and save new files into the directory, but they can't modify existing files.
Change	Users may view and read from the directory and save new files into the directory, they may modify and even delete existing files, and they may change attributes on the directory and even delete the entire directory.
Full Control	Users may view, read, save, modify, or delete the directory and its contents. In addition, users may change permissions on the directory and its contents, even if they don't own the resource. Users also can take ownership at any time.

User permissions define what a user can do based on his user identity. Both the Windows NT and NetWare operating systems use user IDs to differentiate between users. In NT, these IDs are known as Security Identifiers, or SIDs. These are unique values that exist only for that user. Windows NT has two levels of security for protecting your disk resources:

- Share permissions. When a resource, such as a folder, is shared, permissions can be assigned to it that affect all users of that shared resource.

- NTFS permissions. The Windows NT File System (NTFS) lets security attributes be assigned for folders and for individual files on the system.

Windows 98 can't run NTFS on local hard disks, but users on Windows 98 computers connected to a Windows NT domain or workgroup can access shared resources on a Windows NT computer that is running NTFS on its local hard disks. The NTFS permissions assigned to those resources will affect how Windows 98 users can access the shared folders or files.

Implementing Permissions and Security

Once you have shared resources on your Windows 98 computer (see the later section "Creating, Sharing, and Monitoring Resources"), you will want to implement some form of security. You do this using the Access Control tab of the Network properties sheet. By default, share-level security is implemented. At this level, you assign a password to a share. You can assign one of three levels of access to the share: Read-Only, Full Control, or Depends on Password.

On a Windows NT or NetWare network, user-level security can be used. The Windows NT domain controller or the NetWare File Server is used to provide authentication of a user's ID and password. Access rights to shared resources can be assigned to individual users or groups of users. In a Windows NT environment, there are two types of groups: local and global.

Local groups are located locally on a particular Windows NT computer. This computer can be a Windows NT workstation or a Windows NT server that is not a domain controller. Local groups only have meaning to the particular Windows NT computer in question.

Global groups are groups located on a Windows NT domain. These groups have meaning across the whole domain. In a Windows NT domain environment, users are added to global groups, those groups are added to local groups on individual Windows NT computers, and local groups are assigned access rights to shared resources on the particular Windows NT computer. NTFS rights are assigned to individual users or to local groups.

On a Windows 98 computer that is sharing resources using user-level security, global groups are selected from the domain and given access rights to the shared resources on the Windows 98 computer.

At A Glance: NTFS Permissions

Level	Directory Permissions	File Permissions
No Access	None	None
List	RX	Unspecified
Read	RX	RX
Add	WX	Unspecified
Add & Read	RXWD	RX
Change	RXWD	RXWD
Full Control	RXWDPO	RXWDPO

NTFS permissions allow you to assign more-comprehensive security to your computer system. NTFS permissions can protect you at the file level. Share permissions, on the other hand, can be applied only to the directory level. NTFS permissions can affect users logged on locally or across the network to the system where the NTFS permissions are applied. Share permissions are in effect only when the user connects to the resource via the network.

NTFS permissions, when applied at the directory level, can be applied as one of the default assignments listed in Table 3.1.

TABLE 3.1

NTFS DIRECTORY PERMISSIONS

NTFS Permission	*Description*
No Access (none)(none)	The user will have absolutely no access to the directory or its files. This will override any other NTFS permissions the user might have assigned to him through other group memberships.
List (RX) (Not Specified)	Allows the user to view the contents of a directory and navigate its subdirectories. It doesn't grant him access to the files in these directories unless specified in file permissions.
Read (RX) (RX)	Allows the user to navigate the entire directory structure, view the contents of the directory, view the contents of any files in the directory, and execute programs.
Add (WX) (Not Specified)	Allows the user to add new subdirectories and files to the directory. It doesn't give the user access to the files within the directory unless specified in other NTFS permissions.
Add & Read (RWX) (RX)	Allows the user to add new files to the directory structure. Once the file has been added, the user has only read-only access to the files. This permission also allows the user to run programs.
Change (RWXD) (RWXD)	Allows the user to do the most data manipulation. He can view the contents of directories and files, run programs, modify the contents of data files, and delete files.

continues

TABLE 3.1   continued

NTFS Permission	Description
Full Control (All) (All)	Gives the user all the abilities of the Change permission. In addition, the user can change the permissions on that directory or any of its contents. He can also take ownership of the directory or any of its contents.
Special Directory	Can be set as desired to any combination of (R)ead, (W)rite, E(X)ecute, (D)elete, Change (P)ermissions, and Take (O)wnership.

NTFS permissions can also be applied to individual files in directories. The NTFS file permissions are listed in Table 3.2.

TABLE 3.2

NTFS FILE PERMISSIONS

NTFS Permission	Description
No Access (none)	The user will have absolutely no access to that file. This will override any other NTFS directory and file permissions the user might have been assigned through other group memberships.
Read (RX)	Allows the user to view the contents of files but not to make changes to the contents. The user can also execute the file if it's a program.
Change (RWXD)	Allows the user to make any editing changes he wants to a data file, including deleting it.
Full Control (All)	Gives the user all the abilities of the Change permission. The user can also change the permissions on that file and take ownership of the file if he isn't the current owner.
Special File	Can be set as desired to any combination of (R)ead, (W)rite, E(X)ecute, (D)elete, Change (P)ermissions, and Take (O)wnership.

Keep in mind that NTFS permissions or share permissions are cumulative, except when they're combined with each other.

Combining NTFS and Share Permissions

When combining NTFS and share permissions, remember the following tips:

- Users can only be assigned to global groups in the same domain.
- Only global groups from trusted domains can become members of local groups in trusting domains.
- On the exam, NTFS permissions will only be assigned to local groups.
- Only NTFS permissions will give you file-level security.
- When share access permissions and NTFS access permissions conflict, the most restrictive access permissions apply.

Group Permissions

Group permissions are identical to user permissions, except that they are assigned to the user not specifically by user name but by membership in a group. In NetWare and Windows NT, there are only two ways a user gets rights and permissions to resources:

- He is explicitly assigned a right or permission through his account.
- He is a member of a group that has a right or permission.

CREATING, SHARING, AND MONITORING RESOURCES

At A Glance: Shared Resources

Resources that may be shared on a Windows 98 computer	Folders, Printers.
Security models available	Share-level security provides password security for all users of a share.
	User-level security provides a list of access rights that may be assigned to individual users or groups of users. This requires a Windows NT domain controller or a NetWare file server for authentication.

Network service requirements	Requires File and Printer Sharing for Microsoft Networks or File and Printer Sharing for NetWare Networks.
Configured in	Windows Explorer for shared folders.
	Add Printer Wizard in Printers folder for shared printer.

Share-level security allows an administrator to protect his resources from network users. Not only do shares have a level of security, but they are also used as users' entry point into the system. The share permissions that can be created on a Windows 98 machine are Read-Only, Full Control, and Depends on Password:

- Read-Only allows the user to connect to the resource and run programs. He can also view any documents that are stored in the share, but he can't make any changes to them.

- Full Control allows the user to do anything he wants in the share. It also allows him to change the share permissions to affect all users. The Full Control permission generally isn't required for most users.

- Depends on Password allows you to assign two different passwords to a share. One password grants the user Full Control access to the share, and the other grants the user Read-Only access. This is useful when you have many people accessing the share but only a few who need Full Control access.

To share a resource after File and Printer Sharing has been enabled (see Chapter 4, "Integration and Interoperability"), simply right-click the resource and choose Sharing from the context menu. You must assign a share name, the default of which will be the current name of the resource. You can also optionally choose to assign a computer description. The description is only visible to a user when he views the resource with Detail view. Otherwise, it remains unseen.

The two types of resources that a user might wish to connect to remotely—computers and printers—are examined in the following sections.

Connecting to Remote Computers

At A Glance: Connecting to Remote Computers

Connection Method	Procedure
Network Neighborhood	Browse Network Neighborhood for the desired computer.
	Double-click the computer icon to view available resources on that computer.
	Double-click the desired resource to be connected to that resource.
Windows Explorer	Select Tools | Map Network Drive or click the Map Network Drive icon on the toolbar.
	Provide the UNC path to the computer and resource that you wish to use.
	Click OK to be connected.
Command line	Use the NET VIEW \\computername command to view shared resources on the network.
	Use the NET USE X: \\computername\sharename command to connect to a shared folder on a remote computer.
	Use the NET USE X: /delete command to disconnect from a shared folder on a remote computer.

The primary tool for seeing and connecting to remote computers is the Network Neighborhood. When it's first opened, it shows the resources visible within the workgroup or domain, and it has an Entire Network icon at the top. Clicking that icon lets you go beyond the workgroup or domain and see the other available resources.

Clicking a computer in Network Neighborhood updates the view to the resources available on that machine. These will either be folders (shares) or printers. If they are shares, you can open them and proceed down through directories and subdirectories to whatever file(s) you want to interact with, provided that you have the required access rights to that share.

Aside from Network Neighborhood, you can also connect to remote computers and resources through the NET USE commands:

- NET USE *X*: *server**share* will map a drive (*X*) to the share on the server specified. Drive *X* will now appear in My Computer and can be accessed from there as well as from the command line.

- NET USE *X*: /delete will unmap drive *X* from the share on the server specified.

- NET VIEW *server* will show the resources available on the server.

Connecting to Network Printers

The Add Printer Wizard allows you to configure a local or network printer. To add a new network printer to your Windows 98 computer, follow these steps:

1. Select Start | Settings | Printers to open the Printers folder.

2. Double-click the Add Printer icon to start the Add Printer Wizard.

3. Click the Next button to begin the printer installation process.

4. Select Network Printer and click the Next button.

5. Type the UNC path to the printer, or click the Browse button to browse the network for available shared printers.

6. Select Yes or No to specify whether to provide support for MS-DOS applications to print to this printer, and then click Next.

7. Type a name for the network printer and select Yes if you want to use this printer as your default printer. Click Next.

8. Select Yes if you would like to print a test page or No if you don't want to print a test page.

9. Click the Finish button to complete the process.

Once the installation process is finished, you can print a test page if you want to. The connection to the printer is set as permanent, so an attempt will be made to reestablish a connection on each boot.

USER PROFILES AND SYSTEM POLICIES

At A Glance: User Profiles

Local Profiles	*Roaming Profiles*
Stored on the local hard disk under Windows\Profiles*username*	Stored on a network file server
	Saved in the user's HOME directory on a Windows NT domain controller
	Saved in the user's MAIL directory on a NetWare file server
Must be present on each computer with which the user logs in to the network	Available regardless of which computer the user uses to log in to the network
Do not require the network file server to be available	Require the network file server to be available

By default, all users on Windows 98 share the same profile per machine. You can use Control Panel's Passwords applet to let users have their own profiles (saving desktop settings for each user, and so on). When this is enabled, rather than using the common file C:\WINDOWS\USER.DAT as a profile, each user has his own profile under C:\WINDOWS\ PROFILES*username*\USER.DAT.

User profiles store the user portion of the Registry. They can be implemented as either *local profiles* or *roaming profiles*. A local profile is stored locally on the hard disk of the Windows 98 computer. A roaming profile is stored on the network file server. It enables the user portion of each user's configuration to follow him to whatever computer he uses to log in to the Windows NT or NetWare network.

Local Profiles Versus Roaming Profiles

Whenever a user logs in to a system, he creates a local profile on that system. The local profile is implemented as a set of directory structures. This directory structure includes the desktop folder and the Start Menu folder.

When a user logs in to an NT network, his desktop and Start menu are based on the local system that he is logging in to. The desktop will be based on the user's profile directory and the ALL USERS directory. The same is true of the Start Menu directory.

The problem with local profiles is that every workstation the user logs in to will have its own version of the local profile. User configuration settings will have to be set at each workstation that the user logs in to.

To overcome this problem, you must implement roaming profiles. Roaming profiles will have the user portion of the Registry download from a designated system to the system that the user is currently logged in to. Any changes to his settings will be stored in the central location so that they can be retrieved at the next workstation the user logs in to.

Configuring Roaming Profiles in a Windows NT Domain Environment

If you want to configure a user account to use a roaming profile, the first thing to do is set the profile path in the User Manager for Domains for that account. If you're configuring a block of users, the best method to use is to do a group property change by first selecting all the users you want to have roaming profiles and then selecting User | Properties.

The most common setting to use is to have a directory shared with a share name such as *profiles*. It should give the local group USERS the permission of Full Control. With this share, you can set the user's profile path to be \\server\share\%username%. The next time the user logs on, her profile information can be saved to this central profile directory.

Configuring Roaming Profiles in a NetWare Environment

With NetWare, every user created on the NetWare server has a directory beneath MAIL created for them. This directory holds that particular user's login scripts. It is also where you need to place the USER.DAT file so that it can be found and implemented as a roaming profile.

System Policies

At A Glance: System Policies

Created by	System PolicyPolicy Editor Editor (POLEDIT.EXE).
Stored in	NETLOGON share in NT domain.
	PUBLIC directory in NetWare LAN.

Filename	CONFIG.POL.
Policy types	Default policies apply to all users and computers logged into the network.
	Machine policies apply to the specific computer named in the policy.
	User policies apply to the specific user named in the policy.
	Group policies apply to all users who are members of the group named in the policy.
Common uses	Implement defaults for hardware configuration.
	Restrict the changing of specific parameters that affect the hardware configuration.
	Set personal defaults for all users.
	Restrict the user from changing specific areas of his configuration.
	Apply all defaults and restrictions on a group level.

System policies help the network administrator restrict what configuration changes the user can perform to his profile. By combining roaming profiles and system policies, the administrator can give the user a consistent desktop and control what the user can do to that desktop. Likewise, the administrator can be assured that the user can't modify certain settings.

System policies work very much like a merge operation. You can think of system policies as a copy of your Registry. When you log in to the network and the CONFIG.POL file exists on the Windows NT domain controller or NetWare file server, it will merge its settings into your Registry, changing your Registry settings as indicated in the system policy.

The system policy file on an NT-based network is contained within the NETLOGON share. In NetWare, it is placed in the PUBLIC directory.

System policies are created with the System Policy Editor (POLEDIT.EXE), which is found on the Windows 98 CD in the TOOLS\ RESKIT\NETADMIN\POLEDIT directory. System policies can be configured to do the following:

- Implement defaults for hardware configuration for all computers by using the profile or for a specific machine.

- Restrict the changing of specific parameters that affect the hardware configuration of the participating system.

- Set defaults for all users on the areas of their personal settings that they can configure.

- Restrict the user from changing specific areas of his configuration to prevent tampering with the system.

- Apply all defaults and restrictions on a group level rather than just a user level.

The System Policy Editor also can be used to change settings in the Registry of the system that System Policy Editor is being executed on. Many times, it is easier to use the System Policy Editor because it has a better interface for finding common restrictions you might want to place on a Windows 98 workstation.

Implementing System Policies

To create computer, user, and group policies, you must use the System Policy Editor. When you create a new policy file, you will see two default icons within the policy:

- Default Computer is used to configure all machine-specific settings. All property changes within this section affect the HKEY_LOCAL_MACHINE subtree of the Registry. The default computer item will be used for any client that uses the policy and for which a specific machine entry has not been created in the policy file.

- Default User is used to specify default policy settings for all users who will be using the policy. The default user setting will affect the HKEY_CURRENT_USER subtree of the Registry. If the user is configured to use a roaming profile, this information will be stored in his centralized version of USER.DAT in his profile directory.

You can implement computer policies on a computer-by-computer basis by selecting Edit | Add Computer. This will add a new icon to the policy that has that computer's name.

User policies can also be implemented through the System Policy Editor. These policies will affect the HKEY_CURRENT_USER Registry subtree. Each user will be affected individually if a policy exists by his name. Otherwise, the settings for Default User are active for him.

User policies can also be implemented on a user-by-user basis. To create an individual user policy, select Edit | Add User. When a user logs in, CONFIG.POL will be checked to see if there is a policy for the specific user. If there isn't, the default user policy will be used for the login process.

Here are some of the common implementations of user policies:

♦ Lock down display properties to prevent users from changing their monitor's resolution. Display properties can be locked down as a whole or on each individual display's properties page. To lock them down, go to Control Panel's Display applet. Use the Restrict Display option of the Default User properties sheet.

♦ Set a default color scheme or wallpaper. You can do this by using the Desktop option of the Default User properties sheet.

♦ If you want to restrict access to portions of the Start menu or desktop, you can do so via the Shell/Restrictions options of the Default User properties sheet.

♦ If you need to limit what applications can be run at a workstation, you can do so with the System/Restrictions option of the Default User properties sheet. This option can also be used to prevent the user from modifying the Registry.

♦ You can prevent users from mapping or disconnecting network drives by setting the options in the Windows NT Shell/Restrictions area of the Default User properties sheet.

The Zero Administration Kit (ZAK) from Microsoft is aimed at reducing the amount of time an administrator spends administering a system. This is accomplished through a strict set of system policies: By reducing to a bare minimum what a user can do, you are also reducing what you need to administer.

By reducing the amount of time spent on administration, you in essence reduce your total cost of ownership (TCO) for the network. This idea has gained enormous popularity in the past year. Other vendors are coming up with similar approaches—most notably, Novell with its Zero Effort NetWare (ZEN).

If you need to have user settings affect multiple users, you can implement group policies. Group policies add another level of complexity to the processing of policies. Here are some of the additional considerations:

- The System Policy Editor uses global groups for group membership. You must implement appropriate trust relationships to see the necessary global groups.

- Because a user can belong to multiple global groups, the order in which the groups are processed is very important. One group's settings could be the opposite of another group's. You set group order by selecting Options | Group Priority.

Processing Order for System Policies

When a user logs on to a network where system policies have been implemented, the following actions will occur:

1. The user successfully logs in to the network.

2. The user profile is read from the NETLOGON share of the authenticating domain controller.

3. If a predefined policy exists for a user, that policy is merged into the HKEY_CURRENT_USER Registry subtree. The processing then moves to step 6.

4. If no predefined user policy exists, the default user policy is processed.

5. The group priority list is examined. If the user is a member of any of the global groups for which a policy exists, he is processed according to the group priority order. The priority is ordered from bottom to top of the group priority list. Each of the group policies is applied to the HKEY_CURRENT_USER Registry subtree.

6. Once the user and group policies have been processed, the machine policies are determined. If there is a predefined machine policy, that policy is merged with the HKEY_LOCAL_MACHINE Registry subtree. If there is not a predefined machine policy for the system that the user is logging in from, the default machine policy is merged with the HKEY_LOCAL_MACHINE subtree.

BACKING UP AND RESTORING DATA

At A Glance: Microsoft Backup

Installed from	Add/Remove Programs icon in Control Panel
Devices supported	DAT devices
	DC 6000 devices
	TR1, 2, 3, and 4 devices
	DLT devices
	8mm devices
	Removable media such as floppy disks, Jaz drives, and Syquest cartridges
	The following QIC devices: QIC 80 and QIC 80-Wide QIC 3010 and QIC 3010-Wide QIC 3020 and QIC 3020-Wide
Devices no longer supported	QIC 40 devices
Can restore	Backups made with the Windows 98 Backup program
	Backups made with the Windows 95 Backup program
Cannot restore	Backups made with MS-DOS version 6.x or earlier Backup program

Windows 98 provides a utility that lets users back up the valuable data on their hard disk(s) to some other location for archival purposes and for restoration in case of hardware failure or other catastrophic system event. The utility is called Microsoft Backup.

Microsoft Backup isn't installed by default when you run Windows 98 Setup. However, if your computer was upgraded from Windows 95, and Windows 95 Backup was Microsoftinstalled at that time, Windows 98 Setup will install the new Microsoft Backup for Windows 98.

To install Microsoft Backup on your Windows 98 computer, follow these steps:

1. Double-click the Add/Remove Programs icon in Control Panel.

2. Select the Windows Setup tab.

3. Double-click the System Tools icon.

4. Check the Backup check box.

5. Click OK, then Apply, then OK again to complete the installation.

After it's installed, you can run Microsoft Backup by selecting Start | Programs | Accessories | System Tools | Backup. When you first start Microsoft Backup, the Welcome to Microsoft Backup dialog box appears, offering you three options:

- Create a new backup job

- Open an existing backup job

- Restore backed-up files

Select Create a new backup job to start the Backup Wizard. Follow the instructions in the wizard to set up a backup job. A backup job stores all the configuration settings and options you select so that you don't have to select them repeatedly each time you want to back up your data. If you want to back up the same data again with the same options selected, just run the job again. Give the backup job a unique name that doesn't contain any of the following characters: | \ / : * " ? < >

The Backup Wizard will prompt you to provide a unique name for the backup medium you're using (if it doesn't already have one).

NOTE The Backup Wizard can only be used to create a new backup job, not to edit existing backup jobs. If you want to modify the settings for an existing backup job, choose Open an existing backup job in the Welcome to Microsoft Backup dialog box when Microsoft Backup starts. Select the job you want to modify, change the appropriate settings, and resave the job.

If you select Open an existing backup job in the Welcome to Microsoft Backup dialog box, you see a list of the backup jobs that are currently saved on your computer. Select the job you want to run, and click OK. You can click the Start button to begin backing up your data right away. Or, if you want to modify the settings for your backup job, you can make the changes you want and resave the backup job.

Choosing Restore backed up files in the Welcome to Microsoft Backup dialog box starts the Restore Wizard. Follow the instructions to select the appropriate data to restore. When the Operation Completed dialog box appears, you know that the restoration operation was successful.

> **N O T E**
>
> You can restore data from backup jobs created in Microsoft Backup and also from backup jobs created in Windows 95 Backup. You can't restore data from backup jobs created in an MS-DOS version 6.x or earlier Backup utility.

Microsoft Backup can create a report of both Backup and Restore activities. Information in the report can include the number of files backed up, the date and time the backup was run, the size of the file data, and whether or not the job completed successfully. Report files are stored on your hard disk in the Program Files\Accessories\Backup\Reports folder. To set the options you want for your reports, follow these steps:

1. Start Microsoft Backup by selecting Start | Programs | Accessories | System Tools | Backup.

2. Click the Close button in the Welcome to Microsoft Backup dialog box.

3. Click the Options button.

4. Select the Report tab.

5. Select from the following options:

   - List all files that were backed up

   - List files that were not backed up

   - List errors reported while backing up files

   - List warnings reported while backing up files

   - List unattended messages and prompts

   - Show report summary

6. Click OK to save your selections.

The report options for a restore operation are the same as those for a backup operation. Also on the Report tab, you can opt to perform an unattended backup or restoration. If you choose this option, no message boxes or prompts will be displayed during the backup or restore operation.

The Options button leads you to several other tabs, depending on whether you click the Options button from the Backup tab or the Restore tab. The Options button on the Restore tab gives you access to the following three tabs:

- General. On this tab you select the appropriate action for Microsoft Backup to takewhen restoring a file that already exists on your computer:

    - Do not replace the file on my computer

    - Replace the file on my computer only if the file is older

    - Always replace the file on my computer

- Report. This tab allows you to select reporting options for the restore operation. The options are the same as for a backup report, as described earlier in this chapter.

- Advanced. This tab allows you to restore the Registry files if they are present in the selected backup set.

On the Backup tab, the Options button gives you access to the following tabs:

- General. On this tab you can control three elements of Microsoft Backup's behavior during a backup operation. You can do the following:

    - Decide whether to compare the backup files to the original files to determine whether the backup was successful.

    - Decide how to handle data compression. You can disable data compression, compress the data to save time, or compress the data to save space.

    - Decide how to handle media that already contain backup data. You can choose to overwrite the existing backup, append this backup to the media, or to be prompted for a decision when the backup job is run.

- Password. This tab allows you to protect the backup job with a password. Type the password in the Password and Confirm password fields.

◆ Type. This tab allows you to select between a Full backup (All selected files), a Differential backup, and an Incremental backup.

◆ Exclude. This tab allows you to exclude certain file types from the backup job. Click the Add button to add file types to the list. Select a file type and click the Remove button to take it off the list and begin backing up files of that type again.

◆ Report. This tab allows you to specify report options for backup operations. Specific options were described earlier in this chapter.

◆ Advanced. This tab allows you to back up the Registry files.

Selecting the type of backup is an important feature. With Microsoft Backup, you have the option of backing up all your files, which is called a Full backup, or backing up only the new files and files that have changed. If you elect to back up only new and changed files, you have two options with Microsoft Backup. You can run a Differential backup, which backs up new files and files that have changed since the last Full backup, or you can run an Incremental backup, which will back up only those files that are new or that have changed since the last backup—regardless of whether it was a Full or Differential backup.

Often it is more efficient to run a Full backup only once in a while (such as once a month), run Differential backups once a week, and then run Incremental backups each day in between. The decision of how often to run Full backups is really a trade-off between how much risk you can take with your data and how much time you have to run backups. Running a Full backup every night is certainly the safest way to back up your data, but you might not have time to back up all your data every night. In addition, you can conserve media space by running Differential backups (which take up less space) more often and running Full backups periodically.

Of course, if you ever need to restore all your data from backup media, if the most recent backup job run on your system was a Full backup, you need to run only one restore operation. If your most recent Full backup was a week ago, you will need to restore the data from the most recent Full backup, then from each Differential backup job that was run after it, and each Incremental backup that was run after the last Differential backup, in order to bring your data back to its most complete state. Needless to say, this could take considerable time.

For the purpose of taking the exam, it is useful to remember the three types of backups and how the time is spent on each one.

At A Glance: Backup Types

Full backup	Both backups backupsand restorations take a long time and take up much space.
Differential backup	Backups are slower and take up more space. Restorations are usually faster.
Incremental backup	Backups are usually faster and take up less space. Restorations are usually slower.

Microsoft Backup under Windows 98 supports several different types of backup devices and media types:

- DAT devices
- DC 6000 devices
- TR1, 2, 3, and 4 devices
- DLT devices
- 8mm devices
- Removable media such as floppy disks, Iomega Jaz drives, and Syquest cartridges
- QIC 80 and QIC 80-Wide
- QIC 3010 and QIC 3010-Wide
- QIC 3020 and QIC 3020-Wide

> **NOTE**
>
> It's important toQIC note that QIC 40 devices aren't supported by Microsoft Backup. This tape format was supported under Windows 95 but is not supported under Windows 98. This information is useful for the exam.

The Media option on the Microsoft Backup Tools menu provides an assortment of commands you can use to manipulate your backup media:

- Identify. This command identifies the backup device connected to your computer, as well as the media in the device.

- Initialize. This command erases the media and prepares it to accept new backup data. Microsoft Backup prompts you to confirm this operation.

- Format. Quarter Inch Cartridge (QIC) media require that the tape be formatted to a Inch Cartridge (QIC) media require that the tape be formatted ccept data before use. This command accomplishes that task. In the format process, all existing data on the media is lost. Microsoft Backup will prompt you to confirm this operation.

- Retension. This command allows you to rewind the tape. Actually, it fast-forwards the tape and then rewinds it in order to ensure an even tension throughout the length of the tape.

- Rename. This command command allows you to rename the media in the backup device.

As you become familiar with Microsoft Backup, you might decide to perform backup or restore operations manually, without the aid of a wizard. In this case, you might want to disable the Welcome to Microsoft Backup dialog box that appears at startup. To do this, follow these steps:

1. Start Microsoft Backup by selecting Start | Programs | Accessories | System Tools | Backup.

2. Click the Close button on the Welcome to Microsoft Backup dialog box.

3. Select Tools | Preferences.

4. Uncheck the check box called Show startup dialog when Microsoft Backup is started.

5. Click OK. The Welcome to Microsoft Backup dialog box won't appear the next time you start Microsoft Backup.

To run a backup job manually instead of using the Backup Wizard follow these steps:

1. Start Microsoft Backup. Close the Welcome to Microsoft Backup dialog box if it appears.

2. If you want to run an existing backup job, select it from the Backup job drop-down list. If you want to create a new job, select Job | New.

3. Decide whether you want to back up all files or only new and changed files, and then select the appropriate radio button in the What to back up section.

4. On the left side of the What to back up section, select the check box for the drive you want to back up, or click the plus sign next to the drive to expand the view to show folders on the drive.

5. Select the check box for the individual folders you want to back up, or select the folder icon to list the individual files in that folder on the right side of the What to back up section.

6. Select the check boxes for the individual files you want to back up.

7. Under the Where to back up section, select the appropriate destination and media name.

8. Click the Options button to select How to back up configuration options.

9. Select Job | Save and provide a name for the job (if this is a new backup job).

10. Click the Start button to begin running the backup job.

The steps for manually restoring files from a backup without the aid of the Restore Wizard differ slightly from the steps for performing a manual backup. Follow these steps to perform a manual restoration:

1. Start Microsoft Backup. Close the Welcome to Microsoft Backup dialog box if it appears.

2. Select the Restore tab.

3. Answer Yes when prompted to refresh the current view.

4. Select the check box next to the backup job from which you want to restore files, and click OK.

5. In the Restore from section, the correct media type and media name should already be filled in.

6. In the What to restore section, click the plus signs to expand the view until you see the drive(s) or folder(s) from which you want to restore.

7. Select the check box next to the drive(s) or folder(s) you want to restore, or select the drive or folder icon to display the individual files on the right side of the What to restore section.

8. Select the check boxes for the individual files you want to restore.

9. Under Where to restore, select Original Location or Alternate Location from the drop-down list. If you select Alternate location, either type in the path to your desired restore location or browse for it by clicking the folder icon.

10. Click the Options button to select How to restore configuration options.

11. Click the Start button to begin the restore operation. Restore operations are not saved as backup jobs are.

BACKING UP AND RESTORING THE REGISTRY

At A Glance: The Registry Checker

SCANREG.EXE	*SCANREGW.EXE*
DOS command-line interface	GUI interface
Must be used to restore the Registry from a backup	Can't be used to restore the Registry from a backup
Can't be used to compress the Registry backup	Must be used to compress a Registry backup

The Registry is one of the most critical components of your operating system (if not *the* most critical). Backing it up and being able to restore it in the event of a failure is crucial. The Registry Checker (SCANREGW.EXE) can be used to scan the Registry for errors. If no errors are found, it gives you the choice of backing it up.

Choosing Yes creates a CAB file containing the Registry in a hidden directory (C:\Windows\SysBackup). In the event of a failure, you can recover the Registry from here by running

```
scanreg /restore
```

You will be prompted for the backup you want to use. All backups are stored as RB*xxx*.CAB, where *xxx* represents an incremental value. If the Windows 98 operating system was ever started with that version of the Registry, the word Started would appear next to the choice. Otherwise, it reads Not Started.

MANAGING HARD DISKS

For the purposes of the exam, there are four primary components to the managing of hard disks:

- ◆ Disk compression
- ◆ Partitioning
- ◆ Enabling large disk support
- ◆ Converting to FAT32

Each of these is examined in the following sections.

Disk Compression

At A Glance: Disk Compression

Compression utility	DriveSpace3
Drive types supported	Hard disks:
	FAT16 and FAT32 disks
	DoubleSpace compressed drives
	Drives compressed with earlier versions of DriveSpace
	Floppy disks
	Removable media
Compressed Volume File (CFV) name	DRVSPACE.000 or DBLSPACE.000
Compression ratio	Average compression ratio is 2:1. This can be higher, depending on file type and compression type.

Disk compression is accomplished in Windows 98 through the use of the DriveSpace3 utility. When compressed, the entire drive's contents are stored as a *compressed volume file* (CVF). This file, either DRVSPACE.000 or DBLSPACE.000 (numbers increment from 000 to 254), is marked as read-only, system, and hidden. On each boot, the file is extrapolated into a drive to make it appear as if all the files are unchanged.

DriveSpace3 in Windows 98 will work with FAT32 drives but won't compress them. It also works with drives that have been compressed with earlier versions of DriveSpace3 (such as the one that came with Windows 95) and DoubleSpace. The utility can work on hard drives, floppy drives, and removable media. Here are the major changes in this version:

- Support for existing compressed drives

- 20 percent faster than earlier versions

- Can store the file in multiple fragments if necessary

- Enhanced compressions

- Support for drives up to 2GB

- Data is compressed in 32KB blocks (earlier versions used 8KB blocks)

The Compression Agent (CMPAGENT.EXE) allows you to choose when compression should occur. This is useful because the process of compressing files can slow down your computer's performance. If you find that DriveSpace3's on-the-fly compression is slowing down your system's performance, set DriveSpace3's Advanced compression setting to No compression. This will disable DriveSpace3's on-the-fly compression activity. Once you've changed this setting, you will want to make sure that you use the Compression Agent to schedule file compression while your computer is idle.

DriveSpace3 allows you to select from two compression types:

- Standard compression is the compression method used by earlier versions of DriveSpace. It provides an average compression ratio of 2:1.

- HiPack compression compression provides a slightly higher compression ratio but takes a little longer to compress and decompress files.

The Windows 98 Compression Agent allows you to select another compression method—UltraPack compression. UltraPack files are usually much more compressed and thus are much slower to decompress. Infrequently used files are ideal for this, while key files should be left uncompressed or in HiPack format.

Partitioning

At A Glance: Hard Disk Partitions

Created with	FDISK utility
Partition types	Primary Extended Logical
Maximum number per disk	Four partitions are allowed per hard disk—one primary and up to three extended. Four logical partitions are allowed per extended partition.
Boot partition	One partition on each hard disk can be set as active and is used as a boot partition from which to load an operating system.

Partitioning a hard disk involves dividing the available space into separate partitions (or drives). Hard disks are partitioned with the FDISK utility and must be formatted (FAT16 or FAT32) with the FORMAT program before they can be used by Windows 98. You must have a primary MS-DOS partition in order for the system to be bootable. All other partitions can be configured as extended partitions or as a single extended partition with multiple logical partitions.

The rule of thumb is that a drive can be divided into up to four partitions (one primary and the rest extended). An extended partition can be subdivided into up to four logical partitions.

FDISK must be run in MS-DOS mode. When you create hard disk partitions with FDISK, you have the option of using all available disk space or specifying only a portion of the disk space. If you choose to use all the disk space for a partition, and later you want to divide that space into multiple partitions, you must run the FDISK program and delete your existing partition. When you delete a hard disk partition with FDISK, you destroy any existing data on that partition.

To create a primary partition on a new hard disk to hold the Windows 98 operating system, follow these steps:

1. Boot your system from a bootable floppy disk that contains the FDISK utility and the FORMAT program.

2. At the command prompt, type **FDISK** to start the FDISK utility.

3. Press 1 and then Enter to select the Create DOS partition or logical DOS drive option.

4. Press 1 and will then Enter to create a primary partition.

5. If you want to use all the available disk space for the primary partition, press Y and then Enter when prompted. If you don't want to use all the available disk space for the primary partition, press N and Enter. Type the number of megabytes or the percentage of available disk space you want to use for the primary partition, and press Enter.

6. FDISK will create the partition and bring you back to the Create DOS partition or logical DOS drive menu. Press Esc to return to the main menu.

7. Press 2 and then Enter to select the Set active partition option.

8. Press 1 and then Enter to make the first partition (the primary partition you just created) the active partition.

9. Press Esc to return to the main menu.

10. Press Esc to exit the FDISK utility.

11. Your computer will reboot. Boot from the boot floppy again and run the FORMAT program to format your hard disk partition for use by Windows 98.

If you have a hard disk larger than 512MB, FDISK will ask you if you want to enable large disk support. Large disk support is described in detail in the next section.

Enabling Large Disk Support

At A Glance: Large Disk Support

File system format	FAT32
Minimum partition size for large disk support	512MB
Can existing FAT16 partitions be converted?	Yes, with the FAT32 Drive Converter utility
Maximum disk size	2 terabytes

Cluster size	4,096 bytes for disks up to 8GB
	8,192 bytes for disks 8 to 16GB
	16,384 bytes for disks 16 to 32GB
	32,768 bytes for disks 32GB and over
Compatible with older disk utilities?	No
Visible from other operating systems?	No

After creating a partition, you must format it. Windows 98 asks you if you want to enable this partition for large disk support. If you choose Yes, the partition is formatted as FAT32. Otherwise, it becomes a FAT16 partition. If you enable large disk support in FDISK, any partitions you create that are larger than 512MB are automatically formatted as FAT32 partitions. Partitions you create that are smaller than 512MB are formatted as FAT16 partitions.

Existing FAT16 partitions that are larger than 512MB can always be converted to FAT32 without a loss of data (see the next section), but you can't convert from FAT32 to FAT16 without losing all data (back up to tape, format, restore).

Converting to FAT32

The FAT32 Drive Converter allows you to convert an existing FAT16 drive to FAT32. To start Drive Converter (FAT32), choose Start | Programs | Accessories | System Tools. You can also run it from the command line (CVTL.EXE).

CREATING HARDWARE PROFILES

At A Glance: Hardware Profiles

Created in	The Hardware Profiles tab on the System properties sheet is used to manually create new hardware profiles.
	Windows 98 will automatically create a new profile if it finds the computer in a docking station.
Selected by	Windows 98 will attempt to detect the current hardware configuration and use the appropriate hardware profile.
	Windows 98 will display a Hardware Profile menu at startup if it can't determine which hardware profile to use in the current configuration.

Windows 98 supports multiple startup configurations for system hardware using hardware profiles. A hardware profile specifies which hardware devices to use at system startup and supports the use of docking stations for laptop computers. Some hardware profiles are created automatically at system startup. You can also create your own hardware profiles based on existing configurations.

The Windows 98 Startup Process

The Windows 98 startup process consists of four basic phases:

+ Booting the system with the BIOS in control

+ Loading MS-DOS drivers and TSRs

+ Initializing real-mode static VxDs

+ Passing control to the protected-mode OS and loading remaining VxDs

Booting the system with the BIOS in control is the first step of the Windows 98 startup process. When you first turn on the power to your computer, code stored in nonvolatile Read-Only Memory (ROM) loads the computer's Basic Input/Output System (BIOS). The system BIOS performs a number of functions. It checks for system devices such as CPU, memory, hard disks, floppy drives, keyboard, and video adapters. The BIOS tests each of these devices to make sure they are all present and functioning properly. This is called the Power-On Self Test (POST). All devices on the ISA bus are enabled at this time. If the system has a Plug and Play BIOS installed, any Plug and Play devices in the computer are configured as well.

After the POST completes successfully, the system BIOS looks for a boot sector from which to load an operating system. It usually looks to the A: drive first, and then to drive C:, although the boot order is often configurable in the system CMOS. Once a boot sector is found, it is read, and instructions found there are executed. The Windows 98 boot sector contains instructions for loading and running the IO.SYS file.

The IO.SYS file is essentially MS-DOS. It performs the second and third steps in the Windows 98 startup process by loading MS-DOS drivers and TSRs into memory, reading the CONFIG.SYS and AUTOEXEC.BAT files (if they exist), and then reading the Registry and initializing static VxDs in real mode. Before it does any of that, however, it attempts to determine the system hardware configuration.

It does this by initiating a detection process that gathers the following information:

- Interrupt usage

- BIOS ports (serial and parallel)

- BIOS computer identification

- Plug and Play BIOS docking station data

- OEM docking station data

Once the detection process is complete, the current system configuration is saved as a hardware profile. Typical names for hardware profiles created by Windows 98 are docked and undocked. These names refer to whether a laptop computer is in a docking station. Hardware profile names correspond to top-level menu items in the CONFIG.SYS file if CONFIG.SYS has been set up for a multiconfiguration menu. Windows 98 automatically processes the appropriate CONFIG.SYS section for the selected hardware profile name.

NOTE A fully Plug and Play–compliant laptop computer will know whether it is docked or undocked. If your laptop is fully Plug and Play–compliant, it won't be necessary to use multiple hardware profiles. However, you may still use them if you want to enable the use of different combinations of available hardware devices at boot time.

Windows 98 automatically creates a new hardware profile if it finds that the computer is docked in a docking station. It creates a new hardware profile for each different docking station it finds the computer docked in. You can manually create your own hardware profiles as well.

Once the hardware profile has been determined, IO.SYS proceeds with the rest of the Windows 98 startup process. It reads the CONFIG.SYS file and loads any device drivers or TSRs it finds there. It then reads the AUTOEXEC.BAT file, if it exists, and executes any instructions it finds there. Next, the Registry is read, and static VxDs are initialized in real mode.

At this point, WIN.COM is loaded into memory and begins executing. The SYSTEM.INI file is read, any entries that differ from Registry entries are parsed, and necessary VxDs are loaded. VMM32.VXD is loaded, creating virtual machines and initializing each of the VxDs specified in the Registry.

Finally, the Configuration Manager is loaded, and the last phase of the Windows 98 startup process begins. All devices in the system are enumerated, resource conflicts are resolved, and the devices are initialized for use by Windows 98. Then the Windows 98 kernel is loaded into memory (KERNEL32.DLL and KRNL386.EXE), the graphical device interface (GDI32.EXE and GDI.EXE) is loaded, and the user interface is loaded (USER32.EXE and USER.EXE). Last, fonts are loaded into memory, entries in the WIN.INI file are parsed, and the basic desktop is loaded. A login prompt is displayed, and the user can log in to Windows 98.

Creating a New Hardware Profile

Although Windows 98 automatically creates a new hardware profile if it finds the computer in a docking station, it is sometimes useful to create hardware profiles manually.

Hardware profile information is found on the Hardware Profiles tab of the System properties sheet. When creating a new hardware profile, you will base the configuration on an existing hardware profile by copying that profile and saving it under a new name. You then make the appropriate changes to the configuration in that profile. To create a new hardware profile, follow these steps:

1. Right-click the My Computer icon and select Properties to display the System properties sheet.

2. Select the Hardware Profiles tab.

3. Select a hardware profile on which to base your new configuration. Click the Copy button.

4. Enter a name for the new hardware profile, and click OK.

5. Click OK on the System properties sheet to complete the process.

After you have followed these steps, you have a new hardware profile that is identical to the one you selected to base your configuration on. You must now make changes to the configuration in order to distinguish the two profiles from one another. You do this by disabling or removing hardware devices from the hardware profile. Use the Device Manager tab on the System properties sheet to accomplish this.

To remove a device from a hardware profile, or to disable the device in that profile, follow these steps:

1. Right-click the My Computer icon and display the System properties sheet.

2. Select the Device Manager tab.

3. Select the device you want to remove or disable, and click the Properties button.

4. On the device properties sheet, select one of the following options:

- Disable in this hardware profile

- Remove from this hardware profile

- Exists in all hardware profiles

5. Click OK on the device properties sheet to return to the Device Manager tab of the System properties sheet.

6. Perform steps 3, 4, and 5 for each device you want to change.

7. Click OK on the System properties sheet to complete the process.

Windows 98 will attempt to detect the system's hardware configuration at startup and will select the appropriate hardware profile to use at that time. However, if two or more hardware profiles are very similar and Windows 98 can't determine which profile to use, you are promoted to select the hardware profile you want to use.

WHAT IS IMPORTANT TO KNOW

The following list summarizes the chapter and accentuates the key concepts to memorize for the exam:

- Unified Logon means that one password is all you need to access all network resources. It relies on the Windows 98 password to match the password of the primary authenticator and uses .PWL files.

- The Microsoft Family Logon is a client that allows Windows 98 users to quickly load their desktop settings from their local profiles.

- Password caching is the process of storing passwords in .PWL files. It can be disabled through the Registry or with a system policy.

- The Password List Editor can be used to edit and delete entries in .PWL files.

- The Password List Editor doesn't display the actual passwords.

- The Password List Editor only displays the password entries for the user who is currently logged on.

- SETPASS is the NetWare utility used to change passwords.

- File and Printer Sharing allows you to share resources with other users.

- File and Printer Sharing doesn't allow you to share individual files, but it does allow the sharing of folders.

- File and Printer Sharing can use either share-level security or user-level security.

- The File and Printer Sharing for NetWare Networks service must use user-level security.

- Share permissions are Read-Only and Full Control.

- User-level permissions allow specific access rights to be assigned to individual users or groups of users.

- Windows NT can use the NTFS file system, which allows file access rights to be assigned to individual users or groups.

- When share-level access rights and NTFS access rights seem to conflict, the most restrictive access rights apply.

- User profiles are one-half of the Registry—storing the user component.

- User profiles can be local or roaming.

- Local user profiles are stored on the local hard disk in the folder WINDOWS\PROFILES*username*.

◆ Roaming user profiles on a Windows NT domain controller are stored in the users' HOME directories.

◆ Roaming profiles on a Novell NetWare file server are stored in the users' MAIL directories.

◆ System policies restrict what users see and what they can run or change on their workstations.

◆ System policies are contained in the CONFIG.POL file.

◆ On a Windows NT domain controller, the CONFIG.POL file is stored in the NETLOGON share.

◆ On a Novell NetWare file server, the CONFIG.POL file is stored in the PUBLIC directory.

◆ The Registry is backed up with ScanRegW and can be restored with the command `scanreg /restore`.

◆ ScanRegW is the GUI version of the Registry Checker, and ScanReg is the command-line version.

◆ The Registry can only be restored from a backup using the command-line version of the Registry Checker, ScanReg.

◆ The Registry backup can only be compressed using the GUI version of the Registry Checker, ScanRegW.

◆ Disk compression is accomplished with the DriveSpace3 utility and the Compression Agent (CMPAGENT.EXE).

◆ Compression can be in Standard, HiPack, or UltraPack format.

◆ You must be using the Compression Agent in order to use the UltraPack compression method.

◆ Partitioning is done with the FDISK utility.

◆ Hard disks are allowed up to four partitions—one primary and up to three extended.

◆ Each extended hard disk partition is allowed up to four logical partitions.

◆ One hard disk partition should be set to active. Windows 98 boots from the active partition.

◆ Large disk support involves using FAT32, while the absence of it implies FAT16.

◆ FAT16 can be converted to FAT32 without a loss of data by way of the FAT32 Drive Converter (CVTL.EXE). You can't convert from FAT32 to FAT16 without formatting the drive and losing all data.

◆ Windows NT doesn't support the FAT32 file system. FAT32 partitions on local hard disks can't be accessed from within Windows NT.

◆ Windows 98 doesn't support the NTFS file system. NTFS partitions on local hard disks can't be accessed from within Windows 98.

◆ Windows 98 supports multiple hardware configurations using hardware profiles.

◆ Hardware profiles allow a laptop computer to use one set of hardware while in a docking station and another set of hardware while undocked.

◆ Windows 98 automatically creates a new hardware profile if it detects that the computer is in a docking station at startup.

◆ Hardware profiles can be created manually on the Hardware Profiles tab of the System properties sheet.

◆ New hardware profiles are based on copies of existing hardware profiles.

◆ Devices can be disabled in or removed from hardware profiles via the Device Manager tab of the System properties sheet.

▶ Configure a Windows 98 computer as a client computer in a Windows NT network.

▶ Configure a Windows 98 computer as a client computer in a NetWare network.

▶ Configure a Windows 98 computer for remote access by using various methods in a Microsoft environment and a mixed Microsoft and NetWare environment. Methods include the following:
  • Dial-Up Networking
  • 3Proxy Server

CHAPTER 4

Integration and Interoperability

NETWORKING BASICS

At A Glance: Windows 98 Networking Components

Windows 98 Networking Component	Function
Client	Allows a Windows 98 computer to connect to and authenticate with a specific vendor's LAN software.
Adapter	Provides drivers necessary for a specific manufacturer's Network Interface Card to function under Windows 98.
Protocol	Provides a standard communication method for a specific type of network.
Service	Lets Windows 98 computers provide enhanced network functionality for interaction with other computers on the network.

Windows 98 supports many different kinds of networks. In addition to supporting Dial-Up Networking using a modem and connecting to many types of LANs using a network interface card, Windows 98 supports Asynchronous Transfer Mode (ATM) networks as well as direct cable connections and fast infrared network connections. Windows 98 provides a network client for the following types of LANs:

- Microsoft networks. These include the following:

  - Windows 95, 98, and NT networks

  - Windows for Workgroups networks

  - LAN Manager networks

- Novell NetWare networks. These include the following:

  - NetWare 3.x networks

  - NetWare 4.x networks

- Banyan VINES networks

Windows 98 supports version 5 of the Network Device Interface Specification (NDIS 5), which allows it to support ATM as well as ATM LAN Emulation (LANE). A new 32-bit version of the Data Link Control protocol (DLC) is provided with Windows 98 to allow connections to IBM mainframe and AS/400 computers, as well as connections to certain Hewlett-Packard JetDirect network interface cards for printers.

Dial-Up Networking support has been enhanced under Windows 98 to include support for Virtual Private Networking (VPN) using Point-to-Point Tunneling Protocol (PPTP). Support has also been enhanced for the use of Integrated Digital Services Network (ISDN) adapters. Multiple conventional modems can be combined to provide increased bandwidth using Windows 98 support for Multilink Bandwidth Aggregation.

You can configure all your network components when you first install Windows 98, or you can install network components after your Windows 98 installation is complete. If you want to examine how your network components are configured, or make changes to your network configuration, double-click the Network applet in Control Panel to view the Network properties dialog box, shown in Figure 4.1.

Identification Options

Figure 4.2 shows the options available on the Identification tab of the Network properties dialog box. Use this tab to view your computer name and your workgroup or domain name. From here you can change your computer name, or join a workgroup or domain, and enter a description of your computer to help identify it and the resources it contains.

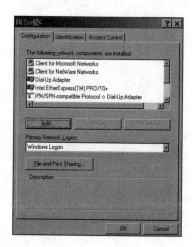

FIGURE 4.1
The Network properties dialog box.

FIGURE 4.2
The Identification tab of the Network properties dialog box.

The maximum length of a computer name, workgroup name, or domain name is 15 characters, and the maximum length of the computer description is 50 characters, although you should try to keep it shorter than that for readability. Your computer name uniquely identifies your computer on the network, so it can't be the same as any other computer name already on the network. The workgroup or domain name identifies a logical group of computers on the network, and resources are shared among members of this group. There can be many such groups on your network, each one with a unique name.

Configuration Options

Use the the Configuration tab of the Network properties dialog box to view and modify the network clients, adapters, protocols, services, and bindings for your computer.

Clicking the Add button allows you to install one of four different types of items:

- Client

- Adapter

- Protocol

- Service

Different clients allow you to authenticate yourself and connect to different types of networks. Here are some clients you might want to add for Windows 98:

- Client for Microsoft Networks
- Client for NetWare Networks
- Banyan DOS/Windows 3.1 client
- Microsoft Family Logon

Each of these clients supports a connection to different networks. The Client for Microsoft networks is used to connect to

- Windows 95, 98, and NT networks
- Windows for Workgroups networks
- LAN Manager networks

The Client for NetWare networks is used to connect to

- NetWare 3.x networks
- NetWare 4.x networks

The Banyan DOS/Windows 3.1 client is used to provide connection support for Banyan VINES networks.

To add a network client to your Windows 98 computer, do the following:

1. Start the Network Control Panel applet and select the Configuration tab.
2. Click the Add button.
3. Choose Client in the dialog box that appears, and click the Add button.
4. Choose the appropriate vendor on the left side of the dialog box that appears, select the appropriate client on the right side, and click OK.
5. Provide the location of the Windows 98 CD, and click OK.
6. Click OK in the Network Properties dialog box.
7. Click Yes to restart the system when prompted to do so.

The Microsoft Family Logon is a client included with Windows 98 that provides a simplified way to log in to Windows 98 using user profiles. It relies on the user profiles that are set up on the Windows 98 computer, so the system must be configured to use profiles. Once Microsoft Family Logon is installed, it should be selected as the primary network logon. Then, whenever the Windows 98 computer is started, a dialog box appears containing a list of users who have profiles stored on the computer. Simply select your name from the list and enter your password, and your settings are loaded from your profile.

Adding the Microsoft Family Logon differs only slightly from adding any other client to your Windows 98 system. To add the Microsoft Family Logon, do the following:

1. Start the Network Control Panel applet.

2. Select the Configuration tab, and click the Add button.

3. Select Client from the dialog box that appears, and click the Add button.

4. Select Microsoft, select Microsoft Family Logon, and click OK.

5. Provide the location of the Windows 98 CD, and click OK.

6. In the Network properties dialog box, select Microsoft Family Logon from the Primary Network Logon drop-down list.

7. Click OK.

8. Select Yes to restart the computer when prompted to do so.

Adapters let you add, remove, view the properties of, or update your network adapter drivers. Windows 98 allows an unlimited number of network adapters. It ships with support for hundreds of different adapters from many different hardware vendors. To install a new adapter in your Windows 98 system, do the following:

1. Start the Network Control Panel applet.

2. Select the Configuration tab in the Network properties dialog box.

3. Click the Add button.

4. Select Adapter from the dialog box that appears, and click the Add button.

5. Select the manufacturer on the left side of the dialog box, select the appropriate network adapter on the right side, and click OK.

6. Provide the location of the Windows 98 CD, and click OK.

7. Click OK in the Network Properties dialog box.

8. Click Yes to restart the computer when prompted to do so.

If you don't see your manufacturer or adapter listed in step 5, you will have to use drivers supplied to you on a disk by the manufacturer of your network adapter. Click the Have Disk button to supply the drivers to Windows 98 for installation.

Use the Protocols selection to view and modify the transport protocols for your computer. Windows 98 allows an unlimited number of network transport protocols. You might want to add some of the following network transport protocols to a Windows 98 workstation:

- ◆ TCP/IP. The default protocol for Windows NT. It is required for Internet connectivity.

- ◆ IPX/SPX-compatible transport. The default protocol for connectivity to NetWare servers.

- ◆ NetBEUI. Typically only allows connectivity to other Microsoft-based computers. Doesn't support routing.

- ◆ 32-bit DLC. This protocol is typically used to connect to IBM mainframe and AS/400 computers, but it can also be used to connect to Hewlett-Packard printers using the HP JetDirect network interface card.

- ◆ Fast infrared protocol. This protocol allows a Windows 98 computer with an infrared port to connect to other infrared-equipped devices, such as printers.

To add a protocol to your Windows 98 computer, do the following:

1. Start the Network Control Panel applet.

2. Select the Configuration tab of the Network properties dialog box.

3. Click the Add button.

4. Select Protocol from the dialog box that appears, and click the Add button.

5. Select the manufacturer on the left side of the dialog box that appears, select the appropriate protocol on the right side, and click OK.

6. Provide the location of the Windows 98 CD.

7. Click OK in the Network Properties dialog box.

8. Select Yes to restart the computer when prompted to do so.

The Internet Packet Exchange/Sequenced Packet Exchange (IPX/SPX) protocol was originally developed by Novell for use with its NetWare network operating system. NetWare networks now also support the TCP/IP protocol, but IPX/SPX is still the default protocol for the NetWare operating system. Microsoft has developed a compatible protocol for use with its Windows operating system. This protocol is referred to as the NWLink IPX/SPX-compatible transport under Windows NT. It's called simply IPX/SPX under Windows 98.

Perhaps the most widely used of the protocols supported by Windows 98 is TCP/IP. TCP/IP is actually a suite of protocols named after the two most important protocols in the suite, Transmission Control Protocol and Internet Protocol.

Microsoft introduced support for TCP/IP in Windows for Workgroups and enhanced its support for the protocol in Windows 95. Microsoft adopted TCP/IP as the default protocol for use with Windows NT 4.0 and has further enhanced support for it in Windows 98. Here are the major enhancements to TCP/IP support in Windows 98:

♦ Support for the new Windows Sockets 2 API. Windows Sockets 2 is a new and improved Application Programming Interface (API) that provides greater efficiency and more features than the Windows Sockets 1 API.

♦ Support for the new Quality Generic Quality of Service (GqoS) and Resource Reservation Protocol (RSVP). This allows applications to request certain characteristics for a network connection, including the following:

- Peak bandwidth

- Latency

- Delay variation

- Support for IP Multicast. Defined in Request For Comments (RFC) 1112, IP Multicast provides a method for the transmission of IP data to a group of hosts simultaneously, rather than to a single host.

- Support for ICMP Router Discovery. This feature allows Windows 98 computers to automatically discover the IP addresses of neighboring routers.

- Support for RIP Listening. This feature is useful for Windows 98 computers that have multiple network interfaces connected to multiple networks (a multihomed host). Windows 98 can use only one default gateway at a time, but multihomed computers need to get routing information from routers on each network they are connected to. RIP listening allows a multihomed computer to listen to RIP messages between routers to discover routes on multiple networks.

You can also add *third-party* transport protocols (ones that haven't been developed by Microsoft), provided that they are compatible with the Transport Data Interface (TDI) and Network Device Interface Specification (NDIS). These are the two network interface standards that are supported under Windows 98, and protocols must be compatible with these standards in order for Windows 98 to be able to use them to communicate with system hardware and software.

The Services selection allows you to install additional services for Windows 98. Here are some services you might wish to install to Windows 98:

- File and Printer Sharing for Microsoft Networks

- File and Printer Sharing for NetWare Networks

- Service for NetWare Directory Services

The File and Printer Sharing services allow you to share files on your hard disk, or printers connected to your computer, with other users on the network. You can load the File and Printer Sharing service for either Microsoft Networks or NetWare Networks, but not both at the same time.

The Service for NetWare Directory Services works with the Microsoft Client for NetWare Networks when you're connected to a Novell NetWare 4.x network. Starting with NetWare 4, Novell introduced NetWare Directory Services (NDS) as a way to manage all users, servers, and other resources on a NetWare network. All resources on the network are referred to as objects, and all objects are managed in a tree-like database known as the Directory. This allows for a single login to provide access to multiple network resources and for a central point of resource administration.

Previous versions of NetWare required the administrator to manage network resources on each file server individually, and users had to have an account on each server that they needed access to. User account information was stored in a database on each server called the Bindery.

The Microsoft Client for NetWare Networks allows for connection to a NetWare 3.x network by authenticating user information with the NetWare file server's Bindery database. When using the client to connect to a NetWare 4.x network, the client requires that the server provide Bindery-like services to it for authentication. This is called bindery emulation. Bindery emulation is enabled on NetWare 4.x servers by default, but it is undesirable because it's resource-intensive. Also, Windows 98 clients can't take advantage of the full benefits of NDS when connecting to the network under bindery emulation. To fix this problem, Microsoft developed the Service for NetWare Directory Services to allow the Microsoft NetWare client to take full advantage of Novell's NDS.

To install a service on your Windows 98 system, follow these steps:

1. Start the Network Control Panel applet and select the Configuration tab.

2. Click the Add button.

3. Choose Service from the dialog box that appears, and click the Add button.

4. Choose the service you wish to install, and click OK.

5. Provide the location of the Windows 98 CD, and click OK.

6. Click OK in the Network Properties dialog box.

7. Click Yes to restart the system when prompted to do so.

Access Control Options

The Access Control tab, shown in Figure 4.3, allows you to choose the type of security in use.

Windows 98 can function as a standalone computer or as a member of a network of computers. Different levels of security are available to Windows 98 users who wish to share resources on their computers, depending on the type of network environment the Windows 98 computer is connected to. Two common networking environments are peer-to-peer and server-based.

In a peer-to-peer network, you simply take the machines currently in existence, install network cards in them, and connect them through some type of cabling. Each machine is known as a peer and can participate in the sharing of files and resources. No dedicated file server is required, so there is no additional cost for a dedicated machine. There is no real security or centralized administration.

Peer-to-peer networks require an operating system (or add-on) that can understand networking and function in this way. Windows 98 can function in a peer-to-peer environment, and in this environment it offers share-level security to users sharing resources with other computers on the network.

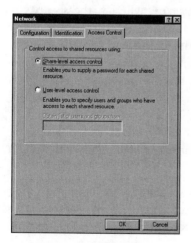

FIGURE 4.3
The Access Control tab of the Network properties dialog box.

Share-Level Security

If File and Printer Sharing has been enabled on a Windows 98 system, you can create a share by selecting a folder and choosing to share it. To share a folder using share-level security, follow these steps:

1. Start Windows Explorer.

2. Select the folder you wish to share.

3. Right-click the folder and select Sharing from the menu that appears.

4. On the Sharing tab, select the Shared As: radio button.

5. Enter a name in the Share Name field. Optionally, enter a description of the share in the Comment field. Share names are limited to 15 characters.

6. Select the appropriate radio button in the Access Type area.

7. Optionally, add a password for access to the share.

By default, no password is associated with the shared resource, but you can choose to assign one that a user must supply in order to access the resource. Access permissions can be Read-Only, Full, or Depends on Password. This is known as *share-level security,* wherein the security is given when a user supplies the correct password to access the share. Each shared resource has its own password. Although these can all be set as the same password, each time a user wants to access a different shared resource, she must supply the password for that resource, even if it is identical to the password for another shared resource that has already been accessed. If you select Depends on Password for the Access Type to a share, you can provide two different passwords for the share—one that gives the user Read-Only access to the share, and another that gives the user Full access to the share.

To enable resource sharing on a peer-to-peer network, you must first install the File and Printer Sharing for Microsoft Networks service. This is done on the Configuration tab of the Network properties dialog box.

To install File and Printer Sharing for Microsoft Networks, follow the instructions presented earlier in this chapter for installing a service, and select File and Printer Sharing for Microsoft Networks in step 4.

Once File and Printer Sharing has been enabled, you will be able to implement share-level access to your files and printers. On the Access Control tab of the Network properties sheet, you will see that Share-level access control has been selected by default.

Peer-to-peer networking works in small environments. If your network grows beyond approximately 15 machines, the administrative overhead of establishing the shares, coupled with the lack of tight security, becomes too difficult to manage effectively. At this point it becomes worth the investment to purchase a dedicated computer to act as a file server and a network operating system, such as Windows NT Server or Novell NetWare.

User-Level Security

In the presence of a file server, be it NetWare or NT, you can implement *user-level security* on your network. With user-level security, permissions are based on how the user logged on and was authenticated by the server. Every user on the network must have an *account* on the file server. The file server stores some kind of database that records the rights and privileges associated with each user account. In this environment, you can assign permissions to shares based on user permissions or group permissions. In short, you must have a server on the network to have user-level security, but can have share-level security with or without a server.

Also known as *client/server networking,* the downside of server-based networking is that it requires a dedicated machine (the server). The upside is that you gain centralized administration and authentication. With centralized administration, you can add all users at one location and control logon scripts, backups, and so on. With centralized authentication, you can identify a user to your entire network based on his logon name and password, not based on each share he attempts to access.

Peer-to-peer networks can exist comfortably within server-based networks, and in many businesses, combinations of the two models are used. A server-based network is used to provide email and other resources to all users, while peer-to-peer networks are established within divisions to share resources among select users.

Microsoft calls peer-to-peer networks *workgroups* and server-based networks *domains.* The terms are used interchangeably in almost all Microsoft documentation and on the test.

Recognizing How the UNC Is Used

The *Universal Naming Convention* (UNC) is a standardized nomenclature for specifying a share name on a particular computer. The computer name is limited to 15 characters, and the share name is usually limited to 15 characters, depending on the network.

The UNC uniquely specifies the path to the share name on a network. The UNC path takes the form of *computername\sharename* [*optional path*]. If a dollar sign ($) is added to the end of the share name, this will prevent the share name from being visible to another computer through a browser, such as Network Neighborhood.

All Windows 98 functions support using a UNC name, including the Run option on the Start menu and the command prompt. NetWare servers, like Windows NT servers, can be accessed through a UNC name.

> NOTE
>
> Share names in Windows 98 can be as long as the involved protocols and user interfaces will allow. However, NetBIOS names can only be 15 characters long and can't contain embedded blanks. Therefore, when establishing share names on your servers, keep them short, don't use spaces within the name, and use 15 or fewer total characters.

CONFIGURING WINDOWS 98 AS AN NT CLIENT

At A Glance: Configuring Windows 98 as an NT Client

Component	Function
TCP/IP protocol	The default communication protocol used by Windows NT for network communications.
Client for Microsoft Networks	Allows a Windows 98 computer to communicate with other Microsoft computers on a network.
File and Printer Sharing for Microsoft Networks	Allows Windows 98 computers to share local resources with other computers on a Microsoft network.

A Windows NT domain contains at least one Windows NT server that acts as the domain controller and maintains a user accounts database. When a Windows 98 computer participates in a domain, it can use user-level security to share and access resources on a per-user account basis. Furthermore, Windows 98 can process Windows NT logon scripts during logon.

A peer workgroup consists of Windows-based computers that are not part of a Windows NT domain. Workgroups must use share-level security, because the clients don't access a central Windows NT or NetWare accounts database.

To configure a Windows 98 computer to participate in a peer-to-peer workgroup, you need to specify only the computer name and workgroup name on the Identification tab of the Network properties dialog box.

To allow other computers on a Microsoft network to access a Windows 98 computer's print queues or files, you need to do the following:

+ Enable the appropriate sharing option(s) in the File and Printer Sharing dialog box of Control Panel's Network applet.

+ If user-level security is to be used, configure that option in the Access Control tab of the Network properties dialog box.

+ The specific directory or printer queue must be shared, and the appropriate access permissions must be granted.

Configuring Windows 98 to Use NT's User-Level Security

To set up Windows 98 to use Windows NT user-level security, you must have Windows 98 running on a Windows NT domain and have Client for Microsoft Networks enabled.

Follow these steps to cause Windows 98 to use Windows NT for user-level security:

1. Start the Network Control Panel applet.

2. Select the Access Control tab in the Network properties dialog box.

3. Select the User-level access control radio button.

4. Enter the path to the NT Domain Controller in the Obtain list of users and groups from field.

5. Click OK.

You can now set up folders and printers to be shared on the Windows 98 client computers using Windows NT domain accounts and groups for user-level security. To share a folder using user-level security, the instructions differ significantly from the instructions presented earlier in this chapter for sharing a folder with share-level security. Follow these steps to share a folder using user-level security:

1. Start Windows Explorer.

2. Select the folder you wish to share.

3. Right-click the folder and select Sharing from the menu that appears.

4. On the Sharing tab, select the Shared As radio button.

5. Enter a name for the shared folder in the Share Name field, and, optionally, enter a description of the shared folder in the Comment field.

6. Click the Add button to display the Add Users dialog box.

7. From the Name list on the left side of the Add Users dialog box, select the users or groups you wish to have access to the shared folder.

8. Click the appropriate button to give the selected users or groups the type of access you want them to have. Choices are Read-Only, Full Access, or Custom.

9. Click OK twice to complete the process.

If you grant Custom access to any users or groups, before you can complete the process, you must select the specific access rights that you wish to grant to those users or groups. A Change Access Rights dialog box appears, and you can select any combination of the following access rights:

- Read Files allows the user to read the contents of a file but not to change those contents.

- Write to Files allows the user to change the contents of a file. This includes the ability to remove all the contents of the file.

- Create Files and Folders allows the user to create new files in the shared folder, as well as create new subfolders inside the shared folder.

- Delete Files allows the user to delete files and subfolders in the shared folder.

- Change File Attributes allows the user to change file attributes on files within the shared folder.

- List Files allows the user to view a directory listing of the names of files in the shared folder but not to access the contents of the file.

- Change Access Control allows the user to change the access rights of users who have rights to the shared folder, including his or her own rights.

If you're sharing a printer using Windows NT user-level security, the steps are similar, except that you can only assign Full Control access to users of the shared printer.

Configuring the Browse Master for Microsoft Networks

When users access the Network Neighborhood, they are viewing a list of computers on the network known as a *browse list*.

Microsoft and NetWare networks can use NetBIOS to distribute browse lists throughout a domain. The browse list contains all NetBIOS computers and shared resources in the domain; it is compiled by the domain's master browser.

When the master browser has compiled the browse list, it distributes the list to the backup browsers. When a client requires access to the browse list, it obtains it from a backup browser so that the master browser doesn't become overloaded with requests from all the computers.

The decision of which computers are master browsers and which are backup browsers is determined through browser elections. Each type of operating system in the network has a different potential to be a browser.

Windows NT computers are more favored to be browsers than Windows 98 computers. If a computer is a preferred browser, it can be chosen to be a browser, depending on the operating system it is running and whether it has been manually configured to be a preferred browser.

When a network client needs to consult a browse list to browse the network, it contacts one of the backup browsers for a copy of the current browse list. The backup browsers periodically receive updated browse lists from the master browser to make sure the browse lists remain current.

You can configure a Windows 98 computer to maintain or not maintain browse lists by configuring the File and Printer Sharing service with one of the following options:

- Automatically decide if the Windows 98 computer is needed as a browser by participating in the browser elections (this is the default setting)

- Disable browse list maintenance so that the Windows 98 computer doesn't compile browse lists

- Be a preferred browser for the browser elections

Normally, you let the browser elections automatically determine which computers are the browsers. However, if you don't want the potential performance load on the Windows 98 computer that can result from browsing, you can configure the computer to never be a browser.

CONFIGURING WINDOWS 98 AS A CLIENT IN A NETWARE NETWORK

Windows 98 clients can easily join existing Novell NetWare networks and share many of the benefits of other NetWare clients. For interoperability with NetWare networks, Windows 98 includes the following components and features:

- The 32-bit Client for NetWare Networks (using the NWREDIR.VXD driver)

- Support for 16-bit Novell NetWare clients, either NETX or VLMs

- A NetWare login script processor

- The IPX/SPX-compatible protocol

- The IPX ODI protocol for compatibility with older NetWare networks

- The File and Printer Sharing for NetWare Networks service

- The Service for NetWare Directory Services

Where possible, the 32-bit Client for NetWare Networks is recommended for interoperability with NetWare networks. The 32-bit client doesn't use any conventional memory. It provides benefits such as unified logon (which requires the same password for all networks) and unified browsing services.

When you install the Client for NetWare Networks, the IPX/SPX-compatible protocol automatically gets installed as well. This protocol must be used with the Client for NetWare Networks, although additional protocols can also be installed.

> **NOTE**
>
> File and Printer Sharing for NetWare Networks must use the user-level security model.

Configuring Windows 98 to Use NetWare's User-Level Security

You can use user-level security when you're running Windows 98 on a NetWare network and you want to have peer services enabled for the Windows 98 clients. When you use user-level security with NetWare networks, security authentication requests are handled using the pass-through security method. This type of security passes the authentication requests to a NetWare server for authentication.

User-level security on NetWare, just as for Windows NT, is used to protect shared network resources by storing a list of users and groups who have access to a network resource. To gain access to a resource, a user must be on the access account list stored in the NetWare server bindery and then have the proper access rights for that resource.

Administrators can set up access rights on a per-user or per-group basis. The rights that can be assigned to a user for a specific resource are the same as those that can be assigned to users in the Windows NT user-level security model (see the list of access rights earlier in this chapter). Attributes are also known as *flags* in the NetWare world, but that term typically is used to refer to file attributes of files stored on the NetWare server.

The File and Printer Sharing for NetWare Networks service is established in protected mode with NWSERVER.VXD, which is supported by the NWSP.VXD, the virtual device driver that handles security for the Windows 98 client computer that shares its files and printers. Because File and Printer Sharing for NetWare Networks depends on the bindery security from the NetWare server, an additional function is necessary to read the NetWare server's bindery. This function is provided through the NWAB32.DLL file, which is responsible for reading the access account list from the NetWare server bindery.

The NetWare utility SYSCON is used by administrators of a NetWare 3.x network to create user accounts and groups. In the NetWare 4.x environment, the NWADMIN utility accomplishes the same tasks. A 32-bit version of the utility, NWADMN95, was released for use with Windows 95 workstations. This version works well under Windows 98 as well.

Configuring the Browse Master for NetWare Networks

The Browser service can be configured on Windows 98 computers that are participating in a NetWare network, the same as those participating in NT networks. The configuration of the service differs from that of a Windows 98 computer participating in a Microsoft network, but the principle is exactly the same.

To implement browsing on a Windows 98 computer participating in a NetWare network, follow these steps:

1. Start the Network Control Panel applet and select the File and Printer Sharing for NetWare Networks service.

2. Click Properties and select the Workgroup Advertising property.

3. Choose one of the following options from the drop-down list:

♦   To have Windows 98 automatically determine if the computer is needed as a browse server, select Enabled: May Be Master for the value.

♦   To prevent the computer from maintaining browse lists for the network, select Enabled: May Not Be Master for the value.

NOTE   The Enabled: May Not Be Master option doesn't prevent the computer from browsing the network resources; it prevents it from maintaining a browse list for itself and other computers. Select the Disabled option to prevent the computer from using the browse service.

♦   To give the computer a higher weighting for the browse elections, select Enabled: Preferred Master for the value. This computer will then be preferred over other Windows 98 computers that have Automatic set for the Browse Master value for the browse elections.

♦   To prevent the computer from using the browser service to browse network resources, select Disabled for the value.

♦   To allow the computer to send SAP broadcasts announcing its presence to real-mode NetWare clients, select the SAP Advertising property and change the value to Enabled.

4. Click OK twice and restart the computer.

Disadvantages of NetWare Servers

Here are some disadvantages of running Windows 98 on a NetWare network:

♦   Long filenames are not supported natively.

♦   The real-mode NetWare driver (ODI and VLM or NETX real-mode shell) uses conventional memory (RAM) that MS-DOS applications could use.

♦   Users of Windows 98 can reassign print queue assignments, among others.

By default, NetWare 3.x file servers don't save long filenames. In order to enable this feature, you must load NAMs (Name Support Modules) on the server. Novell didn't create a name support module for Windows 98. You must load the OS/2 Name Space (OS2.NAM) feature in NetWare 3.x in order for long filenames to be supported on a network with Windows 98 workstations. You must then add the name space to the hard disk volume on the server where you wish to store files that have long filenames. Follow these steps to provide long filename support on a NetWare 3.x file server:

1. Access the NetWare 3.x file server console (the : prompt screen).

2. Enter the Load OS2 command to load the OS2.NAM module.

3. Enter the Add name space OS2 to volume *volumename* command to add the name space to the volume where you wish to store files that have long filenames.

4. Edit the AUTOEXEC.NCF file and add the commands from steps 2 and 3 to provide long filename support each time the file server is rebooted.

In an IntraNetWare 4.11 environment, long filename support is provided by the LONG.NAM module, not the OS2.NAM module. Also, in this environment, long filename support is loaded for each volume by default.

NetWare System Administrators might feel a lack of control when Windows 98 workstations are introduced to their network, because users can use Windows 98's Explorer and Network Neighborhood to access files and remap network drive letters, as well as reassign print queues (they can see whatever print queues the bindery or NDS gives them access to). Not only that, but the user can save drive mappings and print queue assignments as permanent and can reestablish them every time the user logs onto the network and starts Windows 98.

Although administrators can limit what Windows 98 users see through the Network Neighborhood and Explorer, users still might be able to access programs, files, and directories using the MS-DOS prompt or network mapping prompt if they know the server's Universal Naming Convention (UNC).

CONFIGURING WINDOWS 98 TO ACCESS THE INTERNET

Windows 98 supports connecting to the Internet in two ways: through a permanent connection or through a dial-up connection. A *permanent connection* usually means that you will be leasing a dedicated phone line from a local communication provider. This is typically the case in large corporate network environments where all LAN users have access to the Internet. A *dial-up connection* is a connection to an Internet Service Provider made through a modem and an ordinary phone line (or an ISDN line) connected to the Windows 98 computer. You use the TCP/IP networking protocol to connect a Windows 98 computer to the Internet. It must be installed separately, whereas IPX/SPX-compatible and NetBEUI protocols are installed by default when the first network card is placed in the machine.

Dial-Up Connections

Windows 98 uses the same networking protocols for Dial-Up Networking as it does for regular networking connections. Windows 98 essentially treats your modem as a network interface, converting network protocols to line protocols such as Point-to-Point Protocol (PPP) and Serial Line Internet Protocol (SLIP). It converts line protocols to network protocols that use the Windows 98 networking architecture. PPP is installed by default when TCP/IP is installed and is the most common line protocol in use today. If you must connect to an environment where PPP can't be used, SLIP should be used. SLIP is an older line protocol that doesn't support many of the features of PPP (such as automatic addressing), but it doesn't have the overhead that PPP does and is very efficient. For that reason, many network administrators still use it.

Unless you are connected to the Internet through a permanent connection at a company or organization, you probably will gain access through a commercial provider via a dial-up connection using a modem and a regular telephone line. Windows 98 includes the Dial-Up Adapter, which you can set up to connect to an ISP. You then bind this adapter to the TCP/IP protocol, dial into your ISP (using the Dial-Up Networking (DUN) feature), and communicate over the Internet. To set up a connection to an ISP using an ISP account, you will need to know the following:

- The ISP's telephone number

- The line protocol to use (PPP or SLIP)

- Your user name and password

- Your IP address and subnet mask (if this is not dynamically configured each time you connect)

- Your email address

- The SMTP and/or POP3 server name

- The Domain Name Service (DNS) server IP address

Your ISP will provide you with this information.

After you install and configure DUN, you can dial into your ISP, establish an Internet connection, and start using Internet resources. If your network uses the Windows Internet Naming Service (WINS) for the NetBIOS protocol, you need to find out the primary and secondary (optional) WINS server address, the scope ID, and whether the server uses Dynamic Host Configuration Protocol (DHCP) to obtain WINS configuration. This information needs to be entered on the WINS Configuration tab. When enabled, the DNS option requires information on Host, Domain, DNS Server Search Order, and Domain Suffix Search Order.

Proxy Server

A proxy server is a gateway that allows many clients to access the Internet. Rather than requiring each client to have a dedicated phone line to reach the Internet, each client only needs to be able to access the proxy server, which maintains the connections to the Internet.

The proxy server accepts requests from computers on the internal network destined for hosts on the Internet and handles the requests on behalf of the internal computers. Hosts on the Internet communicate with the proxy server and have no knowledge of the computers on the internal network. The proxy server can be configured to store a log of all transactions that take place. This can help an administrator determine whether Internet access is being used inappropriately by internal users. There are many different manufacturers of proxy servers, including Microsoft, which sells a proxy server that runs on its Windows NT operating system.

Installing and Configuring TCP/IP for Use with Windows 98

At A Glance: TCP/IP Parameters

Parameter	Required/Optional	Function
IP Address	Required	Uniquely identifies your Windows 98 computer on the network.
Subnet Mask	Required	Identifies the specific subnet portion of your IP address.
Default Gateway	One gateway is required. Additional gateways are optional.	Identifies the router to send packets to when it is determined that the destination host is not located on the local subnet.
WINS Server Address	Use of the WINS service is optional. If WINS is used, the primary WINS server address is required. The secondary WINS server address is optional.	Provides the IP address of the computer running the WINS service for NetBIOS-name-to-IP-address resolution.
DNS Server Address	Use of the DNS service is optional. If DNS is used, the DNS server address is required.	Provides the IP address of the computer running the DNS service for TCP/IP-host-name-to-IP-address resolution.

Windows 98 comes with the Microsoft 32-bit TCP/IP protocol and related suite connectivity utilities. TCP/IP is the default protocol of choice in enterprise networks. To install it, follow the instructions presented earlier in this chapter for protocol installation. In step 5, select Microsoft as the manufacturer and TCP/IP as the protocol.

Once you have installed TCP/IP in Windows 98, you must configure optional parameters to exploit the full range of the TCP/IP protocol. When you install TCP/IP in Windows 98, you must supply at least three parameters to successfully utilize it:

- The IP address of your computer

- The subnet mask

- The default gateway address

All of these parameters can be configured automatically by using Microsoft's DHCP server. You enter this information by selecting TCP/IP properties from the Network properties dialog box.

The remaining tabs of the TCP/IP properties sheet, discussed in the following sections, contain optional TCP/IP configuration parameters.

Gateway

The default gateway is a router connected to other TCP/IP network segments to which messages are initially sent when it is not known on which segment the destination computer is located. The Gateway tab contains the IP addresses of default gateways that can be used to reach remote hosts and networks.

At least one default gateway must be supplied in order for computers to communicate with other systems that are not connected to the same physical subnet, but optional additional gateways may be added using the Gateway tab.

WINS Configuration

Windows Internet Name Service (WINS) runs on a Microsoft Windows NT server that allows computers on the network to register their NetBIOS names and IP addresses. When a computer first connects to the network, it attempts to register its NetBIOS name with the WINS server, which stores this information in a local database file. The WINS server checks its database, and if no other computer on the network is using the same NetBIOS name, the information is written to the database and the computer is said to be registered with WINS. When users on the network attempt to access resources stored on that computer, it is convenient for them to access the computer using its NetBIOS name rather than its IP address (which might change often).

The WINS database is accessed in that case in order to resolve the NetBIOS name to an IP address that the TCP/IP protocol can use to communicate with the remote computer. Communication using TCP/IP must always use IP addresses. Therefore, a WINS server or some other form of NetBIOS-name-to-IP-address resolution must be used if communication using NetBIOS names is required. An alternative to using a WINS server is to use an LMHOSTS file in the <systemroot> directory, which contains NetBIOS-name-to-IP-address mappings.

The LMHOSTS file is a static table of NetBIOS-name-to-IP-address mappings, which can become difficult to manage in a large network environment where computer names and IP addresses change frequently. Also, when an LMHOSTS file is used to resolve a NetBIOS name, the entire file is read one line at a time until the requested name is found. If the name is at the bottom of a very large LMHOSTS file, reading the file each time the computer needs to resolve the name could make communication very slow. If the LMHOSTS file contained duplicate entries for the same NetBIOS name with different IP addresses, the first listing of that name in the file would be the one used, regardless of whether this was the correct entry. This would make communication with that computer (using the NetBIOS name) impossible until the LMHOSTS file were edited and the erroneous entry removed.

Another problem with using an LMHOSTS file for NetBIOS-name-to-IP-address resolution is that each computer on the network would need to store a copy of the file locally. Changes to the file could be made to a single copy of the file, but that file would then need to be distributed to each computer on the network to ensure that they received the necessary changes. LMHOSTS files can be used effectively in very small workgroup environments but aren't well-suited for use in large network environments. Whenever possible, WINS should be used.

DNS Configuration

Computers running the TCP/IP protocol use IP addresses to communicate with each other, but these addresses can be difficult for humans to memorize, and might change frequently in a large network environment. For this reason, each computer on a TCP/IP network is assigned a TCP/IP host name. This name helps uniquely identify the host on the network and makes accessing resources on the host easier for humans. Groups of TCP/IP hosts can be arranged in a logical structure called a domain.

TCP/IP domains differ from Windows NT domains. There is no resource access control or user ID administration associated with a TCP/IP domain. It is simply a structure used to organize TCP/IP host names. At the top level of the structure are a few large domains, called top-level domains. These domains include the following:

♦ .com is the domain used to organize host names in commercial entities.

- .gov is the domain used to organize host names in government agencies.

- .org is the domain used to organize host names in nonprofit organizations.

- .edu is the domain used to organize host names in educational institutions.

There are several other top-level domains, including a different domain for each country in the world. Organizations within a particular domain have a subdomain representing their enterprise. For example, a company called Widget Inc. in the .com domain would have its own subdomain called widget.com.

Organizations can further divide their subdomain into additional subdomains. For example, Widget Inc. might have one subdomain for the computers in its sales department and another for the computers in its manufacturing department. Computers in each of these departments would belong to either the .sales.widget.com or the .manufacturing. widget.com domain.

Individual computers within each domain will have different host names. A computer in the .sales.widget.com domain might be called promo. The complete name of the computer, promo.sales.widget.com, is called the Fully Qualified Domain Name (FQDN) of that host. A person would enter this name into an application (for instance, a Web browser) to access resources on that computer.

Since computers need to use IP addresses to communicate, they must have a way to resolve the host name specified by the user to an IP address.

The Domain Name Service (DNS) provides address resolution for TCP/IP host and domain names. To access a computer using a host name over TCP/IP, the name must be resolved to an IP address. This can be done using a static HOSTS file in the <systemroot> directory or by accessing a DNS server. The DNS server contains a database that is distributed over an internetwork. The DNS Server Search Order list in the TCP/IP properties sheet lists the order in which DNS servers will be queried for DNS name resolution. The Domain Suffix Search Order lists the order in which domain names can be appended to a host name to try to resolve the resulting FQDN.

CONFIGURING WINDOWS 98 FOR REMOTE ACCESS

Often in large corporate network environments, users need to access company resources while away from the office. Many users carry laptops and travel from site to site. The increasing popularity of telecommuting allows some users to work from home. In each of these cases, there must be a way for users to connect to the corporate network from whatever remote site they may find themselves in. Windows 98 can use Dial-Up Networking to accomplish this.

Different network environments provide remote access to client PCs in different ways. In the Windows NT environment, the most common method is to use Microsoft Remote Access Service (RAS). In a Novell NetWare environment, the most common method is to use Novell's NetWare Connect.

Setting Up a Dial-Up Networking Connection

Before you can use Dial-Up Networking to connect to a remote computer, you must configure a *connection*. A Dial-Up Networking connection specifies all the information required to establish a link with the remote computer, as well as many optional parameters that allow Dial-Up Networking to provide its full functionality and efficiency. To configure a Dial-Up Networking connection, follow these steps:

1. Select Start | Programs | Accessories | Communications | Dial-Up Networking.

2. Within Dial-Up Networking, double-click the Make New Connection icon.

3. The Make New Connection Wizard starts. You are prompted for a name for the connection. Enter the name of the computer you are connecting to, select the modem you will use to make the connection, and click the Next button. If you haven't installed a modem on your system, the Add Modem Wizard will start, and you can set one up at this time.

4. Enter the area code and telephone number for the computer you are connecting to. Select the appropriate country code, and click the Next button.

5. You will see a dialog box informing you that you have successfully created a new Dial-Up Networking connection. Click the Finish button to complete the process.

Once you have created a connection, you can edit the details of that connection to specify the type of connection and the features and parameters you want to use. To edit the details of a Dial-Up Networking connection, start Dial-Up Networking from the Start menu and right-click the icon for the connection you want to edit. You will see the properties sheet for that connection.

A Dial-Up Networking properties sheet has these tabs:

- General

- Server Types

- Scripting

- Multilink

On the General tab, you can edit the area code, phone number, country code, and modem device you selected when you initially configured the connection. You can configure Dial-Up Networking to ignore the area code and country code if your connection is to a local number and you're certain that you don't need that information to complete the call. To accomplish this, deselect the User area code and Dialing Properties checkbox.

You can configure specific modem parameters by clicking the Configure button under your modem selection. From here you can configure the same options you did by running the Modems Control Panel applet. You see an additional tab, Options, on which you can configure the following:

- Whether to bring up a terminal window, and when to bring it up— before or after dialing.

- Whether the call will be operator-assisted or manually dialed.

- Whether to display the modem status while connected to the remote computer.

The Server Types tab lets you specify the environment you're connecting to. Four server types are supported by Dial-Up Networking:

- NRN. NetWare Remote Node is the server type used by NetWare Connect versions 1.0 and 1.1.

- PPP. Point-to-Point Protocol is the server type used by most Internet Service Providers, by RAS running on Windows NT Server versions 3.5 and higher, and by Windows 98 Dial-Up Networking Server.

- SLIP. Serial Line Internet Protocol is the server type used by some UNIX servers.

- Windows for Workgroups and Windows NT 3.1. This is the server type used by the RAS service that runs under Windows for Workgroups and Windows NT 3.1. It is not compatible with the RAS service running on later versions of Windows NT.

After selecting the appropriate server type for the computer you are dialing into, you can select from the following list of advanced options:

- Log on to network specifies whether to provide logon credentials to the remote computer or to simply establish a connection.

- Enable software compression enables or disables data compression implemented in the Dial-Up Networking software (as opposed to the modem hardware).

- Require encrypted password specifies whether to require the password for network logon to be encrypted or sent in plain-text format.

- Require data encryption specifies whether all data for the connection should be encrypted or sent in plain-text format.

- Record a log file for this connection specifies whether to record a log of the connection session.

Some of these options, such as data encryption and password encryption, require that the equivalent option be enabled on the remote computer as well.

Also on the Server Types tab is the Allowed network protocols area, where you specify which network protocols to use for the connection to the remote network. Choices are NetBEUI, IPX/SPX, and TCP/IP (each of which was described earlier in this chapter). If you select TCP/IP as an allowed protocol, you can click the TCP/IP Settings button to specify the following:

- Whether to use a server-assigned IP address or an IP address that you specify

- Whether to use server-assigned addresses for primary and secondary name servers (DNS and WINS) or name server addresses that you specify

- Whether to compress IP packet headers or send the headers uncompressed

- Whether to use the default gateway on the remote network or use a local default gateway

The Scripting tab lets you specify a script file of commands to execute while establishing the connection. You specify the full path to the script file you want to use in the File name field. You can click the Browse button to search for the file, and once you select a script file, you can click the Edit button to open the file in Notepad for editing or review.

Selecting the Step through script check box lets you check your script for errors by executing the script one line at a time while establishing the connection. By default, the script will run in a terminal window that is minimized. Uncheck the Start terminal screen minimized check box to leave the terminal window open while the script runs.

The Multilink tab lets you specify whether to use a single modem for the connection, or to use additional modem devices to increase the total bandwidth for the connection. Select the Use additional devices radio button, and click the Add button to add additional devices to the list. Select a device and click the Remove button to remove it from the list. You must already have additional modem devices set up on your Windows 98 computer in order to use the Multilink feature.

Using Dial-Up Networking to Connect to RAS Servers

RAS is a service running under Windows NT that supports dial-up connections to the Windows NT computer. RAS can run on both Windows NT Workstation and Windows NT Server computers, but the Workstation version supports fewer simultaneous connections. When running on Windows NT Server, RAS can support up to 256 simultaneous connections, while under Windows NT Workstation, RAS can support only one connection.

In a large corporate network environment, RAS is typically set up on a Windows NT server with multiple modems and phone lines connected to it. Remote computers dial into the server using the PPP line protocol. Windows 98 computers use connections configured with Dial-Up Networking. To set up a connection to a RAS server, follow the steps in the preceding section for creating a new Dial-Up Networking connection. Select PPP for the server type (this is the default server type), and configure the remaining options according to the information provided by the administrator of the remote computer.

RAS supports all three of the protocols available in the Allowed protocols section. Select the protocols that you know are available on the server you plan to connect to.

Using Dial-Up Networking to Connect to NetWare Connect Servers

In a Novell NetWare environment, it is typical to use Novell's NetWare Connect remote access software to provide network access to remote workstations. Windows 98 Dial-Up Networking supports connections to NetWare Connect servers.

To dial into a NetWare Connect server using Dial-Up Networking, configure a connection using the instructions provided earlier in this chapter, and select NRN as the server type. When you do so, you will notice that certain advanced options are no longer available, and that the only protocol available is IPX/SPX. This is due to the limited functionality that is supported by NetWare Connect versions 1.0 and 1.1.

WHAT IS IMPORTANT TO KNOW

The following list summarizes the chapter and accentuates the key concepts to memorize for the exam:

◆ TCP/IP is the default protocol used on NT networks.

◆ IPX/SPX is the default protocol used on NetWare networks.

◆ Universal Naming Convention (UNC) paths specify where resources are.

◆ TCP/IP parameters include an IP address, subnet mask, and default gateway.

◆ Windows Internet Name Service (WINS) is used to resolve NetBIOS computer names to IP addresses.

◆ WINS runs only on Windows NT Server.

◆ An LMHOSTS file is a static listing of NetBIOS-name-to-IP-address mappings that is sometimes used instead of WINS in small network environments. Each PC on the network must have its own LMHOSTS file.

◆ Domain Name Service (DNS) is used to resolve TCP/IP host names to IP addresses.

◆ A HOSTS file is a static listing of TCP/IP-host-name-to-IP-address mappings that is sometimes used instead of DNS in small network environments. Each PC on the network must have its own HOSTS file.

◆ DNS can run on many different platforms, including Windows NT and UNIX. Microsoft DNS runs only on Windows NT Server.

◆ The Internet can be reached through a dial-up connection or through a proxy server.

◆ Dial-up connections typically use PPP and sometimes SLIP as the line protocol.

◆ Workgroups are peer-to-peer networks that offer share-level security and don't require a server.

◆ Windows NT domains are networks built around a server. They offer user-level security.

◆ File and Printer Sharing allows you to share resources with other users.

◆ File and Printer Sharing doesn't allow you to share individual files, but it does allow you to share folders.

◆ Dial-Up Networking supports connections to PPP, NRN, SLIP, and Windows for Workgroups/Windows NT 3.1 RAS servers.

- Dial-Up Networking supports the encryption of both passwords and data for dial-up connections.

- RAS servers running under Windows NT 3.5 and above support up to 256 simultaneous connections.

- RAS servers running under Windows NT 3.5 and above support the NetBEUI, IPX/SPX, and TCP/IP protocols.

- NetWare Connect is the remote access software supported by Dial-Up Networking that is most often found in Novell NetWare environments.

- NetWare Connect servers versions 1.0 and 1.1 support only the IPX/SPX protocol.

- Windows 98 Dial-Up Networking supports scripting to automate certain tasks while establishing a connection.

- The Windows 98 Multilink feature allows you to combine multiple modems when establishing dial-up connections to increase the total bandwidth available while connected to a remote computer.

- Service for NetWare Directory Services allows a Windows 98 computer running the Client for NetWare Networks to take advantage of NetWare Directory Services used in NetWare 4.x environments.

- Sharing local resources with users on a NetWare network using File and Printer Sharing for NetWare networks requires that you use user-level access control.

▶ Monitor system performance. Tools include the following:

- Net Watcher
- System Monitor
- Resource Meter

▶ Tune and optimize the system in a Microsoft environment and a mixed Microsoft and NetWare environment. Tasks include the following:

- Optimizing the hard disk by using Disk Defragmenter and ScanDisk

- Compressing data by using DriveSpace3 and the Compression Agent

- Updating drivers and applying service packs by using Windows Update and the Signature Verification Tool

- Automating tasks by using Maintenance Wizard

- Scheduling tasks by using Task Scheduler

- Checking for corrupt files and extracting files from the installation media by using the System File Checker

CHAPTER 5

Monitoring and Optimization

MONITORING TOOLS

At A Glance: Utilities and Executables

Utility Name	Executable File
Disk Defragmenter (used to read frequency of file usage during defragmentation by Disk Defragmenter)	DEFRAG.EXE (CVTAPLOG.EXE)
Net Watcher	NETWATCH.EXE
Resource Meter	RSRCMTR.EXE
ScanDisk: DOS version	SCANDISK.EXE
ScanDisk: Windows version	SCANDSKW.EXE
Signature Verification Tool	SIGVERIF.EXE
System File Checker	SFC.EXE
System Monitor	SYSMON.EXE

Monitoring a computer system is an important part of an administrator's job. It could mean the difference between being reactive and being proactive. This chapter discusses the tools in Windows 98 that make monitoring, optimizing, and troubleshooting easier. The tools used for optimization include ScanDisk and Disk Defragmenter. Other tools, like System File Checker and System Verification Tool, help you troubleshoot issues concerning the Windows 98 environment.

In addition to their usefulness in troubleshooting, these tools can be used to provide information about your environment. Some tell you what resources are available, and others provide information about your network and let you monitor and maintain remote computers.

Windows 98 has three primary tools for monitoring system performance:

- Net Watcher
- System Monitor
- Resource Meter

Each of these will be examined in the following sections.

Net Watcher

Net Watcher lets you access a local or remote computer and delete, add, and create shared resources there. You can also monitor the use of those resources, see which are open, and see who is connected. When it's installed, the Net Watcher utility is located under Start | Programs | Accessories | System Tools. It can be used to view connections to the local computer, or to a remote computer, as long as Remote Administration is enabled on the remote computer. Net Watcher is used primarily to display the status of connections to shared folders. Net Watcher's features let an administrator remotely perform the following tasks:

- Create a new, shared folder

- List the shared folders on a server

- Stop sharing a folder

- Show which users are connected to a shared folder

- Show how long a user has been connected to a shared folder and how long the user has been idle

- Close files a user has opened (only available on Microsoft networks)

- Disconnect a user from a shared resource

You can also access Net Watcher through the Network Neighborhood by right-clicking a computer and selecting Properties from the context menu. On the Tools tab, choose Net Watcher to view the shared folders and the users accessing those folders on the selected computer.

To use Net Watcher, the following characteristics must apply:

- File and Printer Sharing must be enabled on the remote computer.

- You can access only remote systems that use the same access control that you are using on your computer. In other words, both computers must be set to user-level access control or share-level access control to use Net Watcher on a remote machine.

- You can only access remote systems using the same type of file and printer sharing service. For example, both computers must be using File and Printer Sharing for Microsoft Networks.

Net Watcher is a useful utility for administrators to use in a peer-to-peer network because it lets one administrator manage the resources on all computers in the workgroup.

When connecting to a remote computer using share-level access control, the password you must use is the one specified in the Remote Administration dialog box.

When connecting to a remote computer using user-level access control, the password is the administrator's account password.

Before you use Net Watcher, it must be installed, and the computer or server you are viewing must be configured for it.

> **NOTE**
>
> Net Watcher is designed to view your machine first by default. That way, you can view and monitor people connected to your Windows 98 machine with one simple utility.

If Net Watcher is installed, it appears under Start | Programs | Accessories | System Tools. If it isn't installed, you can do so by following these steps:

1. Choose Add/Remove Programs from the Control Panel.

2. Click the Windows Setup tab.

3. Choose System Tools, click the Details button, and choose Net Watcher.

4. Click OK.

To configure a computer or server so that Net Watcher can access it, the remote computer must be running File and Printer Services, and remote administration must be turned on. You can add File and Printer Services through the Network properties sheet. You can install File and Printer Services for Microsoft Networks by following these steps:

1. In Control Panel, select the Network icon.

2. The Network Properties Dialog box appears. Click the Add button.

3. Select Services and click Add.

4. In the Select Network Services dialog box, select File and Printer Sharing for Microsoft Networks.

5. Click OK twice and reboot when prompted.

Remote administration must be turned on through the Passwords Properties dialog box found in Control Panel, shown in Figure 5.1.

Additionally, if the computer you are coming from is using share-level security, it can only connect to other computers using share-level security. If the computer you are coming from is using user-level security, you can connect to another computer if it is using user-level or share-level security.

When connecting to a remote computer, you are prompted for a password. For share-level security (as in a workgroup), the password must be the one supplied in the Remote Administration tab of the Password applet in Control Panel (see Figure 5.1).

> **NOTE**
>
> When connecting to a remote computer using user-level security, the password you must provide is that of the domain administrator account or the equivalent.

When you're connected, the remote server looks like Figure 5.2.

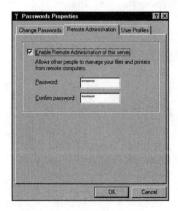

FIGURE 5.1
The Remote Administration tab of the Passwords Properties dialog box.

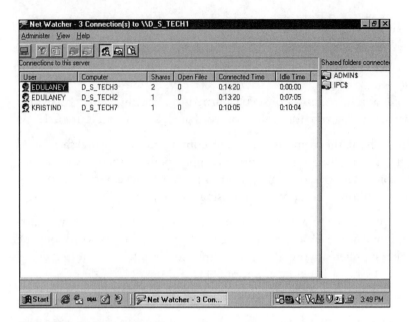

FIGURE 5.2
The Net Watcher initial screen.

You can change the view to see the shared folders on the resource, as shown in Figure 5.3, by clicking the Show Shared Folders button. (Net Watcher is used primarily for viewing the status of shared folders.) From here you can also add a shared folder, stop sharing a folder, and view the properties of the shared folder by right-clicking and choosing Properties (see Figure 5.4).

NOTE — As items change in Net Watcher, you can always press F5 to refresh the display.

NOTE — You can also access Net Watcher by right-clicking a computer in Network Neighborhood and selecting Properties. On the Tools tab, choose Net Watcher.

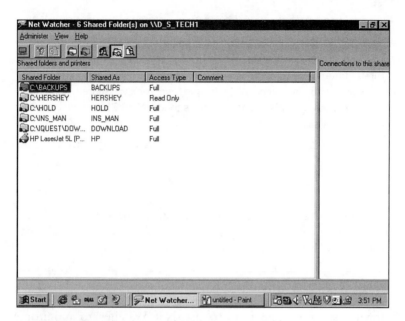

FIGURE 5.3

Viewing the shared folders in Net Watcher.

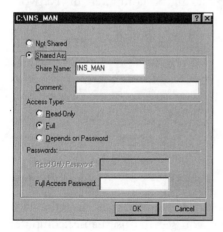

FIGURE 5.4

Viewing the shared folder's properties.

> **NOTE**
>
> When utilized, Net Watcher becomes a powerful tool in reducing the time dedicated to network administration. If your Windows 98 clients are configured for remote administration, either manually or using Batch 98 during installation, you have the ability to add and remove shared resources across the network. This option also adds to Microsoft Zero Administration Kit strategy, similar to Batch 98.

> **NOTE**
>
> For the exam, it is important to distinguish between the monitoring abilities of Net Watcher as opposed to System Monitor. For example, you can't log information with Net Watcher.

The following steps outline how to use Net Watcher to monitor a remote computer:

1. Start Net Watcher by right-clicking a computer in Network Neighborhood and selecting Properties. On the Tools tab, choose Net Watcher. Alternatively, select Start | Programs | Accessories | System Tools | Net Watcher.

2. Select Administer | Select Server. The Select Server dialog box appears.

3. Enter the name of the server (the remote computer) you want to view. Click the Browse button to see a list of the computers to which you can connect.

4. Click OK. A view of the remote computer appears in Net Watcher.

5. Click the Show Users button to see the users connected to the selected computer. On the left, you see the username, computer name, number of shares, number of open files, time of connection, and idle time. On the right, you see the shared folders and the files that are open.

6. Click the Show Shared Folders button to see the names of the shared folders on the selected computer. On the left, you see the shared folder, the name it is shared as, the access type, and a comment associated with the folder. On the right, you see the connections to the share and the files that are open.

7. Click the Show Files button to see the files that have been opened by other users. You see the name of the file, the share it is using, the person accessing the file, and the open mode.

8. Press F5 to refresh the display.

9. Select Administer | Exit to close Net Watcher.

System Monitor

System Monitor is a streamlined version of Windows NT's Performance Monitor. It's essentially the same tool that existed in Windows 95, with the notable exception (read: test fodder) that it now allows for *logging*. If installed, System Monitor appears under Start | Programs | Accessories | System Tools. If it isn't installed, you can do so by following these steps:

1. Choose Add/Remove Programs from the Control Panel.

2. Click the Windows Setup tab.

3. Choose System Tools, click the Details button, and choose System Monitor.

4. Click OK.

System Monitor is used primarily to display data on various performance counters in Windows 98. If both System Monitor and Remote Administration are installed and enabled, you can connect to a remote computer to view their system performance through the System Monitor utility.

You can also quickly enable the monitoring of a remote computer by right-clicking that computer inside Network Neighborhood and selecting Properties from the context menu. Choose System Monitor to start the applet and connect to the selected computer.

System Monitor can be used to monitor the performance of a Windows 98 computer as well as to provide real-time tracking of system activities on a local or remote computer. It is also useful for viewing the effects of configuration or hardware changes on the computer's performance. It can also be used to identify bottlenecks that can affect the computer's performance.

Performance information, including processor usage, the number of reads per second, and the amount of dirty data, can be viewed over time as a line chart, bar chart, or values.

System Monitor lets you look at components of your system with the intent of finding these bottlenecks. The components are broken into seven main categories:

- Dial-Up Adapter
- Disk Cache
- File System
- Kernel
- Memory Manager
- Microsoft Network Client
- Microsoft Network Server

The following table lists the settings—usually with self-explanatory names—that can be viewed in each category:

Dial-Up Adapter	Alignment errors
	Buffer overruns
	Bytes received/second
	Bytes transmitted/second
	Connection speed
	CRC errors
	Frames received/second
	Frames transmitted/second
	Framing errors
	Incomplete frames
	Overrun errors
	Timeout errors

	Total bytes received
	Total bytes transmitted
Disk Cache	Cache buffers
	Cache hits
	Cache misses
	Cache pages
	Failed cache recycles
	LRU cache recycles
	Maximum cache pages
	Minimum cache pages
	Random cache recycles
File System	Bytes read/second
	Bytes written/second
	Dirty data
	Reads/second
	Writes/second
Kernel	Processor usage
	Threads
	Virtual machines
Memory Manager	Allocated memory
	Discards
	Disk cache size
	Instance faults
	Locked memory
	Locked non-cache pages
	Maximum disk cache size
	Mid disk cache size
	Minimum disk cache size
	Other memory
	Page faults
	Page-ins
	Page-outs

continues

	Pages mapped from cache
	Swap file defective
	Swap file in use
	Swap file size
	Swappable memory
	Unused physical memory
Microsoft Network Client	Bytes read/second
	Bytes written/second
	Number of nets
	Open files
	Resources
	Sessions
	Transactions/second
Microsoft Network Server	Buffers
	Bytes read/sec
	Bytes written/sec
	Bytes/sec
	Memory
	NBs
	Server threads

As additional items are added to the operating system, they become visible for monitoring, along with System Monitor's seven main categories. For example, if you are running the IPX/SPX-compatible protocol, it appears as a category with the following items:

- IPX packets lost/second
- IPX packets received/second
- IPX packets sent/second
- Open sockets
- Routing table entries
- SAP table entries
- SPX packets received/second
- SPX packets sent/second

Figure 5.5 shows an example of System Monitor being used to view Kernel: Processor Usage (the default entry) and File System: Bytes read/second.

The default interval for updating the chart is every five seconds, but you can change this from the Options menu. Logging is enabled and disabled from the File menu.

System Monitor can be used to monitor a remote computer as well as the local one. To monitor a remote computer, that computer must be enabled for remote administration, and you must be specified as an authorized user.

When tweaking a system for performance, System Monitor should always be used during normal activity first, to see the routine use of the system before changing any values to test their effect. You should also change only one item at a time to get a true sense of the scope of the change it made. Only after you have seen the full effects of that change should you proceed to make other changes.

> **N O T E**
>
> For the exam, it is important to remember System Monitor's logging capabilities, as well as the ability to remotely monitor another client on the network.

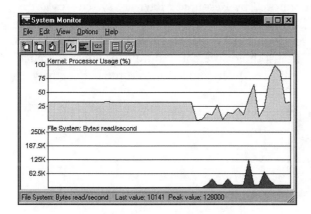

FIGURE 5.5
System Monitor viewing kernel usage and bytes read per second.

To view the effects of a configuration or hardware change on a Windows 98 computer, do the following:

1. Determine which items in System Monitor are to be tracked.

2. Run System Monitor before the change is made to establish the baseline and record the information.

3. Make the desired configuration changes.

4. Run System Monitor again after the change, and view the results of the change.

The results of the change can then be compared to the baseline to see if the change has had a positive or negative effect on system performance.

When establishing the baseline, make sure you run System Monitor during *average* usage. Monitoring the computer's performance while performing abnormal system-intensive tasks will affect System Monitor's values and might not give a true baseline.

In order to monitor a remote computer, Remote Administration must be enabled on the other computer, and the password must be known.

Resource Meter

The three resources monitored by Resource Meter are system resources, user resources, and GDI resources. The Resource Meter is a component similar to Task Manager, found in Windows NT 4.0. It has been scaled down greatly to highlight just three different resources for quick reference. Figure 5.6 shows the Resource Meter coupled with some light activity.

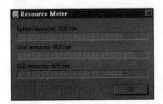

FIGURE 5.6
The Resource Meter.

Using Resource Meter helps you identify system or program flaws. For example, the greater the number displayed as free, the more resources are available to the user. When a program is started, certain resources are needed to run the program. If the available amount of free resources were to remain low, even after the program was closed, this would indicate that the resources were not being turned back over to the operating system. A possible flaw in the program? You decide.

> **NOTE**   For the exam, you should have a clear understanding of the Resource Meter dialog box.

TUNING AND OPTIMIZING WINDOWS 98

There are a number of ways to increase your system's optimization, based on what the potential bottleneck may be. The following table summarizes those that offer the greatest potential gain.

At A Glance: Optimization Considerations

Item	Considerations
Processor	Upgrade the speed Add another processor Upgrade the secondary cache
Memory	Add more RAM
Disk	Replace slow disks Defragment when necessary Upgrade from IDE to SCSI Isolate I/O-intensive tasks to separate disks
Network	Get a faster network card Divide the network into multiple networks

Tuning the operating system is accomplished in many different ways. Microsoft recognizes six major categories:

- Disk Defragmenter and ScanDisk
- Compressing data

- Updating drivers
- Automating tasks with Maintenance Wizard
- Using the Task Scheduler
- Checking for corruption with System File Checker

Compressing data with DriveSpace3 and the Compression Agent was discussed in Chapter 3, "Configuring and Managing Resource Access," in the section "Disk Compression." All the other categories are covered in the following sections.

Disk Defragmenter and ScanDisk

The Disk Defragmenter (DEFRAG.EXE), also known as Disk Optimizer, is shown in Figure 5.7. It places all files in contiguous space on the disk. Then, whenever a file is read, the system finds it in one place rather than having to search and collect it from multiple locations on the hard drive. This speeds up read and write time and makes the system appear (and act) more responsive.

Chapter 1, "Planning," said that the File Allocation Table (FAT) is similar to a library's catalog cards or computerized database of books. When a person enters a library to find a book, she usually heads for the catalog card display or computer terminal. Once there, she can find the exact location of the book or resource she wants. Can you imagine locating a book by simply walking up and down the aisles of the library? Although computers process information at very high speeds, it would take a tremendous amount of additional time to locate resources on a hard disk.

Let's take this example a step further. Normally when you go to the library to find reference material, a complete set of encyclopedias is in the same section. If the books in the set were scattered all over the library, obviously it would take more time and effort to gather the necessary information.

Every application you use in Windows 98 is logged (via Task Monitor) to the %SystemRoot%\Windows\Applog directory. When Disk Defragmenter runs, it views those log files and arranges the data files in the order they appear in the logs to make the system start quicker. The log files also indicate how many times an application is used. Thus, those that are used more frequently are given priority over those that are not.

FIGURE 5.7
The Disk Defragmenter.

The log files have this syntax:

application.lg*drive*

Thus, the log file for RegAdminTool, if it is located on the C: drive, would be

REGADMINTOOL.LGC

If the file were on drive D:, the file would be

REGADMINTOOL.LGD

When started, Disk Defragmenter uses CVTAPLOG.EXE to view the log files and build a single file per drive it can use with the name APPLOG.DTN.

Other items running when Disk Defragmenter begins can cause serious performance problems. Most noticeably, performance-intensive screen savers can bring it to its knees. It is recommended that no other programs be running and that Screen Saver be set to None.

Using Disk Defragmenter to defragment files and free space on a hard disk is easy. You will be able to see the different options available to you, and watch to see how the Defragmenter works:

1. Run the Disk Defragmenter by selecting Start | Programs | Accessories | System Tools | Disk Defragmenter.

2. From the drop-down list, choose a hard drive on your computer, and click the OK button.

3. Click the Settings button. A dialog box with advanced options appears. You can select the defragmentation and whether or not you want to do error checking at the same time. Select Rearrange Program files so my programs start faster, and click OK.

4. A dialog box will appear, showing you the utility's progress.

5. Click the Show Details button. You will see a mapping of your hard drive that shows how each cluster on the hard drive is being used. This might take several seconds to appear.

6. If you want to see a legend describing what the different colors mean for each cluster, click the Legend button.

7. Depending on the size of your hard drive and the speed of your computer, disk defragmentation can take a considerable amount of time. If you want to stop the process, click the Stop button and exit the application.

ScanDisk, shown in Figure 5.8, is used to check a disk for errors and fix any that it finds. It works with RAM drives, floppy drives, FAT16 and FAT32 hard drives, as well as compressed and uncompressed drives. Two versions of this utility are included with Windows 98:

◆ SCANDISK.EXE is the tool used outside of Windows.

◆ SCANDSKW.EXE is the tool used inside Windows.

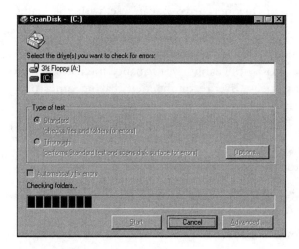

FIGURE 5.8
The ScanDisk utility.

If you run ScanDisk in the command window while the GUI is still loaded, it will call SCANDSKW.EXE even though you aren't currently in the graphical interface.

ScanDisk can find and fix problems related to long filenames, file system structure (cross-linked files and lost clusters), directory structure, bad sectors, and compression problems (DriveSpace3 and DoubleSpace).

Under any FAT-based file system, files are stored with data placed in *clusters*. Every cluster contains data and a pointer to the location of the next cluster in a chain. Whenever a user accesses a file, the file system uses the directory tree to find the first cluster for the file. It reads the data there and the pointer to the next cluster. It jumps about in this noncontiguous fashion until all the data comprising the file has been found.

Going back to our earlier example, when you go to the library and look for a set of resource books, they are normally found together in the same section. Fragmentation is similar to these books being scattered throughout the library.

If the next cluster is corrupted, problems in the process of events can occur. Assume that file ABC.DAT has the majority of its data in cluster 70, along with a pointer to cluster 99 for the rest of it. Assume that file DEF.DAT has the majority of its data in cluster 75, along with a pointer to cluster 99 for the rest of it.

Cluster 99 can't hold the data for both files, so this cluster is considered to be *cross-linked*—a logical inconsistency in the integrity of the drive's file structure has occurred. ScanDisk can identify the problem, but it can't ascertain which file the data really belongs to. It makes a copy of the cluster so that it can be read by the user and deletes both references to it.

ScanDisk can perform two levels of testing on hard drives: Standard and Thorough. Standard mode is best used on a daily basis, whereas Thorough mode is best used when you suspect a problem with the hard drive. In Standard mode, ScanDisk performs logical tests against the file system's file allocation table (FAT), checking for the logical inconsistencies outlined earlier. In addition, the Standard scan checks for various other potential problems, such as invalid filenames and invalid date and time stamps.

In Thorough mode, ScanDisk not only performs all the tests included in Standard mode, but also performs a surface scan. Each cluster on the drive is checked for physical defects that would make the cluster in question unsafe for data storage. A surface scan is performed by reading the information from the cluster and rewriting it to the same cluster. If the information matches what ScanDisk read the first time, the cluster is likely to be safe. If the data is different, a media problem might exist, in which case ScanDisk marks the cluster as bad.

ScanDisk contains a number of additional features. Here is a rundown and a recap:

- ScanDisk can be run from the command line, with parameters to specify how it will run, or from the Windows 98 interface.

- ScanDisk can fix problems on hard drives, floppy disks, RAM drives, and removable media.

- ScanDisk can detect and repair errors in long filenames.

- ScanDisk can be used to test and maintain the integrity of DoubleSpace and DriveSpace volumes.

- ScanDisk can log its activities. The results of the scan are stored in the SCANDISK.LOG file, located in the root of the drive that has been examined.

- ScanDisk can't fix errors on CD-ROMs, network drives, drives created by the DOS command INTERLINK, or drives referenced via MS-DOS commands such as ASSIGN, JOIN, and SUBST.

- As with Disk Defragmenter, it is possible to multitask with ScanDisk. However, if any disk-write activity occurs, ScanDisk might be forced to restart the testing process.

- If Windows 98 is shut down improperly, SCANDISK.EXE, the tool used outside of Windows, will run automatically the next time the system is rebooted.

Complete the following steps to run ScanDisk on a hard disk drive:

1. Run the ScanDisk utility by selecting Start | Programs | Accessories | System Tools | ScanDisk.

2. The ScanDisk dialog box appears. Select a hard drive on your computer to scan for errors.

3. You can select other options from this window. The first is whether you want to do a Standard or a Thorough scan. A Thorough scan checks for all errors that a Standard scan does, and it also scans the physical surface of the drive. Thorough scans take substantially longer to perform. Select Standard or Thorough, based on your preference.

4. Click the Advanced button to see other options that are available to you. Select Always display summary. This will give you a report of ScanDisk's results. Click OK to continue.

5. Click the Start button to begin the scan. Remember not to do other work while ScanDisk is running. If the work you're doing writes information to the drive that is being scanned, ScanDisk might have to start over from the beginning.

6. Wait for ScanDisk to finish, and then look at the results that are displayed.

NOTE

Neither ScanDisk nor Disk Defragmenter will work on drives created with ASSIGN, JOIN, or SUBST. They also won't work on CD-ROM and network drives, because they aren't *true* drives, or because they are read-only drives.

Disk Compression

Windows 98 implements a form of disk compression known as *on-the-fly compression*. This means that the compression/decompression process occurs automatically in the background and is transparent to the user. On-the-fly compression is the process of intercepting normal MS-DOS read/write calls and compressing the data before writing it to the hard disk so that the data consumes less space. Similarly, when the data is read back, it is automatically uncompressed before being transferred to the application or process that requested it.

Microsoft's disk compression, called DoubleSpace, was first introduced in version 6.0 of MS-DOS. It was later re-released as DriveSpace in version 6.2 with some changes to the compression routines and with a new feature: the capability to uncompress a drive. The compression structure has remained fairly consistent. Windows 98 comes with the latest version, called DriveSpace3, also found in the Windows 95 Plus pack. DriveSpace3 is installed automatically during the installation of Windows 98.

After disk compression is installed and the files are initially compressed, the files are stored in the compressed volume file (CVF), a large hidden file that sits on the physical C drive. When the system boots up, the CVF is assigned the drive letter C and is known as the compressed drive. The physical C drive, which now contains only a few files due to the fact that everything else is in a compressed state inside the CVF, is assigned a higher drive letter, typically H, and is known as the host drive. The process of switching drive letters and making the CVF available for viewing in MS-DOS and Windows is called *mounting*. From this point on, any file operation is handled through the disk compression routines, which are responsible for compressing and uncompressing files as disk I/O requests are made by the operating system.

Updating Drivers

The Windows Update utility, found under the Start menu, is used to install new drivers and service packs when they become available. It is the primary tool for keeping the operating system up-to-date. It accesses http://www.microsoft.com/windowsupdate to see what new items have become available, as shown in Figure 5.9.

SIGVERIF.EXE is the Signature Verification Tool, included with Windows 98 (see Figure 5.10). It can ascertain if a file has been assigned a digital signature by Microsoft, and if that file has been modified afterward. You can open this tool by running SIGVERIF.EXE. You can also find it by selecting Tools | System Information.

Together, these two utilities are the backbone of Microsoft's plan to keep the operating system as up-to-date as possible.

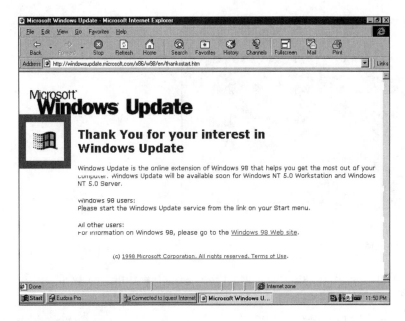

FIGURE 5.9
The Update Web site.

FIGURE 5.10
The Signature Verification Tool.

Maintenance Wizard and Task Scheduler

The Maintenance Wizard, shown in Figure 5.11, lets you take tools used to optimize the system and run them automatically at routine intervals. Select Start | Programs | Accessories | System Tools. When you first start Maintenance Wizard, it asks you whether you want to use the most common settings or create your own.

FIGURE 5.11
Starting the Maintenance Wizard.

If you choose Express, there are three possible time periods during which the programs can run:

- Nights: Midnight to 3:00 a.m.
- Days: Noon to 3:00 p.m.
- Evenings: 8:00 p.m. to 11:00 p.m.

Here are the items it will attempt to add by default:

- Speed up your most frequently used programs (Defrag)
- Check hard disk for errors (ScanDisk)
- Delete unnecessary files from hard disk (Disk Cleanup)

The Task Scheduler, shown in Figure 5.12, is what actually takes the tasks from Maintenance Wizard (and anything else that schedules tasks) and executes them.

You can see the contents of Task Scheduler's queue by selecting Start | Programs | Accessories | System Tools | Scheduled Tasks. You can remove items from the list, change their execution time and parameters, and add items.

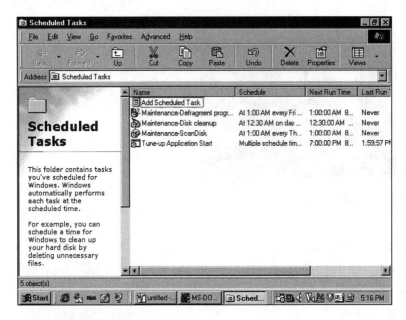

FIGURE 5.12
The list of scheduled tasks.

System File Checker

Two additional utilities enhance performance and maintenance in a Windows 98 environment: System File Checker and Version Conflict Manager. Both can be found under Tools | System Information.

System File Checker (SFC.EXE), shown in Figure 5.13, is a wonderful utility that can be used to scan Windows 98 system files for corruption or deletion and restore them. The completed scan is compared to the DEFAULT.SFC file, which is included on the Windows 98 installation CD. This file contains information about the date, time, and size of each file, as well as version number and Cyclical Redundancy Check (CRC). This helps ensure a smooth-running system, to say the least.

The Version Conflict Manager, another great utility, is discussed in Chapter 6, "Troubleshooting."

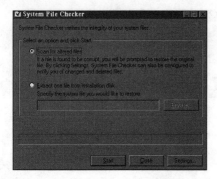

FIGURE 5.13
The System File Checker.

NOTE It is important to note that along with System Verification Tools, the exam might cover different scenarios presenting you with issues regarding both System File Checker and Version Conflict Manager.

Located under Start | Programs | Accessories | System Tools, the System File Checker can update the baseline file if you choose to update verification information or extract a single file from the installation CD.

WHAT IS IMPORTANT TO KNOW

The following list summarizes the chapter and accentuates the key concepts to memorize for the exam:

- Net Watcher lets you use your own machine to view and monitor people connected to your Windows 98 machine.

- Net Watcher also lets you monitor connections and shares remotely. You can also add, remove, and modify shares.

- To use Net Watcher, Remote Administration and File and Print Sharing must be enabled on the machine you will monitor.

- System Monitor divides the system into categories. Each category is divided into items.

- System Monitor can be used to monitor a remote computer if Remote Administration has been enabled.

- New to Windows 98, System Monitor allows the creation of log files.

- In System Monitor, the default category and item viewed are Kernel: Processor Usage.

- The default interval for chart updates in System Monitor is every five seconds.

- Resource Meter is a scaled-down version of Task Manager found on Windows NT. It allows you to view system, user, and GDI resources.

- Disk Defragmenter uses log files of application access to see which programs are used most and what files they need to run and places them contiguously to speed access performance.

- ScanDisk looks for and fixes errors on most writable media.

- The Maintenance Wizard schedules tasks to run automatically in unattended mode.

- The Task Scheduler submits jobs that Maintenance Wizard has chosen, as well as all other unattended jobs, for processing. The queue can be viewed by selecting Start | Programs | Accessories | System Tools | Scheduled Tasks.

- The System File Checker is used to look for corruption, deletion, or modification of the core Windows 98 operating system files. It uses a base file to make comparisons to what should be there. It can be used to restore a file from the media or to update the base file.

► Diagnose and resolve installation failures. Tasks include the following:
  - Resolve file and driver version conflicts by using Version Conflict Manager and the Microsoft System Information utility

► Diagnose and resolve boot process failures. Tasks include the following:
  - Editing configuration files by using the System Configuration utility

► Diagnose and resolve connectivity problems in a Microsoft environment and a mixed Microsoft and NetWare environment. Tools include the following:
  - WinIPCfg
  - Net Watcher
  - Ping
  - Tracert

► Diagnose and resolve printing problems in a Microsoft environment and a mixed Microsoft and NetWare environment.

► Diagnose and resolve file system problems.

► Diagnose and resolve resource access problems in a Microsoft environment and a mixed Microsoft and NetWare environment.

► Diagnose and resolve hardware device and device driver problems. Tasks include the following:
  - Checking for corrupt Registry files by using ScanReg and ScanRegW

C H A P T E R 6

Troubleshooting

DIAGNOSING INSTALLATION FAILURES

At A Glance: Installation Problem Resolution

Installation Problem	Symptom(s)	Resolution
Hardware identification problems	Computer locks up during Setup and no longer responds.	Cold boot the computer. Setup uses the DETCRASH.LOG file to locate the source of the problem and skips the offending device.
File version conflict problems	Computer hangs at startup. Computer starts but crashes with a General Protection Fault or Illegal Operation error when some programs are run.	Version Conflict Manager will replace system files with known-good baseline Windows 98 system files.

During the installation of Windows 98, two ASCII text files are created, detailing the progress of the installation: DETLOG.TXT and SETUPLOG.TXT. SETUPLOG.TXT is created in the root directory and is a log file of events (successful and unsuccessful) during setup.

Additionally, a binary hidden file, DETCRASH.LOG, is created temporarily in the root directory. It details where the installation is in terms of hardware recognition. To a point, DETCRASH.LOG is a binary mirror of the text file DETLOG.TXT.

If the installation proceeds smoothly, DETCRASH.LOG will be removed at the end of it. If the installation fails, when setup starts again after a reboot, it will find DETCRASH.LOG in existence and will skip detection of the device that caused the problem and continue the setup from the next major point beyond the last entry.

That way, it is possible for Windows 98 to install without having successfully recognized all your hardware. A problem with a single piece of hardware won't prevent you from installing Windows 98 halfway through the process, rendering your computer virtually useless. It's better to get the operating system up and running and then solve the problem rather than be stuck at a point that you can't get past.

Two utilities that can help identify and resolve installation problems are Version Conflict Manager and the Microsoft System Information utility.

Version Conflict Manager

The nature of Windows software architecture is modular. Software programs are made up of several components, and each component provides a specific functionality to the program. When a certain functionality needs to be enhanced or modified, only the components that pertain to that specific functionality need to be updated. This allows software developers to update and enhance their products at will without having to rewrite the entire program from scratch each time. Modular architecture also allows several programs that require similar functionality to share the components that provide that functionality rather than install a separate set of files for each program—each set duplicating the other's function. Software components such as these are usually Dynamic Link Library files (DLLs). The Windows 98 operating system provides a suite of DLL files that developers can rely on to provide much of the functionality needed for their programs to work with the operating system. Programs that are written to run under Windows 98 can share these common DLLs, and they can also ship with newer versions of these files that the software developers have enhanced to provide any special functionality that their program might need.

Problems can arise when a DLL, or other shared component that a software vendor has enhanced, replaces a previous version of that file on the system. The software vendor can't always predict how other software vendors might use the functionality provided in that library, and sometimes their enhancements cause the library functions to behave differently than another vendor expects it to. Users typically notice this type of problem when they receive a General Protection Fault or Illegal Operation error message and their system crashes.

The Version Conflict Manager (VCMUI.EXE) automatically overwrites newer files that may be on the hard drive with the Windows 98 system files. This is completely opposite of the way most program and operating system installations occur (it is usually thought that the newer files are the *better* files). But by operating in this fashion, Windows 98 ensures that it has the files it needs to run properly during installation.

> **NOTE**
>
> While Windows 98 will overwrite newer files with older ones, it does so according to the date and time stamp of the file. Version Conflict Manager does adhere to the standard rules of looking at a file version. Newer files (per version) are never overwritten with older ones.

Version Conflict Manager is located on the Tools menu of the System Information utility, which is covered in detail next.

Microsoft System Information Utility

The Microsoft System Information utility (Msinfo32) is one of the best diagnostic utilities to come along in a very long time. It has been included as a smaller tool with Microsoft Office as a shared component for quite some time, and it's now a part of the operating system.

When you select Start | Program Files | Accessories | System Tools | System Information, you see the screen shown in Figure 6.1.

There are three key categories of information it can look at:

- Hardware Resources

- Components

- Software Environment

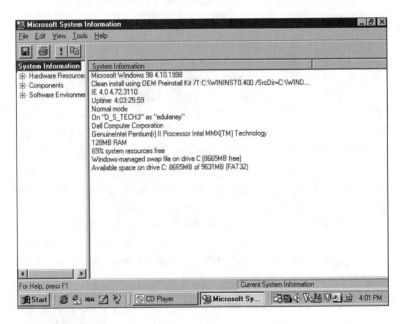

FIGURE 6.1
The System Information utility.

The Hardware Resources section is useful for finding device settings and looking for conflicts with other devices. Listed in the Hardware Resources section are the following items:

- Conflicts/Sharing. This area lists any devices in the computer that are sharing resources or that are in conflict for a particular resource.

- DMA. This area lists the resources that are using Direct Memory Access channels and shows which channels are in use by those devices.

- Forced Hardware. This area lists any devices that require the use of specific resources. These devices are typically older devices that rely on jumpers or switches to statically configure the resources they will use.

- I/O. This area lists the memory addresses that devices in the system are using for input/output.

- IRQs. This area lists the system Interrupt Request lines and shows which devices are using them. Some of the IRQs might be shared by multiple devices.

- Memory. This section lists any Memory Address Spaces reserved for use by system devices.

The Components area shows information that pertains to the configuration of Windows 98 and lists the following items:

- Multimedia
- Display
- Infrared
- Input
- Miscellaneous
- Modem
- Network
- Ports
- Storage
- Printing

- Problem devices

- Universal Serial Bus (USB)

- History

- System

The information provided in the Components area lists in detail the status of your system device drivers for multimedia, networking, and other system devices. You can choose from one of three views: Basic information, Advanced information, and History.

The Basic information view shows an abbreviated list of the resources in use by the selected device. This information includes the driver name, date and time, and any IRQs and I/O memory addresses used by the device.

The Advanced information view expands the information provided in the Basic information view with such fields as Boot resources (resources assigned to the device at boot time), Alloc resources (resources allocated to the device dynamically), and Registry keys (which store parameters required for the device to function properly).

The History view is very useful for troubleshooting problems with devices. It tracks changes to your Windows 98 configuration over time. It can be helpful in determining which information has changed for a device that isn't working now but used to.

Software Environment shows the software settings of items currently loaded into memory. It breaks these down into the following categories:

- Drivers. These are further divided into three subcategories:

  - Kernel Drivers

  - MS-DOS Drivers

  - User-Mode Drivers

- 16- and 32-bit Modules Loaded.

- Running Tasks.

- Startup Programs.

- System Hooks.

- ◆ OLE Registration. This section is further divided into two sub-categories:

  - INI File

  - Registry

The System Information utility shows only the Name and Type information for MS-DOS drivers. For other drivers and modules loaded into memory, as well as for running tasks, the System Information utility shows many important details:

- ◆ Driver. The driver or module name.

- ◆ Version. The version or revision number of the driver or module.

- ◆ Manufacturer. The manufacturer of the driver or module.

- ◆ Description. A brief description of the driver's or module's function.

- ◆ Path. The path where the driver or module file is stored on disk.

- ◆ Loaded From. The origin of the command that caused the driver or module to be loaded.

- ◆ Type. The type of driver or module. Drivers and modules are either static or dynamic.

- ◆ Part of. The software or device that the driver or module belongs to. Many drivers and modules are part of the Windows 98 operating system itself.

For startup programs, the System Information utility shows the name of the program, the location of the command that started the program, and the command itself.

The information in the Software Environment area is useful for troubleshooting in many ways. Often, when you're troubleshooting a system device failure or a problem with software, you will want to verify that the versions of the drivers and modules loaded to support the device or software are the ones you expect. If two different versions of the same file exist on the system, it's possible that the wrong version of the file has been loaded into memory and is causing a problem.

You will also want to verify the location of the files that are loaded into memory to ensure that multiple copies of a file are not present on the disk. Some software applications depend on initialization files that reside in the same directory as the drivers and modules that it loads into memory. If multiple copies of the drivers and module files exist in different locations on the hard disk, even if they are the same version, the initialization files accompanying them might not have the same settings, or an initialization might not be present at all in one of the directories. If that is the case, the drivers and modules won't load into memory with the configuration parameters you expect and probably won't behave the way you want them to.

The Running Tasks section can be helpful in determining if a process is still running, or if it has terminated. You can use this information when troubleshooting software problems or evaluating software performance.

Equally as important as the information it provides, the System Information tool is also the starting point for 10 other diagnostic tools or wizards. The following tools and wizards are loaded from the Tools menu:

- Windows Report tool
- Update Wizard Uninstall
- System File Checker
- Signature Verification tool
- Registry Checker
- Automatic Skip Driver Agent
- Dr. Watson
- System Configuration utility
- ScanDisk
- Version Conflict Manager

Some of these tools—such as ScanDisk—can be found in other locations, such as under Start | Programs | Accessories | System Tools, or on the Tools tab of the properties sheet for a hard disk. Many are located here only.

The information provided by the System Information utility can be saved to a file (with an .NFO extension) for later review at another Windows 98 computer. The information can also be exported to a text file for troubleshooting, for review from a system that doesn't support the System Information utility, or for import into a database where the information for many computers can be compiled for statistical analysis or reporting.

RESOLVING BOOT FAILURES

Startup/boot problems can fall into three main categories: miscellaneous problems with booting, a failure to boot, and programs starting that you don't want started.

Miscellaneous Problems with Booting

The System Configuration utility (MSCONFIG.EXE), shown in Figure 6.2, is the main tool for configuring startup parameters and looking for miscellaneous problems that occur. The interface for this tool consists of a set of tabs used to access information contained in a number of system files.

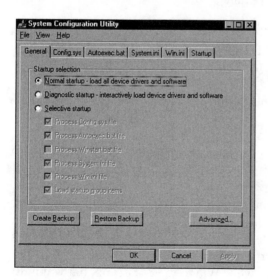

FIGURE 6.2
The System Configuration utility.

It is accessed from the Tools menu of the System Information utility. It allows you to view and edit the following items:

- CONFIG.SYS
- AUTOEXEC.BAT
- SYSTEM.INI
- WIN.INI
- Startup

In addition, the General tab of the System Configuration utility allows you to create a backup of your system configuration information (by clicking the Create Backup button), restore your system configuration from a backup (by clicking the Restore Backup button), and set the startup mode for your system. Startup mode selections include the following:

- Normal startup. Load all device drivers and software.
- Diagnostic startup. Interactively load device drivers and software.
- Selective startup. Options include the following:
  - Process CONFIG.SYS file
  - Process AUTOEXEC.BAT file
  - Process WINSTART.BAT file
  - Process SYSTEM.INI file
  - Process WIN.INI file
  - Load startup group items

Choosing Diagnostic startup causes the Windows 98 boot menu to appear. From there, you can choose Step by Step and watch the processing of all startup items to see where your problems are occurring. This is similar to pressing the F8 key to display the boot menu under Windows 95. That functionality is still available under Windows 98, but since Windows 98 doesn't display a Starting Windows 98 message, it is difficult to know when to press F8. You can also access the boot menu by holding down the Ctrl key while Windows 98 starts up, but you must hold down the Ctrl key until you see the boot menu, because, again, it is difficult to know exactly when to press the key.

If you want to determine if the problem is isolated to an entry in a particular startup file, you can choose not to run that file with the Selective startup option. Try this with one file at a time. Once you can boot without a problem, you can examine the file you excluded from the boot process to identify the exact source of the problem. Using the different startup modes in this way can help you more quickly eliminate variables in the troubleshooting process and identify the configuration parameter(s) that is causing your boot problems.

Also on the General tab of the System Configuration utility, you can enable or disable many advanced troubleshooting settings. Click the Advanced button to bring up the Advanced Troubleshooting Settings dialog box, shown in Figure 6.3.

This dialog box has 12 check boxes from which you can enable or disable the following advanced troubleshooting settings:

- Disable System ROM Breakpoint. This option prevents Windows 98 from using the ROM address space between 000:0000 and 1MB for a breakpoint. Setting the `SystemROMBreakPoint=false` line in the `[386Enh]` section of the SYSTEM.INI file accomplishes the same thing.

- Disable Virtual HD IRQ. This setting specifies that interrupts from the hard disk controller are handled directly by the system ROM rather than by a virtual device. This is the same as setting the `VirtualHDIRQ=false` option in the SYSTEM.INI file.

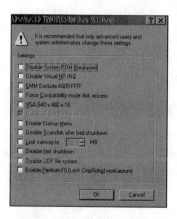

FIGURE 6.3

The Advanced Troubleshooting Settings dialog box.

- EMM Exclude A000-FFFF. This setting prevents Windows 98 from accessing any of the Upper Memory area. This is the same as setting the EMMExclude=A000-FFFF line in the SYSTEM.INI file.

- Force Compatibility mode disk access. This option forces all disk I/O to be done in real mode instead of protected mode.

- VGA 640×480×16. This setting forces the system to use the VGA driver. Enabling this option is the same as setting the Display.drv=Vga.drv line in the SYSTEM.INI file. If the VGA driver was already loaded when you started the System Configuration utility, you won't be able to clear this check box.

- Use SCSI Double-buffering. If you have a SCSI controller in your system, this option will enable the loading of a double-buffering device driver for that controller. If Windows 98 enabled SCSI double buffering during setup, or if you enabled it manually by editing the MSDOS.SYS file before running the System Configuration utility, you won't be able to clear this check box.

- Enable Startup Menu. Checking this option will cause Windows 98 to automatically display the Startup menu at boot time. There will be no need to press the Ctrl key to access this menu. This saves you from having to manually edit the MSDOS.SYS file.

- Disable Scandisk after bad shutdown. Normally, if Windows 98 isn't shut down properly, ScanDisk is run at the next boot time in order to ensure disk integrity. Checking this option disables that feature.

- Limit memory to *xx*MB. This option specifies the maximum amount of memory available for Windows 98. Replace *xx* with the amount of memory you want Windows 98 to use. Using this option can help you troubleshoot if you suspect that defective physical memory is causing Fatal Exception errors.

NOTE

Be careful when using the Limit memory setting. If you set this value below 16MB, Windows 98 might not be able to start at all. If you experience this problem, restart the computer. Access the Startup menu by holding down the Ctrl key during startup, and select Safe Mode. Run the System Configuration utility and deselect this option, or reset the memory limit to a value of 16MB or above.

+ Disable fast shutdown. Windows 98 includes performance enhancements over Windows 95 for faster system shutdown. If you suspect that these enhancements are causing problems with system shutdown, check this feature to help troubleshoot the problem.

+ Disable UDF file system. This option disables support for the Universal Disk Format file system used by DVD movie players. If you are experiencing problems with a DVD movie player, it might not be compatible with UDF. Check this feature to troubleshoot the problem.

+ Enable Pentium F0 (Lock CmpXchg) work around. Some Intel Pentium and Pentium MMX processors can have their operation disrupted by the use of certain instruction sequences. Enabling this feature will allow Windows 98 to work around the problem. If you are debugging an application, this check box should be cleared.

The Config.sys, Autoexec.bat, System.ini, and Win.ini tabs display the contents of the corresponding file. Check boxes are placed to the left of each line of the file, and you can enable or disable each line by checking or clearing the appropriate box. This is the same as *commenting out* the line, but it is easier to do in this graphical interface because the process is consistent. You simply check or clear the check box, as opposed to using the REM keyword in your AUTOEXEC.BAT and CONFIG.SYS files and using the semicolon (;) delimiter in your SYSTEM.INI and WIN.INI files. Each file has its own tab within the interface, so you can edit each file from one place rather than opening multiple files in a text editor.

To edit a particular line in one of these files using the System Configuration utility, you can select the line and click the Edit button, or you can simply double-click the line. You can change the location of a line within the file by selecting the line and clicking the Move Up or Move Down button. This is easier than using cut and paste.

On the last tab of the System Configuration utility, the Startup tab, you can select or deselect the programs that will run automatically when Windows 98 starts. The list of items that appear on this tab is created from the items found in the Startup folder and any items scheduled to run at startup in the Registry.

The View menu of the System Configuration utility lets you access the entire Control Panel, or the following applets from within the Control Panel:

- Device Manager
- Printers Folder
- Display Settings
- Multimedia Settings
- Fonts Folder

With its many features, its streamlined interface, and quick access to Control Panel applets, the System Configuration utility is a very handy troubleshooting tool. It's a vast improvement over the SYSEDIT utility that ran under Windows 3.1 and Windows 95.

Failure to Boot

If the system fails to boot altogether, try booting the system with a startup disk to see if you can diagnose where the system activity fails. The startup disk in Windows 98 is created from the Startup Disk tab of the Add/Remove Programs applet in Control Panel.

If the system doesn't even get to the point where it reads the startup disk, this could be an indication of hardware failure. Try some of the following steps to determine the point of failure. If you answer no to any of the questions along the way, take the appropriate corrective action and try the system again.

Determine if the system is getting power by answering the following questions:

- Do the LEDs on the system (if any are present) light up when you turn on the power switch?
- Does the fan on the power supply spin when you turn on the power switch?
- Are the wires connecting the power supply to the motherboard securely and correctly attached?

If the system is getting power, establish that all required components are present and are functioning by answering the following questions:

- Is there a CPU on the motherboard, and is it securely and correctly installed?

- Is there RAM installed in the computer, and is it securely and correctly installed?

- Is there a BIOS chip securely and correctly installed on the motherboard?

If essential components are installed and seem to be functioning properly, check to see if the computer display is active by answering the following questions:

- Is there a display adapter securely installed in the system?

- Is the monitor properly connected to the system, and does it work?

If the display is functioning correctly, try removing optional components, such as network cards or sound cards, from the system one at a time until the system starts, and then replace them in the opposite order from which you removed them. Usually, the last device that you're left with is the offending device.

Undesired Programs Starting

If applications automatically start when they aren't supposed to, there could be several causes:

- Entries (shortcuts) in the Startup group. If you have enabled user profiles on the system, go to the Windows\Profiles*Username*\Start Menu\Programs\Startup folder to remove the unwanted shortcuts. Otherwise, the shortcuts will be in the Windows\Profiles\All Users folder.

- The Registry key `HKEY_LOCAL_MACHINE\SOFTWARE\Microsoft\Windows\` `CurrentVersion\Run` starts all applications listed beneath it on each boot. Remove values from this key that you don't want to run at system startup.

- The Registry key HKEY_LOCAL_MACHINE\SOFTWARE\Microsoft\Windows\ CurrentVersion\RunOnce starts all applications listed beneath it on the next boot only. Remove values from this key that you don't want to run at system startup.

- The Registry key HKEY_LOCAL_MACHINE\SOFTWARE\Microsoft\Windows\ CurrentVersion\RunServices starts all applications and services listed beneath it on each boot. Remove values from this key that you don't want to run at system startup.

- If it exists, entries in a file named WINSTART.BAT are processed and started as Windows boots.

- The Startup configuration of the System Configuration utility, discussed earlier in this chapter. This is a master set of the items just described, and any settings in INI files and elsewhere.

Entries in any of these locations can cause unwanted applications to start when you boot Windows 98.

RESOLVING CONNECTIVITY PROBLEMS

Connectivity problems can run the gamut from the simple to the complex, based on a number of criteria. When considering a problem in this category, always approach it with a few simple questions first:

- Has there ever been connectivity?

- When was the last time it worked properly?

- What has changed since then?

As simple as these steps sound, forgetting to ask them can cost untold hours of grief. If connectivity was never there before (this workstation can't communicate with the server), find out what needs to be done to the workstation to make it like the others that are working successfully.

Determining the last time it worked properly can be crucial. If this workstation can't communicate with the server but once did, when did it work last? Was it a year ago, before you took NetBEUI off the server? Or was it yesterday?

What has changed since the last time there was connectivity is a question you never want to ask a user, because the answer will always be "Nothing. I didn't do anything." You can then look at the system and see that networked versions of Johnny Deadly were installed yesterday.

There are a couple of tools to use when trying to solve connectivity problems. Net Watcher is one; it was discussed in detail in Chapter 5, "Monitoring and Optimization." WinIPCfg is another. It's shown in Figure 6.4.

This utility is used to see your machine's TCP/IP configuration and any related DHCP information. It is available from Start | Run, or it can be entered as a command in a DOS window.

The WinIPCfg utility displays all your TCP/IP settings for each network adapter in your system. If you're using DHCP for automatic TCP/IP configuration, the WinIPCfg utility allows you to release and/or renew your IP address lease. If the computer has been relocated from one physical subnet to another, you might need to release the lease of the previous IP address and establish a new lease with a new address on the local subnet. The Release button will release the previous IP address lease.

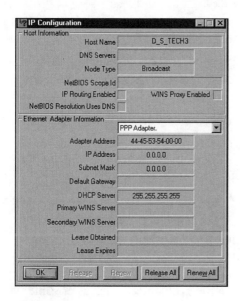

FIGURE 6.4
The WinIPCfg utility.

The Renew button will send a request to the DHCP server for a new IP address lease. It's a good idea to release an IP address lease before moving a Windows 98 system to another subnet, and then to renew the lease when the system is installed in its new location. However, often this step is overlooked, and connectivity problems can be the result.

Problems to Look for in a Microsoft Environment

At A Glance: Common Problems in a Microsoft Network Environment

Problem	Troubleshooting Steps
Can't see other computers in Network Neighborhood	Check the Identification tab on the Network Properties sheet. Ensure that the computer is a member of the correct workgroup or domain.
Can't connect to other computers on the network using NetBIOS names	Verify that the correct address is specified for primary and secondary WINS servers, and that those servers are available.
Can't log in to the domain	Verify that the Client for Microsoft Networks is installed.
	Verify the user's account and password in User Manager for Domains.
	Verify that at least one domain controller is accessible on the network.
Can't access shared resources on other computers connected to the network	Verify that the remote computer is accessible on the network.
	Verify that the user has access to the shared resource through either a share password or an explicit access assignment through user-level security.

When there are problems connecting to a Microsoft network, verify that the correct protocols are employed (NT 4.0 uses TCP/IP as the default). Check the workstation's log files for problems, paying particular attention to NETLOG.TXT, and try to isolate the problem as much as possible.

Here are some typical problems experienced in a Microsoft environment:

- The computer can't see other computers in Network Neighborhood.

- The computer can't connect to other computers on the network using NetBIOS names.

- The user can't log in to the domain.

- The user can't access shared resources on other computers connected to the network.

Sometimes a computer connected to a network can't see any computer other than itself listed in the Network Neighborhood. Usually when this problem occurs, it is due to an incorrect entry in the Workgroup field on the Identification tab of the Network properties sheet. Verify that the computer is a member of the correct workgroup or domain by checking this entry.

Microsoft Windows NT networks use the TCP/IP protocol by default. In a TCP/IP environment, sometimes a computer can connect to another computer by using the IP address but not by using the NetBIOS name of the remote computer. This problem is usually caused by an incorrect or missing entry for the primary WINS server on the WINS Configuration tab of the TCP/IP properties sheet. If you're using WINS for NetBIOS name resolution, verify that this entry is present and correct. Also verify that the WINS server is accessible on the network.

If a user can't log in to the Windows NT domain, check to see if she is being prompted to log in to the domain. If not, chances are that the Client for Microsoft Networks isn't installed on the computer. After installing the Client for Microsoft Networks, you should also verify that the user has a valid account in the domain and that at least one domain controller is available on the network to authenticate the user's login request.

If a user can't access shared resources located on other computers connected to the network, first verify that the remote computer is actually up and running. Then verify that the user has the appropriate access to the resource in question. If share-level security is being used, verify the password being used to access the shared resource. If user-level security is being used, verify that the user has been granted access to the shared resource either directly or through membership to a group that has been granted the appropriate access rights.

Other problems might arise that are more difficult to troubleshoot. Try to limit the variables that might complicate the troubleshooting process. Remove protocols from the system that are not required to access the resource in question. Try to verify that each component involved in the process of connecting to the network (hardware or software) is functioning properly.

When you have the problem narrowed down to its smallest component, consult the Microsoft-recognized help resources. These include, but are not limited to, the following:

+ TechNet. A monthly CD-ROM that is available by subscription.

+ The Windows 98 Resource Kit. A publication of Microsoft Press that contains valuable information that is designed for use by IS professionals.

+ Microsoft Web site. A World Wide Web site that Microsoft maintains at `http://www.microsoft.com/support`.

+ Microsoft download libraries. An electronic bulletin board service maintained by Microsoft that you can dial into by modem. Check with Microsoft for the current phone number and modem settings. They are subject to change periodically without notice.

Problems to Look for in a NetWare Environment

At A Glance: Common Problems in a NetWare Network Environment

Problem	Troubleshooting Steps
Can't log in to the NetWare network.	Verify that the Client for NetWare Networks is installed.
	Verify that the preferred sever name is correct and that the server is available in the network.
	If NDS is used, verify that the Service for NetWare Directory Services is installed.
	Verify that the user has a valid account on the file server or in the NDS.
Login script doesn't run.	Set the correct preferred server and Enable Login Script Processing on the Client for NetWare Networks properties sheet.

NetWare server(s) can't be found.	Check the frame type specified in the Advanced properties for the IPX/SPX-compatible protocol.
The user is prompted for a Windows 98 password and a NetWare password separately.	Set the Windows 98 password to match the NetWare password. Once they match, you will be prompted for a password only once.

Microsoft Client for NetWare Networks can experience four kinds of problems:

- The user can't log in to the NetWare network.
- The NetWare Login Script doesn't run.
- The NetWare file server(s) on the network can't be found.
- The user is prompted for a Windows 98 password and a NetWare password separately.

If a user can't log in to the NetWare network, first verify that she is being prompted to do so. On the Network properties sheet, check to see that the Client for NetWare Networks has been installed. Verify that the Preferred Server entry on the Client for NetWare Networks properties sheet is the correct file server and that the file server is accessible on the network. Next, make sure that the user has a valid account on the file server. If the network is running NetWare Directory Services (NDS), verify that the user has a valid account in the directory.

Sometimes a user will log in to a NetWare network and the login script won't run. If this happens, make sure that the user is logging in to the file server where the expected login script resides. Check the Preferred Server entry on the Client for NetWare Networks properties sheet. Also on this properties sheet, verify that login script processing has been enabled by checking the Enable login script processing check box.

If no NetWare file servers can be found on the network, verify that the Windows 98 computer is running the correct frame type on the Advanced tab of the IPX/SPX-compatible protocol properties sheet. Setting the value of this option to Auto will usually eliminate problems, but you can also set it to the specific frame type that you want to use.

This eliminates problems that can arise if multiple frame types are present on your network and the frame type you want to use isn't the one detected by the Auto setting. Here are the possible values for IPX/SPX-compatible protocol frame types:

- Auto. Automatically listens to the network and detects the frame type that is in use. This setting can sometimes be unreliable if multiple frame types are in use on the same network.

- Ethernet 802.2. This is the default frame type used by NetWare version 3.12 and above for Ethernet networks.

- Ethernet 802.3. This is the default frame type used by NetWare version 3.11 and earlier for Ethernet networks.

- Ethernet II. This frame type is usually found in Ethernet networks running the TCP/IP protocol, but it is also supported by Novell's IPX/SPX protocol and Microsoft's IPX/SPX-compatible protocol.

- Token Ring. This is the default frame type found in Token Ring network environments.

- Token Ring SNAP. The Token Ring Sub-Network Access Protocol frame type is usually found in a Token Ring network that runs the TCP/IP protocol, but it is also supported by Novell's IPX/SPX protocol and Microsoft's IPX/SPX-compatible protocol.

If the user's password for Windows 98 differs from his NetWare password, each time he logs in to the computer, he is prompted for the Windows 98 password and the NetWare password separately. Many users find this annoying. In order to simplify the login process and eliminate multiple password prompts, set the Windows 98 password to match the NetWare password. This is done in the Passwords applet in Control Panel.

RESOLVING PRINTING PROBLEMS

At A Glance: Printing Problems

Printing Problem	*Troubleshooting Steps*
Can't print to a locally connected printer	Check that the printer is online.
	Check that the printer cable is properly connected to the computer and the printer.

	Check for adequate disk space on the hard disk.
	Clear the TEMP directory.
	Try printing directly to the printer.
	Reboot the Windows 98 computer and try again.
Can't print to a shared printer	Check that the remote printer is online on the network.
	Check that network cables are properly connected.
	Check for adequate free space on the print server's hard disk.
	Delete orphaned print jobs from the spool folder.
	Stop and restart the print spooler service on the print server.
	Reboot the Windows 98 computer and try again.

You can print to a locally connected printer, to a Windows NT network, or to a NetWare network. Problems associated with a local printer are typically easy to diagnose and resolve compared to those on the network. We will primarily look at the NT environment and deviate from it for NetWare when necessary.

Windows NT lets you define network printers that are available as shared resources for Windows 98, Windows 95, and Windows NT Workstations to print to. Any client or server on a network can serve as the print server to a network printer. Additionally, you can have local printers that are not shared resources to other network computers but that need to be managed and troubleshot by their owner.

A single standardized print model under Windows replaces the individual print models of applications under MS-DOS. While this simplifies the process nicely, the downside is that when problems do arise, they affect your entire application suite and maybe an entire workgroup.

Windows still retains the older model for printing for MS-DOS applications that run in Windows NT Workstation or Windows 98 from the command prompt. These applications require their own printer drivers in order to print anything other than ASCII output. If you're using WordPerfect 5.1, for example, you must have both a WordPerfect printer driver and a Windows 98 printer driver installed. Some MS-DOS applications might require that you turn on, or capture, the printer port by using a command such as the following before printing:

```
NET USE LPT1: \\servername\printername
```

Understanding the Windows Print Subsystem

The printing subsystem is modular and works hand-in-hand with other subsystems to provide printing services. When a printer is a local printer and a print job is specified by an application, data is sent to the Graphics Device Interface (GDI) for rendering into a print job in the print device's printer language. The GDI is a module between the printing subsystem and the application requesting the printing services. This print job is passed to the spooler, which is a DLL. The print job is written to disk as a temporary file so that it can survive a power outage or your computer's reboot. Print jobs can be spooled using either the RAW or Enhanced Metafile (EMF) printer languages.

The client side of the print spooler is WINSPOOL.DRV, and that driver makes a Remote Procedure Call (RPC) to SPOOLSS.EXE, the server side of the spooler. When the printer is attached to the same computer, both files are located on the same computer. When the printer is attached to a remote computer in a peer-to-peer relationship, those files are located on different computers.

SPOOLSS.EXE calls an API that sends the print job to a route (SPOOLSS.DLL). SPOOLSS.DLL then sends the print job to the computer with the local printer. Finally, the LOCALSPL.DLL library writes the file to disk as a spooled file. At this point, the printer is polled by LOCALSPL.DLL to determine whether the spooled print job can be processed by the printer, and the print job is altered if required.

The print job is then turned over to a separator page processor and despooled to the print monitor. The print device receives the print job, and the raster image processes it to a bitmap file that is then sent to the print engine to output.

Network Printer Process

For network printers, the process is very much the same, but client requests and server services are more clearly defined and separate. The routers found in the spooler modules—WINSPOOL.DRV, SPOOLSS.EXE, and SPOOLSS.DLL—are identical to the ones used for a local printer. A local print provider on the client LOCALSPL.DLL is matched to a remote print provider on the server side—WIN32SP.DLL for Windows print servers or NWPROVAU.DLL for NetWare print servers.

In a network printer process, the print processors and print monitors may use several different server DLLs, each one required by a supported operating system.

Multiple Virtual Printer Setup

You generally install a printer using the Add Printer Wizard. You can find it under Start | Settings | Printers. After you step through the wizard, you create a virtual printer with a name that you provide. You can create any number of virtual (or logical, if you will) printers that use the same physical printer for a number of purposes. If you want to print to a different printer, have different security schemes, or provide different access times, having multiple virtual printers provides a means to do this. You manipulate printers by doing the following:

- Double-clicking the printer to see any spooled jobs (provided that you have the privilege to do so). Access privileges are covered in detail in Chapter 3, "Configuring and Managing Resource Access."

- Right-clicking a printer to view a shortcut menu that provides several actions. You can use this menu to delete a printer that no longer exists, for example. You can use the Default Printer command to set the default printer for a Windows 98 computer from the shortcut menu.

- Right-clicking a printer and selecting the Properties command from the shortcut menu to access the Printer properties sheet and control any number of settings.

Printers as Shared Resources

Network printers are shared resources. You must either own the printer (have created or installed it), be an administrator, or be assigned the rights to the printer to be able to view, modify, and use it. A printer owner or administrator can assign different levels of rights to different users. You assign shared rights by using the Sharing command on a printer's shortcut menu. This brings up the Sharing tab of the Printer Properties dialog box.

Creating additional printer shares for the same physical printer proves useful for the following reasons:

- Each share can have different printer setups.

- If you are a member of a Microsoft Windows NT domain or a NetWare network and are using user-level security, it lets you assign different access privileges to groups of users.

- You can use one share for a network printer and another share name for a local printer.

If users can't see a network printer, they might not have been given the right to access that printer. Conversely, if users don't have the right to print to a printer, they should still see it in the Printers folder but not be able to print to it.

If you have MS-DOS clients on the network and you want them to see a printer share, you must use a file naming convention that DOS recognizes. Names can be up to 12 characters long and can't contain spaces or any of the following characters:

? * # | \ / = > < %

To hide a printer share, add a dollar sign to the end of the share name, as in *sharename*$. Any printer with that kind of name won't show up in the Connect To Printer dialog box that is one of the steps in the Add Printer Wizard. A user must know that this printer share exists and must be able to enter the correct name and path to the printer share to connect to that printer.

Solving Print Spooler Problems

Any print job spooled to a printer is written as a temporary file to the Windows\Spool\Printers folder. The Spool folder is a hidden folder, so it normally doesn't appear in a directory listing. The temporary print job file is deleted after the printer indicates that the job has been printed. The primary print spool problem encountered is a lack of available disk space. If you print high-resolution graphics, you might have print jobs as large as 20 to 80MB per file for a 32-bit image at standard page size.

When you print to the spooler, you create two files for each print job. The .SPL file is the actual print job spool file. You also create a shadow file, which is given an .SHD extension. The shadow file contains additional information about the print job that is not part of the print job itself, such as owner, priority, and so forth. If your computer crashes, .SPL and .SHD files remain in the default spool folder until the service restarts and they are processed and printed. After being printed, these files are deleted from disk. Should your spooled files become corrupted, they will be orphaned and remain in the spool folder, taking up valuable space. You should check your Spool directory periodically to look for any orphaned print jobs and delete them from the disk to prevent them from using up valuable hard disk space.

You can print directly to a printer from your application by turning off the print spooling feature. Before you print, open the Scheduling tab of the Printer Properties dialog box and select the Print directly to the printer radio button. When the printer next becomes available, your document prints. Until that point, you can't use the application that originates the print job. You can task-switch to another application and continue working until your printing application becomes available. Sometimes this can be an effective step in troubleshooting the print process. If you can print directly to the printer but not when you use print spooling, there is a problem with the print spooling process. This problem could be caused by lack of hard disk space, driver file incompatibilities, or other issues.

When all else fails, stop and restart the printer spooler service. This effectively shuts it down and restarts it, thus clearing anything that might have been hung. You can do this on a Windows NT computer from the Services applet in Control Panel. On a Windows 98 computer, you must reboot the system.

Using the Print Troubleshooter

To help you solve printer problems, Windows 98 comes with an interactive print troubleshooting aid as part of the online Help system. To access the Print Troubleshooter, complete the following steps:

1. Choose Start | Help.

2. Click the Index tab and enter **printers troubleshooting** in the box.

3. Select the appropriate problem type, click the Next button, and follow the instructions in the Help system.

Printers are one of the most important network resources in many organizations. Therefore, you will often be called on to solve problems that crop up with printer shares and printer hardware.

RESOLVING FILE SYSTEM PROBLEMS

This section discusses two key problems and one primary tool. Here are the problems:

- File sharing. If you have an older program that requires the use of SHARE.EXE, you can choose the Disable new file sharing and locking semantics setting to modify the way that file sharing and locking on hard disk occurs. To do this, follow these steps:

  1. Right-click the My Computer icon and select Properties.

  2. Select the Performance tab, and click the File System button.

  3. Select the Troubleshooting tab on the File System properties sheet.

  4. Check the Disable new file sharing and locking semantics check box.

  5. Click OK twice to complete the process.

- Write-behind caching. Although this greatly improves system performance by caching information that an application wants to save and saving it when the system is less busy, it can create problems with critical data. Checking the Disable write-behind caching for all drives option ensures that all data is continually flushed to the hard disk. Follow these steps:

  1. Right-click the My Computer icon and select Properties.

  2. Select the Performance tab, and click the File System button.

  3. Select the Troubleshooting tab on the File System properties sheet.

  4. Check the Disable write-behind caching for all drives check box.

  5. Click OK twice to complete the process.

The primary tool for fixing file system problems is ScanDisk (SCANDISK.EXE). ScanDisk analyzes your hard disk for errors and can repair any errors that are found. The following are areas on which ScanDisk checks and fixes errors:

- File system structure, including lost clusters and cross-linked files
- Long filenames
- File Allocation Table
- Physical surface of the drive
- Directory tree structure
- DriveSpace or DoubleSpace volumes

Under a FAT file system, such as that of MS-DOS and Windows 98, data is stored on a hard drive in such a way that the clusters (an allocation) containing data pertaining to a certain file are not necessarily stored contiguously on the drive. Often, the clusters for a specific file are scattered throughout the drive. Each cluster for a file contains both data and a pointer to the location of the next cluster in the chain. When a file is requested, the file system looks up the name of the file in the directory tree (which tells where the first cluster for the file is located) and begins reading through the various clusters, collecting the file's data.

Problems can occur when the pointer to the next cluster becomes corrupted. If, for example, file A has a cluster with some data and a pointer to cluster 12, and file B has a cluster that also points to cluster 12, these files are said to be cross-linked. The data at cluster 12 can't belong to both files, so there is a logical inconsistency in the drive's file structure. ScanDisk can detect such inconsistencies, but it is unable to determine to which file the cluster truly belongs. ScanDisk defaults to making a copy of the cluster so that each file can make use of the information in the cluster. This increases the chances that at least one of the two files in question can be salvaged.

Another associated problem is that the clusters that should have been in the chain after the corrupted cluster are no longer referenced by any file and thus are *orphaned* or lost. These clusters may still contain valid data, but they no longer are part of any file on the drive. ScanDisk can find these clusters and either save them as files to be examined later or mark the clusters as available to the file system, thus freeing up space on the drive.

Operation Modes

ScanDisk can perform two levels of testing on hard drives: standard and thorough. Standard mode is best used on a daily basis, whereas thorough mode is best used when you suspect a problem with the hard drive.

In standard mode, ScanDisk performs logical tests against the file system's File Allocation Table (FAT), checking for the logical inconsistencies outlined earlier. In addition, the standard scan checks for various other potential problems, such as invalid filenames and invalid date and time stamps.

In thorough mode, ScanDisk performs all the tests included in standard mode and also performs a surface scan. Each cluster on the drive is checked for physical defects that would make the cluster in question unsafe for data storage. A surface scan is performed by reading the information from the cluster and rewriting it to the same cluster. If the information matches what ScanDisk read the first time, the cluster is probably safe. If the data is different, a media problem might exist, in which case ScanDisk marks the cluster as bad.

Notes on ScanDisk

Here's some additional information that you should keep in mind when using the ScanDisk utility:

- ScanDisk can detect and repair errors in long filenames (LFNs).

- ScanDisk can be used to test and maintain the integrity of DoubleSpace and DriveSpace volumes if the volumes are mounted. If they aren't, they can be tested from the command-line version of ScanDisk.

- It is possible to have ScanDisk log activities. The results of the scan are stored in the file SCANDISK.LOG in the root of the drive that has been examined.

- ScanDisk can't fix errors on CD-ROMs, network drives, drives created by the DOS command INTERLNK, or drives referenced via MS-DOS commands (such as ASSIGN, JOIN, and SUBST).

- It is possible to multitask with ScanDisk, but if any disk write activity occurs, ScanDisk might be forced to restart the testing process.

RESOLVING RESOURCE PROBLEMS

At A Glance: Resource Problems

Resource	Environment	Common Problems
Shared folder on a Windows 98 computer	Workgroup	Incorrect password.
	Share-level security	Network connectivity problems.
Shared printer on a Windows 98 computer	Workgroup	Incorrect password.
	Share-level security	Network connectivity problems.
		Printer offline.
Shared folder on a Windows 98 computer or a shared folder on a network file server	Domain	User doesn't have rights to the folder.
	User-level security	User is a member of several groups that have conflicting rights to the folder.
		User is not authenticated to the network.
		Network connectivity problems.
Shared printer on a Windows 98 computer or a shared printer on a network print server	Domain	User doesn't have rights to the printer.
	User-level security	User is a member of several groups that have conflicting rights to the printer.
		User is not authenticated to the network.
		Network connectivity issues.
		Printer is offline.

When you're using Windows 98 to connect to Windows NT, Windows NT's security system controls access to network resources through user and machine accounts. Your logon to a particular domain is validated by a domain controller and provides you with certain privileges and rights that are registered in the Security Accounts Manager (SAM) database.

When you log on to the Windows NT domain controller, the system provides a Security Access Token (SAT) based on your user name and password. This SAT is a key that lets you access objects that Windows NT manages by maintaining a Security Descriptor (SD) file. That SD file contains the Access Control List (ACL) for each resource.

Two types of accounts are created and managed in Windows NT: machine accounts and user accounts. A machine account is assigned to Windows NT computers, servers, and workstations, which participate in Domain security. A user account is assigned to each user who will log in to the Windows NT domain. Both of these types of accounts are stored in the Security Account Manager (SAM) database stored on the primary domain controller (PDC) and replicated to any backup domain controllers (BDC) on the system. Accounts are assigned a unique, internally held System Identification number (SID).

On the NT Server, machine accounts are created in the domain with the Server Manager utility. The administrator creates and manages user accounts in the User Manager for Domains utility. An account is specified by the domain and user name, as in *domainname\username*.

A *group* is an account that contains other accounts. Every Windows NT computer contains a Users group to which all user accounts belong. There is also a Guest group that allows limited privileges to users who log in without a password (if you allow it).

The logon process provides the definition of your group membership and other properties assigned to you. Access privileges to resources are assigned to a group as a whole, and all group members (which can include users as well as other groups) are given the same access rights to those resources.

Local groups can be created to provide control over resource access. Local groups have meaning only to the Windows NT computer on which they were created. Windows NT also comes with some prebuilt global groups that are available system-wide and that have meaning within the context of the entire Windows NT domain. You can also define additional local or global groups. Users, groups, and domains offer a flexible system for managing resource access through security settings that you make either in the file system or on your desktop for various system objects.

Under Windows NT, access privileges are cumulative when you're combining Share permissions (permissions assigned at the share level) or when you're combining Local permissions (permissions assigned to local groups). When you combine Share permissions with Local permissions, however, the most restrictive environment applies. This means that if a user is a member of a group that has been assigned full access rights to a shared resource, but access to that resource has been limited for that person's user account at the share level, the most restrictive set of access rights will be allowed. This is referred to as the effective rights to that resource. This also applies to Share permissions and NTFS permissions under Windows NT. If a user has been granted Full Control at the share level but has been restricted through NTFS permissions, the most restrictive access rights will be the user's effective rights to the shared resource.

Due to the complexity of the Windows security architecture, resource access problems can often arise. When troubleshooting resource access problems, try to answer the following questions:

+ Does the user have a valid account?

+ Has the user's account been authenticated to the network?

+ Has the user been assigned access rights to the resource, either directly to the user's account or to a group in which the user is a member?

+ Have conflicting sets of resource access rights been assigned at different levels (one set to a group and a different set to the user at the share level)?

+ Is the user providing the correct password (for share-level security)?

It is often difficult to troubleshoot resource access problems, but these questions can help narrow down the possible causes of the problem to further isolate the exact source of the problem.

Password Issues

Passwords allow you to log on to a particular user account. To log on successfully, you must know both the user name and the exact password. The important thing to know about passwords is that they are *case-sensitive* under Windows NT. Therefore, one of the most commonly encountered errors is when the Caps Lock key is pressed accidentally.

A user can enter the correct password and still have his entry to the system denied because the password was entered in uppercase.

To protect passwords, Windows NT has an option that lets you retire a password after a certain period. You can also set an option that requires Windows 98 users to change the assigned password the first time they log on to the system. Users logging on after that time are required to change their password. Windows NT also allows a *no password* password for anonymous access that provides limited access to system resources. This password is used for a Web server running an FTP service. One example of its use is allowing a user to access a PUB folder.

Windows NT supports a feature called Account Lockout. The Windows NT computer will *lock out* an account after a certain number of failed login attempts. The account won't be able to log in to the system at all, even if the correct password is provided, until a certain period of time has elapsed. If your server is set to use the Account Lockout feature, there is a parameter called Lockout Duration. If failed login attempts have locked out an account, the account can be used again after the Lockout Duration has expired. If you are highly concerned about security, set this value to Forever, which will not unlock an account until an administrator does so manually. You will be able to keep track of most break-in attempts—at least those that fail. To configure Account Lockout in the User Manager utility, select Policies | Account.

Troubleshooting Profiles and System Policies

A user profile is created whenever a user logs on to Windows 98 the first time. User profiles can be created that provide a specific configuration of the desktop, programs, accessories, printers, a taskbar and Start menu configuration, Help system bookmarks, and options in the Windows Explorer. This lets an administrator provide a default profile that is used as a standard template for all users in a domain.

Profiles offer a method of creating an environment based on the user account. Profiles can be stored on the server and retrieved as a cached copy on a local machine when a user logs on. A stored local profile can be used when a problem occurs with a network connection or logon. To let a user have his profile and configuration travel with him regardless of which workstation he logs on to in the domain, you can create *roaming profiles*.

These are simply profiles stored on the file server in the user's home directory (or in the MAIL directory on a NetWare server) so that they are available to the user from any workstation on the network.

You can find user profile settings in the Windows 98 Registry in the HKEY_CURRENT_USER key. If you want to modify your user profiles, you can find them in the Profiles folder for each user. Each user profile folder contains a directory of shortcuts or link (.LNK) files to desktop items and the USER.DAT file. The following shortcuts are contained in these folders:

- Application Data. Contains any application data and settings.

- Cookies. This folder stores cookies that are left on your hard drive by the Web sites you visit. Information such as your specific preferences for that site or your user ID at that site is stored in these files.

- Desktop. Shortcuts to files or folders are contained in the Desktop folder. Any icon that you have on your desktop will have an associated .LNK file that is stored in this folder.

- Favorites. Contains shortcuts to programs, folders, and favorite locations on the Web.

- NetHood. This hidden folder stores shortcuts to Network Neighborhood objects.

- Personal. This folder contains program items.

- PrintHood. This hidden folder contains network printer connections and settings.

- Recent. The files that appear on the Documents menu are stored as shortcuts in this hidden folder.

- SendTo. This contains shortcuts to document items. Different destinations that would be appropriate to send a document to can be stored here, such as a shortcut to Notepad or to your email or fax software. By default, a shortcut to your Desktop folder, to your My Documents folder, and to your floppy drive are added to this folder. Windows 98 might add other shortcuts, such as to your email or fax software, if you had such software installed when you upgraded to Windows 98. You can always add such shortcuts manually.

- Start Menu. Any items that appear on the Start menu are stored in this folder.

- Templates. Any template items stored to disk by a user are contained in this hidden folder.

- Temporary Internet Files. Images embedded in Web pages are downloaded to your browser and stored here for easy reloading the next time you visit the page. HTML pages are also sometimes stored here, as well as different media files, such as sound or video files.

A user profile can't be opened and read in any text editor, because a .DAT file is a compiled binary file. It can be opened with REGEDIT.EXE. The information contained in the *USERNAME*\USER.DAT file is stored in the following subkeys of HKEY_CURRENT_USER:

- AppEvents. If your system is configured with a sound card, the configuration information that tells Windows 98 which sounds to play for certain Windows events, such as startup or shutdown, is stored here.

- Control Panel. This subkey stores information that determines which Control Panel applets are accessible and what their current settings are.

- Keyboard Layout. Your default keyboard layout and any custom keyboard mappings are stored in this subkey.

- Network. Persistent network connections and paths to any recently accessed network drives (in UNC format) are stored here.

- Remote Access. Configuration information for any connections you have configured in Dial-Up Networking is stored in this subkey.

- Software. The software applications that are available and the settings and other configuration information for each application are stored in this subkey.

Working with System Policies

At A Glance: System Policies

Policy Type	Characteristics
User Policy	Applies only to the specific user.
	Controls the system environment for that user, regardless of which workstation the user logs in to the network with.

Group Policy	Applies to all members of the specified group.
	Controls the system environment for those users, regardless of which workstations they log in to the network with.
	Requires the GROUPPOL.DLL file to be installed on each Windows 98 computer.
Default Policy	Applies to all users who log in to the network.
	Controls the system environment for all users, regardless of which workstations they log in to the network with.
	System Policy Editor comes with two default policies—Default User and Default Computer.

To enforce a set of rules on a computer, a network administrator can create a system policy that applies to a single user, a group of users, or all users who log in to the network. You create a specific policy with custom options in the System Policy Editor. This utility lets you edit portions of the Windows 98 Registry or a system policy. Policies that you see in the System Policy Editor are contained in the system policy template files. Template files are a set of stored Registry entries. You can modify a template file in the System Policy Editor, or create new template files.

You install the System Policy Editor from the Windows 98 CD. It is stored in the Windows\Tools\Policy folder. The System Policy editor can be run in one of two modes: Registry mode or Policy File mode. System policy settings are stored in the Windows 98 Registry in the HKEY_CURRENT_USER and HKEY_LOCAL_MACHINE keys. When you open the System Policy Editor in Registry mode, you expose various keys in this area of the Registry.

A system policy can restrict network logon or access, customize the desktop, or limit access to settings in the Control Panel. A system policy can be applied to a single user, a group of users, or all the users who log in to the network. Windows 98 comes with two standard policies: Default Computer and Default User, both of which control options applied to all computers and users who log in to the network. You can create and enforce additional system policies.

With the System Policy Editor in Policy File mode, you create or modify system policy files (.POL) for the domain. Any modifications you make for a user, group, or computer in the system policy are written as an entry into the CONFIG.POL file. To enforced them, you must save this file in the NETLOGON share on all domain controllers, or to the Public directory on your NetWare file servers.

Accessing Shared Resources

Failure to access a share is one of the most common problems requiring resolution by an administrator. Files, shared folders (or simply shares), printer shares, and other shared resources require resource permissions. To create a share for an object, typically you right-click the object and select Sharing. You must first have File and Printer Sharing installed on the computer. In many instances, the object's Sharing tab appears and lets you specify users, groups, and access privileges that are allowed.

The person who creates the resource "owns" the resource and has full privileges to it. The administrator also has full access to resources and can take ownership of them. When an administrator takes ownership of a resource, access to the resource from the original owner is denied. This is a safety mechanism to make it obvious that ownership has been removed and that the resource has been fully taken over.

When a user can't access a shared resource, he might not have the privileges required to do so. Try logging on under a different account to attempt to access the resource. If the resource has been accessed in the past under a particular user account, make sure that the resource name is spelled correctly and that it has been located properly—on the correct computer or with the correct UNC path.

You should check the Network Control Panel to ascertain whether the network bindings are correct. Follow these steps to view and edit bindings:

1. Start the Network Control Panel applet.

2. On the Configuration tab, select the adapter or protocol whose bindings you want to view or edit.

3. Click the Properties button.

4. Select the Bindings tab from the adapter or protocol's properties sheet.

5. You see a list of possible bindings for the adapter or protocol. Boxes that are checked show bindings that are currently active. To remove a binding, uncheck the corresponding check box.

6. Click OK when you're done, and click OK again on the Network properties sheet.

Administrators sometimes remove certain bindings for security reasons. For example, the binding of File and Printer Sharing for Microsoft Networks to the TCP/IP protocol on the dial-up adapter is often removed to prevent users on the entire Internet from being able to access shared directories on the local drive(s) while the computer is connected to the Internet using a modem. This subject is covered on the exam.

Inadvertent or even intentional changes to a user's group memberships in the User Manager or a change in system policy can also lead to denied access to resources that were previously permitted. Always try to determine what, if anything, has changed since the user last had access to the resource. Often you will find that the user was recently removed from a group or that a new system policy was implemented recently.

RESOLVING HARDWARE PROBLEMS

Several problems may be directly related to Registry errors. Here are the most common:

- ◆ Your computer won't boot properly or at all.

- ◆ Your computer looks or works differently than it once did.

- ◆ Your computer won't shut down correctly.

- ◆ A software or hardware component that operated correctly stops working without any physical changes having been made to the files or the device.

- ◆ Something stops working after you add new software or hardware, and the two aren't known to be incompatible with one another.

The first complete Registry appeared in Windows NT version 3.1. The Registry also appeared in Windows 95, and it was expanded with Windows 98. The Windows NT Registry and the Windows 95/98 Registry provide the same functionality but aren't compatible. The basic hierarchical nature of the Registry is the same in both versions, but the root keys (the keys at the top level of the Registry) are different.

The Registry is a database of settings and parameters. Among the features set by the Registry are the nature of the interface, operating system hardware and software settings, and user preferences. Prior to the Registry's appearance in Windows 95/98 and NT, these settings appeared as sections and lines in various .INI files.

The Registry is hierarchical. Each branch is referred to as a hive. Individual subbranches are called keys, which are binary files. The top or first key of a hive is the primary key, and each key is composed of subkeys that take value entries. Most Registry entries are permanent, although some are session-dependent, transient, and never written to disk.

When you install software—either a program or a part of the operating system, such as a device driver or service—new subkeys and value entries are written to the Registry. Uninstall these components to remove the information. Subkeys and value entries store information about hardware settings, driver files, environmental variables that need to be restored—anything the application developer requires reference to.

Changing the Registry

At A Glance: Changing the Registry

Control Panel Applets	*Registry Editor (REGEDIT.EXE)*
GUI interfaces for changing Registry settings specific to related devices	Global interface for changing all Registry settings
Only allows the user to enter values within a certain appropriate range	Allows the user to enter any value
Allows the user to back out of changes by clicking the Cancel button before changes are saved	Changes are immediate—no Undo or Cancel feature
Microsoft-recommended method of changing Registry settings most of the time	Required method of adding Registry entries that are not created by default
	Sometimes required to make changes for system recovery

You use the Registry Editor (REGEDIT.EXE) to view and modify the Windows 98 Registry. This program isn't listed on the Start menu and isn't found in the System Tools folder, where you might expect to find it.

If you want to, you can add it to your Start menu or run it by selecting Start | Run.

Whenever you change a setting in the Control Panel or alter your desktop, you are writing changes to the Registry associated with the user account profile with which you logged on. Microsoft recommends that you use the interfaces provided by the Control Panel applets to modify the Registry whenever possible (which is most of the time).

When you alter a value in the Registry directly by using the Registry Editor, the changes you can make are unlimited and can be hazardous to your computer's health. If you delete or modify a required key or value, you could cause your computer to malfunction. You'll notice (or you should notice) that there is no Undo option on the Registry Editor's Edit menu. This means that unless you have a backup of your Registry files, the changes you make are permanent.

Registry Keys

The six root keys and their subtrees are as follows:

- HKEY_CLASSES_ROOT. This subtree stores OLE, file, class, and other associations that let a program launch when a data file is opened. Although HKEY_CLASSES_ROOT is displayed as a root key, it is actually a pointer to a subkey of HKEY_LOCAL_MACHINE\Software.

- HKEY_CURRENT_USER. All user settings, profiles, environment variables, interface settings, program groups, printer connections, application preferences, and network connections for the currently logged-in user are stored in the subkeys of this root key.

- HKEY_LOCAL_MACHINE. This subkey contains information that identifies the computer on which the Registry is stored. Information in this key includes settings for hardware such as memory, disk drives, network adapters, and peripheral devices. Any software that supports hardware—device drivers, system services, system boot parameters, and other data—is contained in this subkey.

- HKEY_USERS. All data on individual user profiles is contained in this subkey.

- HKEY_CURRENT_CONFIG. The current configuration for software and any machine values are contained in this key. Among the settings stored in this root key are display device setup and control values required to restore the configuration when the program launches or your computer starts up.

- HKEY_DYN_DATA. Transient or dynamic data is stored in this last key in the Windows Registry. This key is actually stored in memory and is never written to the hard disk.

When the system loads the Registry, most of the data is contained in the HKEY_LOCAL_MACHINE and HKEY_CURRENT_USER keys. As an example of the kinds of changes you can make, individual settings that you make in the Control Panel are written back to different keys in the Registry. You can modify those settings directly. When you make a mistake, however, and delete a key or value in the Registry Editor, you can't use an Undo command to recover from this error.

Sometimes your Registry files can become corrupt, and inconsistencies in the files can cause serious problems with the operation of your computer. Under Windows 95, there was no utility to guard against such corruption or to detect it and recover from it. Under Windows 98, Microsoft has introduced a new utility, with both a GUI interface and a command-line interface, that can help you prevent and recover from Registry file corruption. It is called the Registry Checker.

ScanReg and ScanRegW

At A Glance: The Registry Checker

ScanReg	*ScanRegW*
DOS-based utility	GUI-based utility
Runs in real mode and in Safe mode	Runs in protected mode
Can't be used to compress a backup of the Registry	Must be used to compress a backup of the Registry
Must be used to restore the Registry from a backup	Can't be used to restore the Registry from a backup

The Registry Checker is used to find and fix Registry problems as well as back up Registry files. It can be run in GUI mode from the Tools menu of the System Information utility, or you can enter **scanregw** after selecting Start | Run. It can be run in MS-DOS mode or Safe mode from a command line with the command scanreg. When the Registry Checker is run, it scans the Registry files for errors. If no errors are found during the search, it will give you the choice of backing up the Registry.

Choosing Yes creates a CAB file containing the Registry in a hidden directory (C:\Windows\SysBackup). In the event of a failure, you can recover the Registry from this directory by entering

```
scanreg /restore
```

You will be asked which backup you want to use. All backups are stored as RB*xxx*.CAB, where *xxx* represents an incrementing value. If the Windows 98 operating system has ever been started with that version of the Registry, the word Started will appear next to the choice. Otherwise, it will read Not Started.

ScanReg is the DOS-based version of the tool, while ScanRegW is the Windows-based version. The differences between them include the fact that ScanReg runs in real mode and Safe mode, while ScanRegW runs in protected mode; ScanReg can't be used to compress the backup; and ScanRegW can't be used to restore the backup. Applying common sense to the two tools makes memorizing their differences simple: ScanRegW is the tool of choice most of the time. ScanReg is used when there is a serious problem and ScanRegW isn't available. Thus, it offers the functions that are needed to get the system back up and running.

WHAT IS IMPORTANT TO KNOW

The following list summarizes the chapter and accentuates the key concepts to memorize for the exam:

- The ASCII logs created during installation (SETUPLOG.TXT and DETLOG.TXT) can be the first clue to solving installation problems.

- DETCRASH.LOG is a binary file created during installation to allow Windows 98 Setup to get around crash problems should they occur.

- Version Conflict Manager automatically overwrites newer files with Windows 98 system files.

- The Microsoft System Information utility is used to view system information and provide a launch pad for system tools.

- The System Configuration utility can be used to change startup files and modes.

- The WinIPCfg utility displays the TCP/IP information for the Windows 98 computer.

- If the Windows 98 computer is configured to use DHCP for automatic TCP/IP configuration, the WinIPCfg utility can be used to release and/or renew IP address leases.

- Connectivity problems can be caused by incorrect protocols or frame types.

- Bindings for network adapters, protocols, and services can be viewed or edited on the properties sheet for the adapter or protocol.

- The binding for File and Printer Sharing for Microsoft to TCP/IP on the dial-up adapter is usually removed for security reasons.

- DOS programs can use printers when mapped to them via the NET USE commands.

- ScanDisk looks for and fixes errors on most writable media.

- ScanDisk can't fix errors on CDs or network drives.

- The System Policy Editor (POLEDIT.EXE) is used to edit system policies.

- System policies are stored in the CONFIG.POL file, on the NETLOGON share on a Windows NT domain controller, or in the Public directory on a NetWare file server.

- The Windows 98 user profile is the user's USER.DAT file.

- Registry settings are usually changed through the interfaces provided by the various Control Panel applets, but they may also be edited directly using the Registry Editor (regedit).

- The Registry Editor does *not* have an Undo feature.

- ScanRegW can't be used to restore a backup of the Registry.

- ScanReg can't be used to compress a backup of the Registry.

- ScanReg is the DOS version of the Registry Checker, while ScanRegW is the Windows version of the same tool.

- ScanRegW runs in protected mode, while ScanReg runs in real mode and Safe mode.

INSIDE EXAM 70-098

Part II of this book is designed to round out your exam preparation by providing you with chapters that do the following:

- "Fast Facts Review" is a digest of all "What Is Important to Know" sections from all Part I chapters. Use this chapter to review just before you take the exam: It's all here, in an easily reviewable format.

- "Hotlist of Exam-Critical Concepts" is your resource for cross-checking your tech terms. Although you're probably up to speed on most of this material already, double-check yourself anytime you run across an item you're not 100% certain about; it could make a difference at exam time.

- "Sample Test Questions" provides a full-length practice exam that tests you on the actual material covered in Part I. If you mastered the material there, you should be able to pass with flying colors here.

- "Insider's Spin on Exam 70-098" grounds you in the particulars for preparing mentally for this examination and for Microsoft testing in general.

- "Did You Know?" is the last-day-of-class bonus chapter: A brief touching-upon of peripheral information designed to be helpful and of interest to anyone using this technology to the point that they wish to be certified in its mastery.

CHAPTER 7

Fast Facts Review

WHAT TO STUDY

This chapter is a review of the key topics discussed in the preceding six chapters. After you are certain that you understand the principles discussed in those six chapters, study these key points on the day of the exam prior to taking it.

Planning

The minimum Intel-based hardware requirements for Windows 98 are a 468DX/66 processor with 16MB of RAM and 140MB of hard disk space. Although a CD-ROM is recommended, you can request Windows 98 on 1.44MB floppy disks from Microsoft. Either FAT16 or FAT32 file systems can be used, but FAT16 must be used for compatibility with almost anything else (including Windows NT). FAT32 has many more features than FAT16 but is not compatible with Windows NT or many other operating systems. If you want to dual-boot a system with both Windows 98 and Windows NT, FAT16 is required. You can convert FAT16 to FAT32 without losing data, but you can't convert FAT32 to FAT16 without reformatting and losing all data. The contrast of hard disk space necessary to install Windows 98 is reflected in the recommended size of 225MB for FAT16 versus only 175 for FAT32 in a typical installation. Workgroups are peer-to-peer networks that offer share-level security and that don't require a server. Domains are networks built around a server, and they offer user-level security. File and Printer Sharing allows you to share resources with other users. File and Printer Sharing doesn't let you share individual files, but it does let you share folders. When you're planning a network with NetWare as the authentication provider, user-level access control is required.

User profiles are stored in USER.DAT files and hold the configuration information for each user. If the ability to save settings is turned on, each user will have his own USER.DAT file. The USER.DAT file can be stored locally or on the server, in which case it is called a roaming profile. Each user account set up with a roaming profile must be configured to point to the server where the user's USER.DAT is stored. This is done inside User Manager for Domains in a Windows NT environment. In a NetWare environment, if user profiles have been enabled, the USER.DAT file is stored on the user's preferred server in his Mail directory. Whenever he logs in and out of the NetWare server, the user profile is automatically copied and stored on the NetWare server.

System policies are restrictions held within a CONFIG.POL file to prevent users from performing certain actions. By default, there can be only one system policy on the network for all users, but it can contain as many computers, users, or groups as you wish. The group portion of a system policy doesn't work for Windows 98 users unless the GROUPPOL.DLL file has been installed on the machine. System policies are stored in the NetLogon share in a Windows NT environment and in the Public folder in a NetWare environment.

Installation and Configuration

The NETSETUP program, which existed in Windows 95 for installing over a network, is not included with Windows 98. Batch 98 is used to create .INF files to install Windows 98 from a server or another location.

The four setup types are

- Typical
- Custom
- Portable
- Compact

You uninstall Windows 98 using the Add/Remove Programs applet in Control Panel. The option to uninstall Windows 98 is available only if the system has been upgraded. New installations and migrations don't have the uninstall option.

A subset of Microsoft's Internet Information Server (which runs on Windows NT Server) is available for Windows 98, where it is known as Personal Web Server (PWS). Personal Web Server can report statistics such as requests per day or hour and visitors per day or hour. Microsoft Backup utility is used to create and restore backups. It doesn't work with QIC-40 tapes. The Backup Wizard can create and view backup jobs but not change them. Backup strategies are important in understanding Full, Incremental, and Differential backups, along with the benefits of each.

USB provides Plug and Play compatibility for external devices. IEEE 1394 FireWire provides for bus support of high-bandwidth external devices such as video cameras. Some printers currently on the market can take advantage of USB Plug and Play support.

Configuring and Managing Resource Access

Unified Logon in Windows 98 means that you need only one password to access all network resources. It configures the Windows 98 password to match the password of the primary authenticator. Password caching is the process of storing passwords in .PWL files on the local hard disk. It can be disabled through the Registry or with a system policy. The Password List Editor can be used to edit and delete entries in .PWL files. Only the password entries of the currently logged-in user can be seen with the Password List Editor. SETPASS is the NetWare utility used to change passwords for NetWare user accounts. The Microsoft Family Logon offers a simplified method of providing desktop settings using profiles. Once profiles are configured on a Windows 98 computer, the Microsoft Family Logon client can be installed and set as the Primary Network Login. The Microsoft Family Logon displays a list of users who have profiles configured on the Windows 98 computer. Simply select your login ID from the list and provide your password, and your desktop settings are loaded from your local profile.

Windows 98 supports two security models: share-level access and user-level access. Workgroup environments can support only share-level security. Domain environments can support share-level or user-level security. File and Printer Sharing for NetWare Networks must use user-level security. Share-level security involves assigning a password to a shared resource and selecting permissions for the share. The assigned permissions affect all users of the share. User-level security involves using either a Windows NT domain controller or a Novell NetWare file server to authenticate a user's credentials (user ID and password). User-level permissions can be assigned to specific individuals or groups of users.

Share permissions are Read-Only and Full Control. User-level permissions include Read-Only, Full Control, and Custom. Custom user-level permissions allow for any combination of the following access rights: Read, Write, Create, Delete, Change Attributes, List, and Change Access Control.

User profiles are one half of the Registry—storing the user component. User preferences for wallpaper, color scheme, sounds, application settings, and so on are stored in user profiles. User profiles can be local or roaming. Local profiles are stored in the Windows\Profiles folder under a subdirectory specific to each user of the computer. Roaming profiles are stored in the network file server in the user's Home directory on a Windows NT domain controller and in the user's Mail directory on a NetWare file server. Roaming profiles allow a user to keep the same preferences no matter which workstation he uses to log in to the network. Local profiles apply only to the particular Windows 98 computer on which they reside.

System policies restrict what users can do and are stored as a file named CONFIG.POL. The CONFIG.POL file is stored on the NetLogon share on a Windows NT domain controller and in the Public directory on a NetWare file server. Default Computer and Default User are two system policies that apply to every user who logs in to the network. System policies allow an administrator to provide a standard Windows 98 environment for all network users. Individual user policies can also be set up, as well as group policies, that differ from the default policies. These policies are named after the user or group they apply to. Group policies require that the GROUPPOL.DLL file be copied to all Windows 98 workstations. System policies work by merging changes into the Windows 98 Registry when the user logs in to the network.

Configuration settings and system parameters are stored in the Windows 98 Registry. The Registry is made up of two files, USER.DAT and SYSTEM.DAT. These files are sometimes subject to corruption and errors, which causes problems with the operation of the Windows 98 computer. The Registry Checker can check the Registry files for errors and fix them. The Registry Checker has a GUI interface (ScanRegW) and a command-line interface (ScanReg). The Registry is backed up with ScanRegW and can be restored using ScanReg | Restore.

Disk compression is accomplished with the DriveSpace3 utility and the Compression Agent (CMPAGENT.EXE). Compression can be in either Standard, HiPack, or UltraPack format. You must use the Compression Agent to use the UltraPack format. Disk compression averages a 2-to-1 compression ratio, depending on the file type and the method of compression used.

Hard disk partitioning is done with FDISK. Hard disks can have up to four partitions: one primary and up to three extended partitions. Extended partitions can be divided into up to four logical partitions. FDISK must be run in MS-DOS mode. Hard disk partitions must be formatted before they can be used by Windows 98.

Large disk support involves using FAT32, while the absence of it implies FAT16. FAT16 can be converted to FAT32 without a loss of data using the FAT32 drive converter (CVTL.EXE). You can't convert from FAT32 to FAT16 without reformatting the drive and losing all data. Windows NT 4.0 doesn't support the FAT32 file system. Windows NT can use its own file system, NTFS, but no other operating system supports NTFS. Dual-boot computers that run both the Windows 98 operating system and the Windows NT operating system need to run the FAT16 file system on all drives in order for all drives to be accessible to both operating systems. Windows 98 won't be able to access any drives that are formatted with the NTFS file system. Likewise, Windows NT won't be able to access any drives formatted with the FAT32 file system.

Windows 98 supports multiple hardware configurations by using hardware profiles. Hardware profiles allow a laptop computer to use one set of hardware when loaded in a docking station and another when undocked. Windows will create a new hardware profile automatically if it detects that the computer is in a docking station. At system startup, Windows 98 attempts to detect the current hardware configuration and will select the appropriate hardware profile to use at that time. If Windows 98 can't determine the appropriate hardware profile to use, it will display a Hardware Profile menu prompting the user to select which hardware profile to use.

Integration and Interoperability

TCP/IP is the default protocol used on NT networks. TCP/IP parameters include an IP address, subnet mask, and default gateway. Communication between TCP/IP hosts occurs using IP addresses. All TCP/IP hosts must have a unique IP address. Hosts are also assigned host names to make it easier for humans to access them. The Domain Name Service (DNS) provides a way to resolve host names to IP addresses. The IP address of the DNS server must be supplied in order to use this service. In the absence of a DNS server, hosts may have their names and IP addresses entered into a HOSTS file that is stored locally on each TCP/IP host computer. Windows computers are also assigned NetBIOS names. It is often more convenient to the user to refer to a computer by its NetBIOS name rather than by its IP address. Windows Internet Naming Service (WINS) provides a way to resolve NetBIOS names to IP addresses. The IP address of the primary WINS server must be supplied in order to use the WINS service. The IP address of a secondary WINS server may also be supplied but is not required. IP addresses must be unique for each TCP/IP host. Because host computers leave and join the network, and because they are often moved from one subnet to another, managing IP address assignments can be difficult. Dynamic Host Configuration Protocol (DHCP) provides a way to assign IP addresses to TCP/IP hosts automatically. All other TCP/IP parameters can be supplied to the host by the DHCP server as well.

IPX/SPX is the default protocol used on NetWare networks. When you install the Client for NetWare Networks on a Windows 98 computer, the IPX/SPX-compatible protocol is also installed if it isn't already present. The IPX/SPX-compatible protocol supports many different frame types. The frame type used by the Windows 98 computer must be the same as the frame type used by the NetWare file server in order for the two computers to communicate.

Universal Naming Convention (UNC) paths specify where resources are. UNC names are in this format: *computer_name\resource_name*.

The Internet can be reached through a dial-up connection or through a proxy server. A proxy server is a computer that has a connection to an Internet Service Provider (ISP) that acts on the behalf of other computers on the local network to access resources located on computers on the Internet. Dial-Up Networking uses a modem and a conventional phone line to connect a Windows 98 computer to an ISP or to another remote computer. Dial-Up Networking can support the PPP, SLIP, NRN, and Windows NT 3.1 (or Windows for Workgroups) RAS line protocols. Point-to-Point Protocol (PPP) is the line protocol most often used to connect to an ISP and is also used to connect to a Windows NT 4.0 RAS server. Serial Line Internet Protocol (SLIP) is older, more stable, and less feature-rich than PPP. It is still in use, mostly by older UNIX operating systems. NetWare Remote Node is the line protocol used to connect to NetWare Connect, a remote access server found in NetWare network environments. Windows NT 3.1 and Windows for Workgroups used a different line protocol for the RAS service that ran on those operating systems. This line protocol is also supported by Windows 98 Dial-Up Networking.

Workgroups are peer-to-peer networks that offer share-level security and that don't require a dedicated file server. Domains are networks built around a server, and they offer user-level security. Novell NetWare networks are also built around file servers and offer user-level security.

Monitoring and Optimization

Net Watcher allows you to monitor connections and shares not only on your local machine, but remotely as well. You can also add, remove, and modify shares. To use Net Watcher on a remote machine, Remote Administration must be enabled on the machine you will monitor, as well as File and Printer Sharing. System Monitor divides the system into categories, and each category is divided into items. New to Windows 98, the System Monitor allows the creation of log files. In System Monitor, the default category and item viewed is Kernel - Processor usage. The default interval for chart updates in System Monitor is every five seconds.

Resource Meter lets you quickly assess resource utilization. Located under Start | Programs | Accessories | System Tools, Resource Meter allows you to view system, user, and GDI resources. The newfound ability to quickly determine whether a program is releasing resources when closed is paramount to developers.

Disk Defragmenter uses log files of application access to see which programs are used most and what files they need to run and places them contiguously to speed access performance. ScanDisk looks for and fixes errors on most writeable media.

The Maintenance Wizard schedules tasks to run automatically in unattended mode. The Task Scheduler submits the jobs that Maintenance Wizard has chosen and all other unattended jobs for processing. The queue can be viewed by selecting Start | Programs | Accessories | System Tools | Scheduled Tasks.

The System File Checker is used to look for corruption, deletion, or modification to the core Windows 98 operating system files. It uses a base file to make the comparisons to what should be there. It can be used to restore a file from the media or to update the base file.

Troubleshooting

The ASCII logs created during installation (SETUPLOG.TXT and DETLOG.TXT) can be the first clue to solving installation problems. DETCRASH.LOG is a binary file created during installation to help Windows 98 Setup get around crash problems. If Windows 98 Setup crashes or hangs, reboot the computer and run Setup again. The Setup program will detect the presence of DETCRASH.LOG and will skip the section of hardware detection that caused the problem, allowing the Windows 98 installation to continue.

Version Conflict Manager automatically overwrites newer files with Windows 98 system files. It decides which files are newer by examining the file's version information, not its date/time stamp.

The Microsoft System Information utility is used to view system information and provide a launch pad for other system tools. Some system tools can only be accessed from the Tools menu of the System Information utility. The System Information utility has three main views: Hardware Resources, Components, and Software Environment. The Hardware Resources view shows the system resources that are in use by the various hardware devices in the computer. Resources such as IRQs, I/O ports, DMA addresses, and reserved memory addresses are shown. The Components view lists in detail the status of your system device drivers for multimedia, networking, and other system devices. The Software Environment view shows the name, size, date/time stamp, version information, and path on disk to device drivers and system modules loaded in memory.

The System Configuration utility can be used to change startup files and modes. It provides a graphical interface and a simpler way to access system configuration file settings than the older SYSEDIT program. With the System Configuration utility, you can edit the CONFIG.SYS, AUTOEXEC.BAT, SYSTEM.INI, and WIN.INI files all in one place. You can also select the Windows 98 Startup mode and enable or disable programs that are run at system startup from within the System Configuration utility.

Connectivity problems can be caused by incorrect protocols or frame types. DOS programs can use printers when mapped to them via the NET USE commands.

The WinIPCfg utility displays the computer's TCP/IP configuration information. You can view the IP address, subnet mask, default gateway, DNS server address, and primary and secondary WINS server addresses with WinIPCfg. If DHCP is used, you can view the DHCP server address, as well as release or renew the workstation's IP address lease. You can also view the computer's MAC address and NetBIOS information.

Microsoft offers several resources with valuable information for troubleshooting problems with Windows 98, including Microsoft TechNet, the Windows 98 Resource Kit, and the Microsoft Support Web site at www.microsoft.com/support.

The Print Troubleshooter is part of the Windows 98 online Help system that can be used to help troubleshoot basic printing problems. To access the Print Troubleshooter, enter the keyword **printers troubleshooting** on the Index tab of the Windows 98 Help system. Select the appropriate problem type, click the Next button, and follow the instructions in the Help system to troubleshoot your printing problem.

ScanDisk looks for and fixes errors on most writable media. ScanDisk is most often used to repair cross-linked files. ScanDisk can be run in Standard Mode or Thorough Mode. In Standard Mode, ScanDisk performs logical tests against the file system's File Allocation Table (FAT), checking for the logical inconsistencies outlined earlier. In addition, the standard scan checks for various other potential problems, such as invalid filenames and invalid date/time stamps. In Thorough Mode, ScanDisk performs all the tests included in Standard Mode and also performs a surface scan.

Windows 98 users can share the resources on their computers with other users on the network, as well as access shared resources located on other computers on the network. Shared resources may be folders or printers located on other Windows 98 computers, on Windows NT workstations or servers, or on Novell NetWare file servers. Different access rights apply to the different operating systems employed. Windows 98 can offer share-level security, in which a password is applied to a shared resource and access rights affect everyone who knows the password. In a Windows NT domain or NetWare file server environment, Windows 98 can offer user-level security, in which the Windows NT domain controller or the NetWare file server authenticates the user's ID and password, and access to shared resources can be assigned to individual users or groups of users.

Windows NT computers use two types of groups: local and global. Local groups are located only on the particular Windows NT computer and have no meaning to other computers on the network. Global groups are located on a Windows NT domain controller and have meaning to all computers in the NT domain. User IDs are placed in global groups, global groups are placed in the local groups on each Windows NT computer that has shared resources, and access rights to those resources are assigned to the local groups.

Windows NT computers can use the NTFS file system. It lets access permissions be set on folders and individual files within the directory structure. Where NTFS permissions and share permissions conflict, the most restrictive access rights apply.

The Registry is one of the most important components of the Windows 98 operating system. Corruption in the Registry files can cause the computer to malfunction. Windows 98 provides a utility called the Registry Checker, which you can use to check the Registry files for errors, repair them, and make backup copies of the Registry. ScanReg is the DOS version of the Registry Checker, and ScanRegW is the Windows version. ScanRegW must be used in order to compress the backup copy of the Registry. ScanReg must be used to restore the Registry from a backup copy. To restore the Registry from a backup copy, use the ScanReg | Restore command.

CHAPTER 8

Hotlist of
Exam-Critical Concepts

Term	*Definition*
Active open	An action taken by a client to initiate a TCP connection with a server.
Address classes	A grouping of IP addresses with each class, defining the maximum number of networks and hosts available. The first octet of the address determines the class.
Address mask	A 32-bit binary number used to select bits from an IP address for subnet masking.
Analog	A form of electronic communication using a continuous electromagnetic wave, such as television or radio. Any continuous waveform, as opposed to digital on/off transmissions.
API	Application Programming Interface. A language and message format that lets a programmer use functions in another program or in the hardware.
ARP	Address Resolution Protocol. A protocol in the TCP/IP suite used to bind an IP address to a physical hardware (MAC) address.
ARPA	Advanced Research Projects Agency. A government agency that originally funded research on the ARPANET (which became DARPA in the mid-1970s).
ARPANET	The first network of computers funded by the U.S. Department of Defense Advanced Research Projects Agency. An experimental communications network funded by the government that eventually developed into the Internet.
ASCII	American Standard Code for Information Interchange. Data that is limited to letters, numbers, and punctuation.
ATM	Asynchronous Transfer Mode. Broadband technology that increases transfer speeds.
Backbone	Generally very high-speed T3 telephone lines that connect remote ends of networks to networks. Only service providers are connected to the Internet in this way.
Baseband	A network technology that requires all nodes attached to the network to participate in every transmission. Ethernet, for example, is a baseband technology.

Term	*Definition*
BOOTP	Bootstrap protocol. A protocol used to configure systems with an IP address, subnet mask, and default gateway across internetworks.
Bps	Bits per second. A measurement that expresses the speed at which data is transferred between computers.
Bridge	A device that connects one physical section of a network to another, often providing isolation.
Broadband	A network technology that multiplexes multiple network carriers into a single cable.
Broadcast	A packet destined for all hosts on the network.
Brouter	A computer device that works as both a bridge and a router. Some network traffic may be bridged, while other traffic is routed.
Buffer	A storage area used to hold input or output data.
Checksumming	A service performed by UDP that checks to see if packets were changed during transmission.
Connectionless service	A delivery service that treats each packet as a separate entity. Often results in lost packets or packets delivered out of sequence.
CRC	Cyclic Redundancy Check. A computation about a frame in which the result is a small integer. The value is appended to the end of the frame and recalculated when the frame is received. If the results differ from the appended value, the frame has presumably been corrupted and is therefore discarded. It is used to detect errors in transmission.
CSMA	Carrier Sense Multiple Access. A simple media access control protocol that allows multiple stations to contend for access to the medium. If no traffic is detected on the medium, the station may send a transmission.
CSMA/CD	Carrier Sense Multiple Access with Collision Detection. A characteristic of network hardware that uses CSMA in conjunction with a process that detects when two stations transmit simultaneously. If that happens, both back off and retry the transmission after a random period of time has elapsed.

Term	*Definition*
DARPA	Defense Advanced Research Projects Agency. Originally called ARPA. The government agency that funded the research that developed the ARPANET.
Datagram	A packet of data and delivery information.
DHCP	Dynamic Host Configuration Protocol. A protocol that provides dynamic address allocation and automatic TCP/IP configuration.
Digital	The type of communication used by computers, consisting of individual on-and-off pulses. Compare to analog.
Directed broadcast address	An IP address that specifies all hosts on the network.
Domain	The highest subdivision of the Internet, for the most part by country (except in the U.S., where it's by type of organization, such as educational, commercial, and government). Usually the last part of a host name. For example, the domain part of ibm.com is .com, which represents the domain of commercial sites in the U.S. Can also be the network governed by a Primary Domain Controller (PDC) in the Windows NT world.
Domain Name System (DNS)	The system that translates between Internet IP address and Internet host names.
Ethernet	A type of local area network hardware. Many TCP/IP networks are Ethernet based.
FDDI	Fiber Distributed Data Interface. The formal name for fiber wiring.
Firewall	A device placed on a network to prevent unauthorized traffic from entering the network.
FQDN	Fully Qualified Domain Name. A combination of the host name and the domain name.

Term	*Definition*
Frame	Packets as transmitted across a medium. Differing frame types have unique characteristics.
Frame relay	A type of digital data communications protocol.
FTP	File Transfer Protocol. A popular Internet communications protocol that allows you to transfer files between hosts on the Internet.
Gateway	A device that interfaces two networks using different protocols.
Hardware address	The physical address of a host used by networks.
Host	A server using TCP/IP and/or connected to the Internet.
Host address	A unique number assigned to identify a host on the Internet. Also called IP address or dot address. This address is usually represented as four numbers between 1 and 254, separated by periods. For example, 192.58.107.230.
Host ID	The portion of an IP address that identifies the host in a particular network. It is used in conjunction with network IDs to form a complete IP address.
Host name	A unique name for a host that corresponds to the host address.
HTML	Hypertext Markup Language. The formatting language/protocol used to define various text styles in a hypertext document, including emphasis and bulleted lists.
HTTP	Hypertext Transfer Protocol. The communications protocol used by WWW services to retrieve documents quickly.
ICMP	Internet Control Message Protocol. A maintenance protocol that handles error messages to be sent when datagrams are discarded or when systems experience congestion.
ISDN	Integrated Services Digital Network. A dedicated telephone line connection that transmits digital data at the rate of 64- to 128Kbps.

Term	Definition
LAN	Local Area Network. A network of computers that is usually limited to a small physical area, like a building.
LLC	Logical Link Control. A protocol that provides a common interface point to the MAC layers.
MAC	Media Access Control. A protocol that governs which access method a station has to the network.
MAN	Metropolitan Area Network. A physical communications network that operates across a metropolitan area.
MIME	Multipurpose Internet Mail Extension. A protocol that describes the format of Internet messages.
Name resolution	The process of mapping a computer name to an IP address. LMHosts and WINS are two ways of resolving names.
NIC	Network Interface Card. An add-on card to allow a machine to access a LAN (most commonly an Ethernet card).
Nodes	Individual computers connected to a network.
OSI	Open Systems Interconnection. A set of ISO standards that define the framework for implementing protocols in seven layers.
Packet	The unit of data transmission on the Internet. A packet consists of the data being transferred, along with additional overhead information, such as the transmitting and receiving addresses.
Packet switching	The communications technology that the Internet is based on, where data being sent between computers is transmitted in packets.
Ping	Packet Internet Groper. A utility that sends a packet to an Internet host and waits for a response. Used to check if a host is up.
POP	Point of Presence. Indicates the availability of a local access number to a public data network.

Term	Definition
PPP	Point-to-Point Protocol. A driver that allows you to use a network communications protocol over a phone line. Used with TCP/IP to allow you to have a dial-in Internet host.
PPTP	Point-to-Point Tunneling Protocol. Microsoft's newest protocol to enhance PPP. It offers all the features of PPP, plus security, and is used to create Virtual Private Networks (VPNs).
Protocol	The standard that defines how computers on a network communicate with one another.
RARP	Reverse Address Resolution Protocol. A protocol that lets a computer find its IP address by broadcasting a request. It is usually used by diskless workstations at startup to find their logical IP address.
Repeater	A device that allows you to extend the length of your network by amplifying and repeating the information it receives.
RIP	Routing Information Protocol. A router-to-router protocol used to exchange information between routers. RIP supports dynamic routing.
Router	Equipment that receives an Internet packet and sends it to the next machine in the destination path.
Segment	A protocol data unit consisting of part of a stream of bytes being sent between two machines. It also includes information about the current position in the stream and a checksum value.
Server	A provider of a service. A computer that runs services. This also often refers to a piece of hardware or software that provides access to information requested from it.
Service	An application that processes requests by client applications—for example, storing data or executing an algorithm.
SLIP	Serial Line Internet Protocol. A way of running TCP/IP via phone lines to allow you to have a dialup Internet host.
SMTP	Simple Mail Transport Protocol. The accepted communications protocol standard for the exchange of email between Internet hosts.

Term	*Definition*
SNMP	Simple Network Management Protocol. A communications protocol used to control and monitor devices on a network.
Socket	A means of network communication via special entities.
Subnet	Any lower network that is part of the logical network. Identified by the network ID.
Subnet mask	A 32-bit value that distinguishes the network ID from the host ID in an IP address.
TCP/IP	Transmission Control Protocol/Internet Protocol. A communications protocol suite that allows computers of any make to communicate when running TCP/IP software.
TFTP	Trivial File Transfer Protocol. A basic, standard protocol used to upload or download files with minimal overhead. TFTP depends on UDP and is often used to initialize diskless work-stations, because it has no directory or password capabilities.
Transceiver	A device that connects a host interface to a network. It is used to apply signals to the cable and sense collisions.
UDP	User Datagram Protocol. A simple protocol that lets an application program on one machine send a datagram to an application program on another machine. Delivery is not guaranteed, nor is it guaranteed that the datagrams will be delivered in the proper order.
URL	Uniform Resource Locator. A means of specifying the location of information on the Internet for WWW clients.
WAN	Wide Area Network. A network of computers that are geographically dispersed.
X.25	A CCITT standard for connecting computers to a network that provides a reliable stream transmission service, which can support remote logins.
X.400	A CCITT standard for message transfer and interpersonal messaging, such as electronic mail.

Additional Terms and Concepts

CHAPTER **9**

Sample Test Questions

QUESTIONS

This sample test has 52 questions and covers each of the six objective categories.

1. *You have a computer with two 1.5GB hard disk drives. You want to install Windows 98 on the first one and Windows NT on the second. Both operating systems must be able to see files on either hard drive. Which of the following options is best?*

   A. Format the first drive as FAT32 and install Windows 98. Format the second drive as NTFS and install Windows NT.
   B. Format the first drive as FAT16 and install Windows 98. Format the second drive as NTFS and install Windows NT.
   C. Format the first drive as FAT16 and install Windows 98. Format the second drive as FAT16 and install Windows NT.
   D. Format the first drive as FAT32 and install Windows 98. Format the second drive as FAT32 and install Windows NT.

2. *You upgraded your Windows 95 system to Windows 98. The current file system is FAT16. You need to install Windows NT and dual-boot. How can this be accomplished?*

   A. Install Windows NT in the Windows directory. All the programs accessible from Windows 98 will be accessible in Windows NT.
   B. Install Windows NT in the Winnt directory. All the programs accessible from Windows 98 will be accessible in Windows NT.
   C. Install Windows NT in the Windows directory and reinstall all the programs accessible from Windows 98 through Windows NT.
   D. Install Windows NT in the Winnt directory and reinstall all the programs accessible from Windows 98 through Windows NT.

3. *Dual-booting Windows 98 with Windows NT requires what?*

   A. FAT16
   B. FAT32
   C. NTFS
   D. HPFS

4. *When upgrading Windows NT to Windows 98, what special steps are required? (Select the best answer.)*

   A. Back up the Registry and restore it after the upgrade.

   B. Run the FAT32 Information utility from the Resource Kit Tools to verify the increase of available hard disk space.

   C. There are no special steps required for upgrading Windows NT to Windows 98.

   D. You can't upgrade Windows NT to Windows 98.

5. *While planning the implementation of Windows 98, you decide to include the use of system policies. In a Windows NT domain environment, where would the system policy file be stored by default?*

   A. In the NETLOGON share

   B. In the Mail directory

   C. In the Windows\Profiles directory

   D. In the Public directory

6. *During the configuration of system policies, the sales group was denied the ability to share resources. The marketing group was given the right to share resources. Helen is a member of both groups. How would you give her the right to share resources?*

   A. Add a third group to the system policy, making Helen a member and giving the group the right to share resources.

   B. Set the group priorities so that the marketing group has the higher priority.

   C. Set the user profile so that Helen has the right to share resources.

   D. Set the group priorities so that the sales group has the higher priority.

7. *Which utility would allow you to set restrictions on or enable, disable, or ignore the Remove RUN command from specific users?*

   A. User Profile Editor

   B. Net Watcher

   C. System Policy Editor

   D. Resource Meter

8. *After you upgrade all the machines in the office from Windows 95 to Windows 98, an employee complains that a program no longer works. After troubleshooting the issue with no success, what other step can you take?*

   A. Nothing. Have the employee use a different program.

   B. Uninstall Windows 98.

   C. Use the System Configuration utility to assign the employee permissions to the program files.

   D. Contact the manufacturer and request an updated version of the driver.

9. *While planning the implementation of Windows 98, you decide to include the use of system policies. In a NetWare environment, where would the system policy file be stored by default?*

   A. In the NETLOGON share

   B. In the Mail directory

   C. In the Windows\Profiles directory

   D. In the Public directory

10. *What is the system policy name for Windows 98 clients?*

    A. 98.POL

    B. CONFIG.POL

    C. 98CONFIG.POL

    D. POLICY.CFG

11. *Which utility allows you to run an automated setup of Windows 98?*

    A. System Policy Editor

    B. Batch 98

    C. Setup 98

    D. Auto 98

12. *When configuring the file to aid in an automated setup, which options are available by default? (Select all that apply.)*

    A. Installation Directory

    B. Setup Prompts

    C. File and Printer Sharing for Microsoft Networks

    D. Digital Certificates

FIGURE 9.1

FIGURE 9.2

13. *After you load a new program, the Resource Meter resembles Figure 9.1. An hour after you close the program, the Resource Meter looks like Figure 9.2. What can you deduce?*

   A. The new program has been executed and is working just fine.

   B. The new program has been executed and has a problem releasing resources.

   C. The new program has been executed and has an optimal effect on system resources.

   D. The new program has been executed and will release the system resources after three hours.

14. *What do you use to uninstall Windows 98?*

   A. SETUP /U

   B. Add/Remove Programs applet

   C. FORMAT

   D. UNINSTALL

15. *You are the administrator of 10 client machines in the sales department workgroup. You have been instructed to implement File and Printer Sharing among the machines. Which level of access control is available? (Select all that apply.)*

    A. Full

    B. User-level

    C. Read-only

    D. Share-level

16. *You are the administrator of a 500-user network. NetWare 4.0 is used to authenticate all users. After installing Windows 98 on a new client machine, you can't access the NetWare server to log in. Which component must be installed?*

    A. File and Printer Sharing for NetWare Networks

    B. File and Printer Sharing for Microsoft Networks

    C. Service for NetWare Directory Services

    D. Service for Microsoft Directory Services

17. *After installing Windows 98 on four client machines in a Windows NT domain, you open Network Neighborhood and find out that none of the new clients are listed. What additional component must be installed to list a client in Network Neighborhood?*

    A. File and Printer Sharing for NetWare Networks

    B. File and Printer Sharing for Microsoft Networks

    C. Service for NetWare Directory Services

    D. Service for Microsoft Directory Services

18. *After installing Microsoft Personal Web Server on your Windows 98 machine, you are asked to monitor the daily activity. Which options are available in PWS? (Select all that apply.)*

    A. Requests per Day

    B. Requests per Minute

    C. Visitors per Day

    D. Visitors per Minute

19. *You want to set up your Windows 98 client machine to be a Dial-Up Server. Which options are available? (Select all that apply.)*

    A. Require Encrypted Password
    B. Enabling Digital Certificates
    C. Server Type
    D. Access Restricted by Protocol

20. *During your watch at the help desk, a user calls and says he can't log in to the NetWare 4.0 server. Which service would you check to make sure it was installed?*

    A. File and Printer Sharing for NetWare Networks
    B. File and Printer Sharing for Microsoft Networks
    C. Service for NetWare Directory Services
    D. Service for Microsoft Directory Services

21. *In a 10-client Windows 98 workgroup, you want to configure one machine to maintain the browse list. How can you accomplish this? (Select the best answer.)*

    A. No additional steps are necessary.
    B. On the Network properties sheet, select Client for Microsoft Networks and change the Browse property for one machine to Enabled and all the others to Disabled.
    C. On the Network properties sheet, select File and Printer Sharing for Microsoft Networks and change the Browse property for one machine to Enabled and all the others to Disabled.
    D. On the Network properties sheet, select File and Printer Sharing for NetWare Networks and change the Browse property for one machine to Enabled and all the others to Disabled.

22. *What provides Plug and Play support for external devices such as a keyboard?*

    A. FireWire
    B. IEEE 1394
    C. USB
    D. QIC

FIGURE 9.3

23. *You just finished installing Windows 98 in a TCP/IP network environment. Your Windows NT Backup Domain Controller also serves as a DHCP server. You installed TCP/IP protocol as shown in Figure 9.3. After rebooting the system, you see a message that there is an IP conflict. What changes can be made to fix this?*

A. Change the IP address to 192.168.10.55.

B. Select Obtain an IP address automatically.

C. Change the default gateway to 192.168.10.1.

D. Change the subnet mask to 255.255.255.240.

24. *You are upgrading the following systems to Windows 98. Which ones require hardware upgrades? (Select all that apply.)*

System	Memory	Disk Space	Operating System
486/33	16MB RAM	250MB hard disk	Windows 3.1
Pentium 133	48MB RAM	100MB hard disk	Windows 95
486/66	32MB RAM	125MB hard disk	Windows 95
486/66	16MB RAM	1.2GB hard disk	Windows 95

A. System 1

B. System 2

C. System 3

D. System 4

25. *Which utility gives you quick access to updated drivers?*

   A. Signature Verification Tool
   B. Windows Update
   C. Maintenance Wizard
   D. System File Checker

26. *Which utility has the ability to log system information collected from a remote client?*

   A. System Monitor
   B. Network Watcher
   C. Resource Meter
   D. Maintenance Wizard

27. *By default, in what two ways does Windows 98 support connecting to the Internet?*

   A. Through a UNIX server
   B. Through a dial-up connection
   C. Through a permanent connection
   D. Through IBM LAN Server

28. *You want to share resources on your Windows 98 computer with other computers in your workgroup, which includes other Windows 98 computers as well as Windows NT Workstation computers. What type of security can you implement to protect your shared resources from unauthorized access?*

   A. Workgroup-level security
   B. Share-level security
   C. Data-level security
   D. User-level security

29. *Danny has a Windows 98 computer that is a member of the Accounting workgroup, which consists of eight PCs, each running Windows 98. Each of those computers also logs in to a NetWare LAN. Danny wants to share resources on his computer with other computers on the network. He installs File and Printer Sharing for NetWare Networks to accomplish this. What security model(s) can he use?*

   A. Workgroup-level security
   B. Share-level security
   C. Data-level security
   D. User-level security

30. *Kevin has enabled user profiles on his Windows 98 computer. Where are these profiles stored by default?*

   A. In the NETLOGON share
   B. In the Mail directory
   C. In the Windows\Profiles directory
   D. In the Public directory

31. *Sharon is using Dial-Up Networking to connect to a remote computer. The computer is running an older version of the UNIX operating system that doesn't support Point-to-Point Protocol. What line protocol should she use to connect to the remote computer?*

   A. SLIP
   B. PPP
   C. UDP
   D. SNMP

32. *David needs to find out the version number and location of the ODBC drivers his machine is using to connect to a remote database. What utility can he use to find this information?*

   A. ScanDisk
   B. Windows Explorer
   C. System Information utility
   D. System Configuration utility

33. *Which utility can you use to view connections to shared resources on your Windows 98 computer?*

   A. Performance Monitor
   B. Net Watcher
   C. Windows Explorer
   D. System Information utility

34. *Which utility can you use to create and manage shares on remote Windows 98 computers?*

   A. Net Watcher
   B. Windows Explorer
   C. System Configuration utility
   D. Remote Administration tool

35. *In order to monitor the performance of a remote Windows 98 computer with the System Monitor tool, what must you install or configure on both the local and the remote machines?*

   A. Microsoft Remote Registry Service
   B. User-level security
   C. Performance tuning
   D. Remote administration

36. *Lauren is administering a number of Windows 98 computers on her network. She wants to be able to do the following:*

   ◆ Browse shares on each computer using Net Watcher.

   ◆ Manage each computer's file system with Net Watcher.

   ◆ Edit each computer's Registry remotely using the Registry Editor.

   ◆ Monitor each computer's performance from her computer using System Monitor.

   She takes the following steps to accomplish her goals:

   ◆ Installs File and Printer Sharing for Microsoft Networks on each computer.

   ◆ Enables user-level security on each computer.

   ◆ Enables remote administration on each computer.

   ◆ Grants remote administration privileges to herself on each computer.

   After performing these steps, which tasks will she be able to accomplish?

   A. Browse shares on each computer using Net Watcher.
   B. Manage each computer's file system with Net Watcher.
   C. Edit each computer's Registry remotely using the Registry Editor.
   D. Monitor each computer's performance from her computer using System Monitor.

37. *Kelly has problems with her Windows 98 computer that she believes are related to Registry file corruption. What command can she use to restore her Registry files from a backup?*

   A. `scanregw -r`
   B. `scanreg /restore`
   C. `scanregw /restore`
   D. `scanreg -r`

38. *Sharon is giving a presentation and is planning to move her Windows 98 computer from her office to a conference room in another building on her corporate campus. The corporate network uses DHCP for automatic IP address configuration. The conference room is wired for network connectivity but is on a different subnet. What should she do to ensure that TCP/IP connectivity will be established when she connects her computer to the network in the conference room?*

   A. Renew her IP address lease using the System Configuration utility when she gets her PC set up in the conference room.
   B. Remove the TCP/IP protocol from her computer and reinstall it when she gets to the conference room.
   C. Release her IP address lease with the WinIPCfg utility before she moves the computer from her office.
   D. Nothing. The DHCP server will automatically change her TCP/IP settings when she logs in to the network from the conference room.

39. *Fred needs to install Windows NT Workstation 4.0 onto his Windows 98 computer in order to dual-boot between either operating system. He has two hard disks in his computer—one formatted as FAT16, and one formatted as FAT32. He wants to be able to access all his data from either operating system. What must he do to accomplish this?*

   A. Convert both drives to FAT32 with the Windows 98 Disk Converter utility.
   B. Convert both drives to NTFS during Windows NT setup.
   C. Back up the data on his FAT32 drive, format the drive using FAT16, and restore his data before installing Windows NT.
   D. Nothing. Both the FAT16 and the FAT32 file systems are supported by each operating system.

40. *Which utility is used to create hard disk partitions for Windows 98?*
    A. FDISK
    B. Partition Manager
    C. Format
    D. ScanDisk

41. *Windows 98 Backup supports which type of backup activities?*
    A. Full
    B. Selective
    C. Incremental
    D. Differential

42. *Which Windows 98 utility checks for Registry file corruption and creates Registry file backups?*
    A. System File Checker
    B. System Configuration utility
    C. Registry Editor
    D. Registry Checker

43. *Under Windows 98, where are new hardware profiles created?*
    A. On the Hardware Profiles tab of the System properties sheet
    B. With the Hardware Profiles utility on the Tools menu of the System Information utility
    C. On the Hardware Profiles tab of the System Configuration utility
    D. With the MSBatch utility

44. *The Client for NetWare Networks uses what protocol by default?*
    A. PPP
    B. SLIP
    C. IPX/SPX-compatible
    D. TCP/IP

45. *System policies allow an administrator to control which Windows 98 features?*
    A. Desktop settings
    B. Modem connection speeds
    C. Programs that appear on the Start menu
    D. Access to the command prompt

46. *Ellen wants to make sure that shared folders on her Windows 98 computer are secure when her computer is connected to the Internet with a Dial-Up Networking connection. What can she do to accomplish this?*

    A. Unbind Client for Microsoft Networks from the TCP/IP protocol on the Dial-Up Adapter.

    B. Unbind the TCP/IP protocol from the Dial-Up Adapter.

    C. Unbind the File and Printer Sharing for Microsoft Networks service from the IPX/SPX protocol on the Dial-Up Adapter.

    D. Unbind the File and Printer Sharing for Microsoft Networks service from the TCP/IP protocol on the Dial-Up Adapter.

47. *Which command is used to convert from FAT16 to FAT32?*

    A. CVT1

    B. MGRT

    C. FRMT

    D. FDISK

48. *A proxy server provides what function on a network?*

    A. It allows users to connect to the Internet without having a direct connection to an ISP for each workstation computer.

    B. It acts on behalf of users' workstations to connect to resources on the Internet.

    C. It resolves host names to IP addresses for computers connected to the Internet.

    D. It allows workstations on the Internet to register their NetBIOS names and IP addresses to a database on a Windows NT domain controller.

49. *The ScanDisk utility fixes which type of file system problems?*

    A. Cross-linked files

    B. Deleted files

    C. Cluster-linked files

    D. Files with crossed sectors

50. *How can you change values to entries in the Windows 98 Registry?*

    A. With Control Panel applets

    B. With the Registry Editor

    C. With system policies

    D. With Notepad

51. *Mark is having trouble connecting to a remote computer on the Internet with his Windows 98 computer. He has installed and configured the TCP/IP protocol and established a dial-up connection to his ISP. What can he do to verify that the remote computer is available on the network?*

    A. Send messages to the remote computer with the PING utility.

    B. Verify that the remote computer has an entry in the LMHOSTS file.

    C. Look for resources on the remote computer with the Net Watcher utility.

    D. Poll the remote computer's TCP/IP configuration with the WinIPCfg utility.

52. *How does the Windows 98 Version Conflict Manager determine which files are older files?*

    A. By examining the file's date and time stamp.

    B. By examining the file's version information.

    C. By reading the entry in the VERSION.INF file.

    D. By reading the version information database stored in the Windows\VCM directory.

ANSWERS AND EXPLANATIONS

1. **C**   To install both Windows 98 and Windows NT so that each operating system can see each partition, you must format the first drive as FAT16 and install Windows 98, and then format the second drive as FAT16 and install Windows NT.

2. **D**   To dual-boot a system and allow programs to be accessible from each operating system, you must install Windows NT in a *new* directory and reinstall all the programs that are accessible from Windows 98 through Windows NT.

3. **A**   FAT16 is the only file format that is accessible from both Windows 98 and Windows NT. FAT32 is accessible only from Windows 95 and 98, while NTFS is accessible only from Windows NT.

4. **D**   You can't upgrade Windows NT to Windows 98.

5. **A**   In a Windows NT domain environment, each Windows 98 client by default looks for the system policy file in the NETLOGON share. In a multiple domain controller environment, it is wise to implement directory replication to replicate the system policy file to each domain controller's NETLOGON share.

6. **B**   You can use the System Policy Editor utility to establish group priority. By selecting Options | Group Priority, you can set group priorities so that the marketing group has the higher priority.

7. **C**   System Policy Editor allows an administrator to set several restrictions and configuration components for computers, users, and groups.

8. **B**   Uninstalling Windows 98 will allow the user to return to Windows 95. During the installation/upgrade to Windows 98, the option to save original files must be selected in order to have the option to uninstall.

9. **D**   In a NetWare environment, each Windows 98 client by default looks for the system policy file in the Public directory.

10. **B** CONFIG.POL is the system policy file used by Windows 95 and Windows 98 clients.

11. **B** Batch 98 is the utility provided in the Windows 98 Resource Tool Kit to help you set up a script file to automate the installation of Windows 98.

12. **A - B - C** Several options are available in Batch 98. The Installation Directory, user setup prompts, and File and Printer Sharing for Microsoft Networks are but a few.

13. **B** The new program has been executed and has a problem releasing resources. Resource Meter detects resources for the system, user, and GDI. If the resources aren't increased when a program is closed, the program appears to retain control of those resources.

14. **B** If you chose Yes when prompted to save the original files during your upgrade, you can uninstall by using the Add/ Remove Programs applet.

15. **D** Share-level access control is available in a workgroup environment.

16. **C** Service for NetWare Directory Services allows a Windows 98 client to utilize NetWare's NDS.

17. **B** File and Printer Sharing for Microsoft Networks. Unless File and Printer Sharing is installed, the server service isn't active on a Windows 98 client. Without the server service active, the browse list never receives any communication from the client to know it is there.

18. **A - C** The options available with PWS on the main page are Requests per Hour, Requests per Day, Visitors per Hour, and Visitors per Day.

19. **A - C** Require Encrypted Password and Server Type are just two options that can be set in the Dial-Up Server settings.

20. **C** Service for NetWare Directory Services allows a Windows 98 client to utilize NetWare's NDS.

21. **C**   On the Network properties sheet, select File and Printer Sharing for Microsoft Networks and change the Browse property for one machine to Enabled and all the others to Disabled. This will instruct one Windows 98 client to always maintain a browse list, while the others do not.

22. **C**   USB (Universal Serial Bus) gives a machine the ability to recognize Plug and Play devices such as printers, keyboards, and mice.

23. **B**   Select Obtain an IP address automatically. This will cause the DHCP server to issue an IP address and maintain IP configuration administration.

24. **A - B - C**   The minimum configuration for Windows 98 is a 486/66 with 16MB of RAM and at least 140MB of hard disk space.

25. **B**   Windows Update allows you to access the Internet and upgrade your Windows 98 operating system, including drivers.

26. **A**   System Monitor for Windows 98 can log information for later diagnosis.

27. **B - C**   Windows 98 supports connecting to the Internet in two ways: You can connect through a permanent connection or through a dial-up connection.

28. **B**   Share-level security is the only security model available in a workgroup environment.

29. **D**   File and Printer Sharing for NetWare Networks must use the user-level security model.

30. **C**   User profiles are stored by default in the Windows\Profiles directory under a subdirectory for each user on the Windows 98 computer.

31. **A**   Serial Line Internet Protocol (SLIP) is a line protocol still in use by some systems, typically older UNIX systems, that don't support PPP.

32. **C**   The System Information utility shows the version and location of drivers and modules loaded in memory.

33. **B**   Net Watcher can be used to view connections to shared resources on your Windows 98 computer.

34. **A**   Net Watcher can also be used to view, create, and manage shares on remote Windows 98 computers.

35. **A - B - D**   In order to monitor the performance of a remote Windows 98 computer with the System Monitor tool, you must install the Microsoft Remote Registry Service and enable user-level security and remote administration on both the remote and the local Windows 98 computers.

36. **A - B**   She can browse shares on each computer using Net Watcher and manage each computer's file system with Net Watcher after performing the steps outlined in the question. In order to accomplish her other goals, she must first install the Remote Registry service on each of the Windows 98 computers.

37. **B**   The scanreg /restore command will restore the Registry files from a backup.

38. **C**   To ensure that TCP/IP connectivity will be working in the new location, she should release her IP address lease with the WinIPCfg utility before she moves the computer from her office. The DHCP server will configure her computer with a new lease on the new subnet when her computer boots and first connects to that subnet.

39. **C**   Windows NT doesn't support FAT32, and there is no conversion utility to convert a FAT32 drive to FAT16. He must back up the data on his FAT32 drive, format the drive using FAT16, and restore his data before installing Windows NT in order for both operating systems to be able to access all of his data.

40. **A**   The FDISK utility is used to create hard disk partitions.

41. **A - C - D**   Windows 98 Backup can perform Full, Incremental, and Differential backups.

42. **D**   The Registry Checker checks the Windows 98 Registry for corruption. If it finds no errors, it makes a backup.

43. **A**   Hardware profiles are created on the Hardware Profiles tab of the System properties sheet.

44. **C**   IPX/SPX-compatible protocol is used with the Client for NetWare Networks by default, although additional protocols also can be installed.

45. **A - C - D**   System policies allow an administrator to control many Windows 98 features, including the user's desktop, the programs that appear on the Start menu, access to the command prompt, access to Control Panel applets, access to the Registry Editor, and more.

46. **D**   In order to protect shared folders on a Windows 98 computer from unauthorized access by users on the Internet, she should unbind the File and Printer Sharing for Microsoft Networks service from the TCP/IP protocol on the Dial-Up Adapter.

47. **A**   You can convert from FAT16 to FAT32 without reformatting, but you can't go in the opposite direction.

48. **A - B**   A proxy server allows users to connect to the Internet without having a direct connection to an ISP for each workstation by acting on behalf of each workstation to connect to resources on computers on the Internet. Only the proxy server itself needs a direct connection to an ISP.

49. **A**   ScanDisk can repair cross-linked files.

50. **A - B - C**   You can alter Registry settings by changing settings in Control Panel applets, by making changes directly through the Registry Editor, or by implementing system policies.

51. **A**   The PING utility is used to verify the availability of a remote host on a TCP/IP network such as the Internet.

52. **B**   The Windows 98 Version Conflict Manager compares version information to determine which files are older.

CHAPTER 10

Insider's Spin on Exam 70-098

At A Glance: Exam Information

Exam number	70-098
Minutes	90
Questions	59
Passing score	709
Single-answer questions	Yes
Multiple-answer with correct number given	Yes
Multiple-answer without correct number given	Yes
Ranking order	No
Choices of A to D	Yes
Choices of A to E	Yes
Objective categories	6

The Windows 98 exam, as it is referred to, is officially known as Implementing and Supporting Microsoft Windows 98. It is computer-administered and intended to measure your ability to implement and administer the product in an enterprise environment. It builds upon basic knowledge and assumes that you have a great deal of experience with the product. There are 59 questions, and you have 90 minutes to answer them with a passing score of at least 709 (roughly translating to passing with 42 right answers).

There are two types of multiple-choice questions on the exam—single-answer (always readily identified by a radio button) and multiple-answer with the number of correct answers given. There are no multiple-answer questions without the number of correct answers given. There are a limited number of "click-on" questions, where you are given a property sheet and told to click on the item that you would choose to meet the specifications given. The questions overall are verbose, include a large number of exhibits, and only have choices from A to D.

Although Microsoft no longer releases specific exam information, at one time it was quoted that 85 percent of all those who take a certification exam fail it. Common logic then indicates that only 15 out of every 100 people who think they know a product know it well enough to pass—a remarkably low number.

Quite often, administrators who *do* know a product very well and use it daily fail certification exams. Is it because they don't know the product as well as they think they do? Sometimes, but more often than not, it is because of other factors:

- They know the product from a real-world perspective, not from Microsoft's perspective.

- They are basing their answers on the product as it currently exists, not on when it was first released.

- They aren't accustomed to so many questions in such a short time, or they aren't accustomed to the electronic test engine.

- They don't use all of the testing tools available to them.

The purpose of this chapter is to try to prepare you for the exam and help you overcome the four items just listed. If you've been taking exams regularly and you don't think you need this information, skim this chapter and go on. Odds are you will still uncover some tips that can help you. On the other hand, if you haven't taken many electronic exams, or if you've been having difficulty passing them by as wide a margin as you should, read this chapter carefully.

GET INTO MICROSOFT'S MINDSET

When taking the exam, remember that Microsoft was responsible for writing the exam. Microsoft employees don't write the exam. Instead, experts in the field are hired on a contract basis to write questions for each exam. However, all questions must adhere to certain standards and be approved by Microsoft before they make it into the actual exam. What this translates into is that Microsoft will never put anything in an exam that reflects negatively on them. They will also use the exam for promotional marketing as much as possible.

Therefore, in order to successfully answer questions and pass the exam, you must put yourself into the Microsoft mindset and see questions from their standpoint. Take the following question, for example:

1. Which network operating system is the easiest to administer in a small real estate office?

   A. NetWare 3.12

   B. SCO UNIX

   C. Windows NT 4.0

   D. LAN Server

Although you could make a sincere argument for at least three of the answers, only one will be correct on the exam. Don't try to read too much between the lines, and don't think that you can put a comment at the end of the exam, arguing why another choice would be better. If you answer anything other than C, you might as well write this one off as a missed question.

UNDERSTAND THE EXAM'S TIMEFRAME

When you take an exam, find out when it was written. In almost all cases, an exam goes live within three months of the final release of the product it's based on. Prior to the exam's release, it goes through a beta process in which all the questions that can be on the exam are written. It is then available for a short time (typically a week), during which scores on each question can be gathered. Questions that exam-takers get right every time are weeded out as being too easy, and those that are too hard are also weeded out.

When you take something like a major operating system (which will remain nameless in this example) and create an exam for it, you end up with a timeframe similar to the following:

1. The product goes into early beta.

2. A survey is done (mostly of beta testers) to find out which components of the product they spend the most time with and consider the most important. Their findings are used to generate the objectives and the weighting for each.

3. The product goes to final beta.

4. Contract writers are hired to write questions about the product using the findings from the survey.

5. The product goes live.

6. The exam is beta-tested for one to two weeks. After that, the results for each question are evaluated, and the final question pool is chosen.

7. The service pack for the product is released.

8. The exam goes live.

9. Another service pack is released. It fixes problems from the first service pack and adds additional functionality.

10. Yet another service pack comes out.

11. An option pack that incorporates service packs is released.

12. You take the exam.

Now suppose the product happens to be NT Server 4.0, and you see a question such as this:

1. What is the maximum number of processors that NT Server 4.0 can handle?

   A. 2

   B. 4

   C. 8

   D. 16

In the real world, the answer would be C or D, depending on how you look at it: The end-user license agreement states that eight is the limit, but NCR and other vendors make SMP servers that can run NT on 16. When NT 4.0 first came out, however, the answer was B. Since the original exam questions were written to the final beta, the answer then was B, and now is B. Microsoft has maintained that they will only test on core products, not add-ons. Service packs, option packs, and the like are considered something other than core product.

With this in mind, you must *always* answer every question as if you were addressing the product as it exists when you pull it from the box, and before you do anything else with it—because that is exactly what the exam is written to. You must get into this mindset and understand the timeframe in which the exam was written, or you will fail the exam consistently.

GET USED TO ANSWERING QUESTIONS QUICKLY

Every exam has a different number of questions, and most stick with the 90-minute timeframe. If you run out of time, every question you haven't answered is graded as a wrong answer. Therefore, keep the following in mind:

- Always answer every question; never leave any unanswered. If you start running out of time, answer all the remaining questions with the same letter (such as C or D), and then go back and start reading them. Using the law of averages, if you do run out of time, you should get 25 percent of the remaining questions correct.

- Time yourself carefully. A clock runs at the top right of each screen. Mark all questions that require lots of reading or that have exhibits, and come back to them after you've answered all the shorter questions.

- Practice, practice, practice. Get accustomed to electronic questioning and answering questions in a short period of time. With as many exam simulators as there are available, there is no reason for anyone not to run through one or two before plunking down $100 for the real test. Some simulators aren't worth the code they're written in, and others are so close in style to the actual exam that they prepare you very well. If money is an issue, and it should be, look for demos and freebies on Web sites. http://www.MeasureUp.com is an excellent place to try some sample exams online. At http://www.ds-technical.com, you'll find ways to turn on the Tip-of-the-Day feature in Windows to display items you need to memorize for the exam.

If you do run out of time, spend as much time as you want on the last question. You will never time out with a question in front of you. You will time out only when you click Next to go from that question to the next one.

TAKING THE TEST

An enormous amount of common sense is important here, and much of that common sense only comes as you get more used to the testing procedure. Here's a summary of a typical sequence of events:

1. You study for an exam for a considerable period of time.

2. You call Sylvan Prometric (1-800-755-EXAM) and register for the exam.

3. You drive to the testing site, sit in your car, and cram on last-minute details.

4. You walk into the center, sign your name, show two forms of ID, and walk to a computer.

5. Someone enters your ID in the computer and leaves. You're left with the computer, two pieces of plain paper, and two #2 pencils.

6. You click the button on the screen to begin the exam, and the 90 minutes begins.

When you call Sylvan, be certain to ask how many questions are on the exam, so you know before you go in. Sylvan is allowed to release very little information (for example, they can't tell you the passing score). This is one of the few pieces of information they can pass along.

The exam begins the minute you click the button to start it. Before that, the 90-minute timeframe hasn't started. Once you walk into the testing center and sit down, you're free (within reason) to do whatever you want to. Why not dump everything from your brain (including those last-minute facts you studied in the parking lot) onto those two sheets of paper before you start the exam? The two sheets provide you with four sides—more than enough to scribble down everything you remember; refer to it during the 90 minutes.

Once you click the start button, the first question appears. There are many types of questions. Figure 10.1 shows one example. Since Microsoft doesn't readily make available the ability to take screen shots of the exams (for obvious reasons), all the figures in this chapter are from a third-party emulator that closely resembles the real thing.

Look at the question briefly, but more importantly, look at the information on-screen. First, you have the ability to mark this question. Doing so lets you see (at the end of the exam) any questions you thought were difficult and jump back to them. Never mark a question and go to the next one without choosing an answer. Even if you don't read the question at all because you're saving it for later, mark it and answer C. That way, if you run out of time, you have a chance of getting it right.

In the top-right corner, you see the question number you're on. On the real exam, you also see the time remaining here. Beneath the question are the possible answers. The radio buttons to the left of each indicate that there can be only one possible answer.

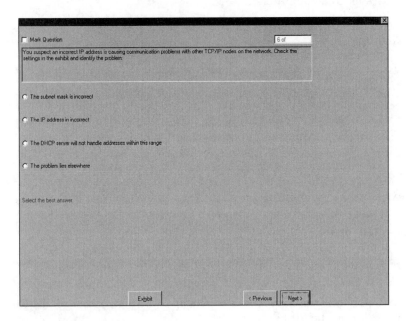

FIGURE 10.1
A sample test question.

Sometimes, when there are four possible answers, one will be so far off the mark as to not even be worth considering, and another will be too much of a gimme to be true. So you're left with two possibilities. Here's an example:

1. In NT Server 4.0, to view the Application log, what tool must you use?

   A. Application Viewer

   B. Event Viewer

   C. Event Observer

   D. Performance Monitor

In this case, choice A is the gimme of a nonexistent tool that fits the question too perfectly. Choice D is the blow-off answer—so far away from what's possible as to not be considered. That leaves choices B and C.

Even if you knew nothing about NT Server, a clue that B and C are legitimate possibilities is the closeness in the wording of each. Anytime you see two answers worded so closely, assume them to be the ones to focus on.

The buttons at the bottom of the screen let you move to the next question or a previous question. The latter is important, because if you ever come across a question where the wording provides the answer to a question you were asked before, always use the Previous button to go back and change or check your first answer. Never walk away from a sure thing.

If there is an exhibit associated with the question, the command button for it will be displayed as well. The problem with exhibits is that they layer on top of the question or can be tiled in such a way that you can't see either. Whenever you have an exhibit, read the question carefully, open the exhibit, memorize what is there (or scribble information about it on one of your sheets of paper), close the exhibit, and answer the question.

Figure 10.2 is an example of a question with more than one correct answer—a fact made obvious by check boxes appearing to the left of the choices instead of radio buttons.

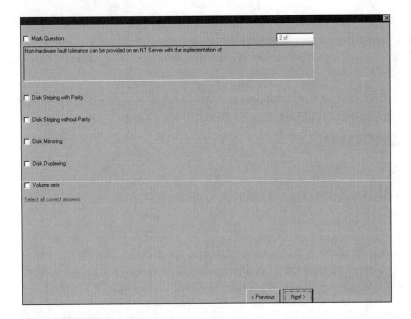

FIGURE 10.2
Another sample test question.

There are two types of these questions—ones where you are told how many answers are correct (choose two, choose three, and so on), and ones where you are not. In Figure 10.2, you are told to choose all correct answers, and you don't know if that's two, three, or four. The only thing you do know is that it isn't one or five: The test doesn't use check boxes if radio buttons will work, and the test will never have an all-of-the-above-type answer.

The vast majority of multiple-answer questions offer four possibilities, meaning that you must choose two or three answers. However, five possibilities is not uncommon (as shown in Figure 10.2). With these questions, read the question as carefully as possible, and begin eliminating choices. For example, the question shown in Figure 10.2 specifically says *non-hardware,* and one of the choices is duplexing. Duplexing requires a hardware enhancement over mirroring, so choice D isn't correct. You are now left with four possibilities and must rely on your knowledge to choose the right ones.

The biggest problem with multiple answers is that there is no such thing as partial credit. If you are supposed to choose four items, and you choose only three, the question still counts as being wrong. If you choose two—one right answer and one wrong answer—you miss the whole question. Spend much more time with multiple-answer questions than single-answer questions, and, if time allows, always come back after the exam and reread these questions carefully.

After you complete the exam, if there is time remaining, you see an item review section, similar to the one shown in Figure 10.3.

From here you can see the questions you marked and jump back to them. If you've already chosen an answer on that screen, it remains chosen until you choose something else. (The question also remains marked until you unmark it.) The command buttons at the bottom of the screen now include an Item Review choice to let you jump back to the Item Review screen without going through additional questions.

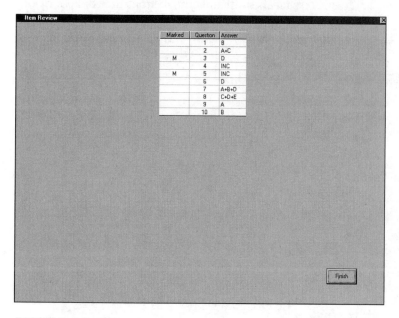

FIGURE 10.3
The Item Review at the completion of the exam.

Use the ability to mark and jump as much as you possibly can. All lengthy questions should be marked and returned to in this manner. Also note all answers that are incomplete. You can't afford to not answer any question, so be certain to go back and fill them in before choosing to finish the exam (or before you run out of time).

After you click Finish, grading is done, and the Examination Score Report appears. The one shown in Figure 10.4 is a bit misleading. Typically, you see only the bar graphs and a message as to whether you passed or failed. The Section Analysis doesn't appear on-screen—only on the printed documentation you walk out of the testing center with. The pass/fail score is based on the beta of the exam and statistics gathered from the performance of those who took it.

If you fail an exam, and everyone will occasionally, *never* be lulled into a false sense of confidence by the Section Analysis. If it says you scored 100% on a particular section, you should still study that section before retaking the exam. Too many test-takers study only the sections they did poorly on.

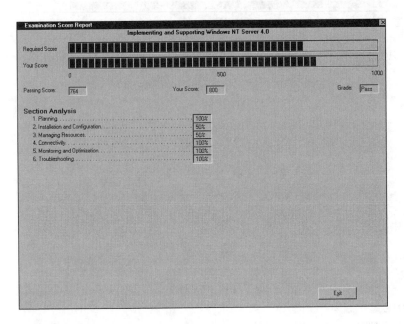

FIGURE 10.4
The Examination Score Report.

That 100% in Monitoring and Optimization could be the result of the first question pool containing only one question, and you had a 25 percent chance of guessing correctly. What happens next time, when there are three questions in the random pool in that category, and you don't know the answers? You're handicapping yourself right off the bat.

A good rule of thumb if you do fail an exam is to rush back to your car and write down all the questions you can remember. Have your study materials in the vehicle with you so you can look up the answers then and there. If you wait until later, you'll forget many of them.

The new policy from Microsoft allows you to retake an exam you fail once without waiting (other than the time it takes you to register, and so on). If you fail it again, however, you must wait 14 days before you can take it a third time (and 14 days from that point for the fourth try, and so on). This is to prevent people from actually memorizing the exam. Do your best to never fall into this category. If you fail an exam once, start all over and study anew before trying it the second time. Make the second attempt within a week of the first, however, so that topics are fresh in your mind.

WHERE THE QUESTIONS COME FROM

Knowing where the questions come from can be as instrumental as anything in knowing how to prepare for the exam. The more you know about the question-creation process, the better your odds of passing. Earlier, I pointed out the timeframe used to create the exam and told you that contract writers are hired for the exam. The contract writers are given a sizable document that details how questions must be written. If you really want to pursue this topic with more fervor, contact Microsoft and inquire about a contract writing position. For now, here are a few tidbits that can be gleaned from multiple-choice authoring:

1. No question should have an all of the above answer. When you see this choice, it's almost always the correct answer, so it isn't a fair representation of a valid multiple-choice question.

2. For the same reason, there should never be a none of the above answer.

3. Scenarios should be used when they will increase the value of the question.

4. No subjective words (such as best and most) should be used.

5. Although there can be only one correct answer for the question, all other possibilities should appear plausible and avoid all rationale or explanations.

6. All single-answer questions must be mutually exclusive (no A and C, B and C, and so on).

7. Negative words such as not and cannot should be avoided.

DIFFERENT FLAVORS OF QUESTIONS

At one time, all questions were either single-answer or multiple-answer. There is a push today to go more toward ranking questions and performance-based questions. Older exams have only the first two question types, but newer ones offer the latter.

Ranking questions provide you with a scenario, a list of required objectives, a list of optional objectives, and a proposed solution, and then ask you to rank how well the solution meets the objectives. Here's a rudimentary example:

1. Evan is a teenager who just got his driver's license. He wants to buy a fast car and ask Betty Lou to the movies on Friday.

Required objectives:	Buy a fast car.
	Ask Betty Lou to the movies.
Optional objectives:	Earn money for the movies.
	Earn money for a car.
Solution:	Take a part-time job at the Qwik-E-
	Mart and buy a classic '67 Cougar.

    Rank the solution in terms of the objectives:

    A. The solution meets all of the required and optional objectives.

    B. The solution meets both required objectives and only the first optional objective.

C. The solution meets both required objectives and only the second optional objective.

D. The solution does not meet the required objectives.

In this over-simplified example, the answer is D. The solution doesn't include asking Betty Lou to the movies, so it doesn't meet the required objectives. With ranking questions, it is often the case that the required objectives are needed in all but the last answer, so read the question backward, if you will, and see if the required objectives are met. If they aren't, you can answer the question quickly without reading any further and go on to the next one.

Performance-based questions have been incorporated into electronic testing for a long time—just not with Microsoft testing. If I really wanted to test how well you knew a product before hiring you, the best way to do so would be to turn you loose with the product and tell you to do something. If you can, I'll hire you. If you can't, I won't.

Representing that scenario in the testing center becomes difficult. First and foremost, you can't be given unrestricted access to the product within the confines of something (a shell) grading your actions. Second, the stability of the operations on most testing centers' antiquated machines is questionable at best. Last, the time allotted can't exceed a reasonable amount, or you will become exhausted, and the testing center won't be able to move as many people through each day.

The solution to many of these problems is to keep the number of performance-based questions to a minimum and to have you work with an emulator of some type. The emulator can come on the screen when you click the button and bring up something that looks similar to the configuration information in the real product, without the time and overhead involved in bringing up the real product.

How do you prepare for performance-based questions? Simple—know your product. Focus on the administrative side of it. If you know how to add new users, sites, servers, and directories, you will have no difficulties. If you're good at guessing multiple-choice answers, but you really don't know the product, these questions will ferret that out. On the other hand, if you know your product extremely well, and you aren't good at multiple-choice guessing, you'll find these questions a godsend.

Regardless of your familiarity with the product (or lack thereof), be very careful with performance-based questions. Although the emulator can load much quicker than the actual product in question, it is still very time-consuming, and the amount of time required to answer each question is far from minute. These questions take *a lot* of time, and you need to budget for them accordingly.

In the Future

The study of test delivery and grading is known as *psychometrics,* and a good many people are employed in this profession. Microsoft uses many of them to help design and implement their exams. It should come as no surprise (if you have any experience with other certifications, such as Novell's) that the next big push will be toward *adaptive* testing.

Under adaptive testing, the amount of time for each exam can be reduced from 90 minutes to somewhere near 30, and the number of questions can drop from 50 to 70 down to 15 or so. This benefits you greatly and also allows more students to be tested each day at the training centers.

The premise behind adaptive testing is fairly simple. The first question you get is totally at random and pulled from a pool. Beyond that first question, every other question presented to you is somehow related to how well you answered the preceding question.

For example, suppose I want to give you a general exam on astronomy. The first question that comes up asks you how many planets are in our solar system. You answer correctly (nine). I now ask you to name the third planet from the sun, and again you answer correctly (Earth). I can now assume that you know your planets very well, so the next question will be about quasars. We'll do this for 15 questions, and if you answer them all correctly, I'll assume that you know astronomy well and pass you.

On the other hand, if you answered Mars to the second question, the next question will be about planets again, giving you a chance to redeem yourself. If you miss that one, I'll probably ask an extremely difficult question about planets to see if you can get it right. If you can't, you don't know planets, so you don't know astronomy, and you'll fail. In some versions of adaptive testing, you bomb out right then, since there is no chance of redemption. With others, you're given bogus questions for the remainder of the exam to make you feel like you're getting your money's worth, even though you're going to fail.

It differs according to style and vendor, but with most adaptive tests, if you answer the 15 questions and haven't passed but are very close to doing so, you can be asked additional questions. The additional questions give you an opportunity to redeem yourself and achieve a passing score.

The key to adaptive testing, besides each question's relationship to the one preceding it, is that every question has a point value. The first questions are of medium value. If you miss a question on a topic, the next one asked will be more difficult, and of a higher point value, to give you a chance at redemption. If you answer the first question correctly, the next question will be of lesser value and lesser difficulty.

There is no item review in adaptive testing, and there is no going back to the preceding question(s). Once you answer a question, you are done with it. You can draw a fair conclusion as to how you did by whether or not the next question is on a similar topic.

Performance-based testing is in its infancy at Microsoft, but it should be rolled out within the year. Again, the best preparation is to know your topic and to spend time with each question, making certain you fully understand what is being asked before answering. With performance-based testing, you are given a task to perform in an emulator of the product you're being tested on. Your performance is graded to see if you accomplished the task in the time and manner in which an administrator should.

CHAPTER 11

Did You Know?

The following are interesting items not relevant to the exam:

1. Microsoft has never supported disk-image copying for Windows 95 (and probably never will). For Windows 98, disk-image copying is supported as long as the Microsoft Windows 98 Image Preparation Tool is used to create the master disk image.

2. While much of the view and many of the utilities have changed from Windows 95 to Windows 98, the architecture of the fundamental networking functions has changed minimally. As a result, all network drivers and software (including add-ons) that worked with Windows 95 should work equally well with Windows 98.

3. While Windows 98 contains all of the features and functions necessary to connect to a Windows NT Server–based network with minimal work, to be on the safe side, you should check user licensing before doing so. You must purchase a network client license for each Windows 98 machine connecting to an NT server to be within the legal bounds of NT's licensing agreement. The Windows 98 CD contains an executable file, EULA.EXE, that brings up the operating system's license agreement.

4. Settings in the Registry are overridden by system policies. The greatest weakness of the System Policy Editor is that it is powerless without templates. The only choices you can make in editing the Registry or creating system policies are the choices allowed within the templates you load. The System Policy Editor is on the CD in the Tools\Reskit\Netadmin\PolEdit directory.

5. If you are a command-line fanatic, you can pull tools from the Windows 98 CD under Tools\OLDMSDOS. Here you will find the latest versions of such utilities as XCOPY, MOVE, and MSD.

6. The WHERE utility located on the CD in Tools\Reskit\File mimics the similar command in UNIX. It will look through your PATH for all occurrences of the executable name you supply so that you can ascertain which one is running for you.

7. The WINDIFF utility located on the CD in Tools\Reskit\File can compare files or directories and tell you what is identical between them and what is different. It works much like the DIFF utility in UNIX.

8. If you move or rename a file and then change your mind, you can undo this action immediately after you perform it by pressing Ctrl+Z. This offers the operating system the same undo feature that most of the Office applications have had for quite some time.

9. You will find several additional utilities on the Windows 98 Resource Kit Tools Sampler that comes with the Windows 98 CD. You can access these utilities through a new interface called Microsoft Management Console. MMC was first introduced with the release of Internet Information Server 4.0 for Windows NT, and it will become the standard interface for Windows management.

10. FAT32 Conversion Information Tool is just one of the useful utilities found in the Resource Kit Tools Sampler. It allows you to determine how much free space would become available if you converted a partition to FAT32. It's a great way to have a "dress rehearsal" prior to the actual conversion with Drive Converter (FAT32).

11. When you delete a file from within Windows Explorer, by default the file is first sent to the Recycle Bin. From there, you can retrieve the file if you find that you deleted it in error, or you can empty the Recycle Bin if you decide that you really don't need the file after all. If you delete the file from within an MS-DOS prompt window, the file is gone. It won't be sent to the Recycle Bin for later purging or recovery.

12. When you use Internet Explorer to surf the Web under Windows 98, you don't have to type the entire URL for the most common Web site addresses. Simply type in the domain and press Ctrl+Enter. Internet Explorer will automatically put `http://www.` in front of the domain name and `.com` at the end. For example, to visit the Microsoft Web site, simply type **microsoft** and press Ctrl+Enter. Internet Explorer will connect automatically to `http://www.microsoft.com`.

13. You can change the order of items on the Start menu. Click Start and select Programs. Click any program item and drag it to the location on the menu where you want it to appear. Windows 98 will reorder the menu items for you. You can do this with program items or program groups.

INDEX

U

MCSE Fast Track: Networking Essentials

1-56205-939-4,
$19.99, 9/98

MCSE Fast Track: TCP/IP

1-56205-937-8,
$19.99, 9/98

MCSE Fast Track: Windows 98

0-7357-0016-8,
$19.99, 12/98

MCSE Fast Track: Internet Information Server 4

1-56205-936-X,
$19.99, 9/98

MCSE Fast Track: Windows NT Server 4

1-56205-935-1,
$19.99, 9/98

MCSD Fast Track: Solution Architectures

0-7357-0029-X,
$19.99, Q2/99

MCSE Fast Track: Windows NT Server 4 Enterprise

1-56205-940-8,
$19.99, 9/98

MCSD Fast Track: Visual Basic 6, Exam 70-175

0-7357-0018-4,
$19.99, 12/98

MCSE Fast Track: Windows NT Workstation 4

1-56205-938-6,
$19.99, 9/98

MCSD Fast Track: Visual Basic 6, Exam 70-176

0-7357-0019-2,
$19.99, 12/98

TRAINING GUIDES

Complete, Innovative,
Accurate, Thorough

Our next generation *Training Guides* have been developed to help you study and retain the essential knowledge that you need to pass the MCSE exams. We know your study time is valuable, and we have made every effort to make the most of it by presenting clear, accurate, and thorough information.

In creating this series, our goal was to raise the bar on how MCSE content is written, developed, and presented. From the two-color design that gives you easy access to content to the new software simulator that allows you to perform tasks in a simulated operating system environment, we are confident that you will be well-prepared for exam success.

Our New Riders Top Score Software Suite is a custom-developed set of full-functioning software applications that work in conjunction with the *Training Guide* by providing you with the following:

Exam Simulator tests your hands-on knowledge with over 150 fact-based and situational-based questions.
Electronic Study Cards really test your knowledge with explanations that are linked to an electronic version of the *Training Guide*.
Electronic Flash Cards help you retain the facts in a time-tested method.
An Electronic Version of the Book provides quick searches and compact, mobile study.
Customizable Software adapts to the way you want to learn.

MCSE Training Guide: Networking Essentials, Second Edition

1-56205-919-X, $49.99, 9/98

MCSE Training Guide: Windows NT Server 4, Second Edition

1-56205-916-5, $49.99, 9/98

MCSE Training Guide: Windows NT Server 4 Enterprise, Second Edition

1-56205-917-3, $49.99, 9/98

MCSE Training Guide: Windows NT Workstation 4, Second Edition

1-56205-918-1, $49.99, 9/98

MCSE Training Guide: Windows 98

1-56205-890-8, $49.99, Q1/99

MCSE Training Guide: TCP/IP, Second Edition

1-56205-920-3, $49.99, 11/98

MCSE Training Guide: SQL Server 7 Administration

0-7357-0003-6, $49.99, Q2/99

MCSE Training Guide: SQL Server 7 Design and Implementation

0-7357-0004-4, $49.99, Q2/99

MCSD Training Guide: Solution Architectures

0-7357-0026-5, $49.99, Q2/99

MCSD Training Guide: Visual Basic 6

0-7357-0002-8, $49.99, Q1/99

TRAINING GUIDES
First Editions

Your Quality Elective Solution

MCSE Training Guide: Systems Management Server 1.2, 1-56205-748-0

MCSE Training Guide: SQL Server 6.5 Administration, 1-56205-726-X

MCSE Training Guide: SQL Server 6.5 Design and Implementation, 1-56205-830-4

MCSE Training Guide: Windows 95, 70-064 Exam, 1-56205-880-0

MCSE Training Guide: Exchange Server 5, 1-56205-824-X

MCSE Training Guide: Internet Explorer 4, 1-56205-889-4

MCSE Training Guide: Microsoft Exchange Server 5.5, 1-56205-899-1

MCSE Training Guide: IIS 4, 1-56205-823-1

MCSD Training Guide: Visual Basic 5, 1-56205-850-9

MCSD Training Guide: Microsoft Access, 1-56205-771-5

TESTPREP SERIES

Practice and cram with the new, revised Second Edition TestPreps

Questions. Questions. And more questions. That's what you'll find in our New Riders *TestPreps*. They're great practice books when you reach the final stage of studying for the exam. We recommend them as supplements to our *Training Guides*.

What makes these study tools unique is that the questions are the primary focus of each book. All the text in these books support and explain the answers to the questions.

Scenario-based questions challenge your experience.

Multiple-choice questions prep you for the exam.

Fact-based questions test your product knowledge.

Exam strategies assist you in test preparation.

Complete yet concise explanations of answers make for better retention.

Two practice exams prepare you for the real thing.

Fast Facts offer you everything you need to review in the testing center parking lot.

MCSE TestPrep: Networking Essentials, Second Edition

0-7357-0010-9, $19.99, 12/98

MCSE TestPrep: Windows 95, Second Edition

0-7357-0011-7, $19.99, 12/98

MCSE TestPrep: Windows NT Server 4, Second Edition

0-7357-0012-5, $19.99, 12/98

MCSE TestPrep: Windows NT Server 4 Enterprise, Second Edition

0-7357-0009-5, $19.99, 11/98

MCSE TestPrep: Windows NT Workstation 4, Second Edition

0-7357-0008-7, $19.99, 12/98

MCSE TestPrep: TCP/IP, Second Edition

0-7357-0025-7, $19.99, 12/98

MCSE TestPrep:
Windows 98

1-56205-922-X, $19.99, 11/98

TESTPREP SERIES
FIRST EDITIONS

MCSE TestPrep: SQL Server 6.5
Administration, 0-7897-1597-X

MCSE TestPrep: SQL Server 6.5 Design
and Implementation, 1-56205-915-7

MCSE TestPrep: Windows 95 70-64
Exam, 0-7897-1609-7

MCSE TestPrep: Internet Explorer 4,
0-7897-1654-2

MCSE TestPrep: Exchange Server 5.5,
0-7897-1611-9

MCSE TestPrep: IIS 4.0, 0-7897-1610-0

How to Contact Us

IF YOU NEED THE LATEST UPDATES ON A TITLE THAT YOU'VE PURCHASED:

1) Visit our Web site at www.newriders.com.

2) Click on the DOWNLOADS link, and enter your book's ISBN number, which is located on the back cover in the bottom right-hand corner.

3) In the DOWNLOADS section, you'll find available updates that are linked to the book page.

IF YOU ARE HAVING TECHNICAL PROBLEMS WITH THE BOOK OR THE CD THAT IS INCLUDED:

1) Check the book's information page on our Web site according to the instructions listed above, or

2) Email us at support@mcp.com, or

3) Fax us at (317) 817-7488 attn: Tech Support.

IF YOU HAVE COMMENTS ABOUT ANY OF OUR CERTIFICATION PRODUCTS THAT ARE NON-SUPPORT RELATED:

1) Email us at certification@mcp.com, or

2) Write to us at New Riders, 201 W. 103rd St., Indianapolis, IN 46290-1097, or

3) Fax us at (317) 581-4663.

IF YOU WISH TO PREVIEW ANY OF OUR CERTIFICATION BOOKS FOR CLASSROOM USE:

Email us at pr@mcp.com. Your message should include your name, title, training company or school, department, address, phone number, office days/hours, text in use, and enrollment Send these details along with your request for desk/examination copies and/or additional information.

IF YOU ARE OUTSIDE THE UNITED STATES AND NEED TO FIND A DISTRIBUTOR IN YOUR AREA:

Please contact our international department at international@mcp.com.

WE WANT TO KNOW WHAT YOU THINK

To better serve you, we would like your opinion on the content and quality of this book. Please complete this card and mail it to us or fax it to 317-581-4663.

Name _____

Address _____

City _____ State_____ Zip _____

Phone _____ Email Address _____

Occupation_____

Which certification exams have you already passed? _____
_____
_____
_____

Which certification exams do you plan to take? __
_____
_____
_____

What influenced your purchase of this book?
❑ Recommendation ❑ Cover Design
❑ Table of Contents ❑ Index
❑ Magazine Review ❑ Advertisement
❑ Publisher's reputation ❑ Author Name

How would you rate the contents of this book?
❑ Excellent ❑ Very Good
❑ Good ❑ Fair
❑ Below Average ❑ Poor

What other types of certification products will you buy/have you bought to help you prepare for the exam?
❑ Quick reference books ❑ Testing software
❑ Study guides ❑ Other

What do you like most about this book? Check all that apply.
❑ Content ❑ Writing Style
❑ Accuracy ❑ Examples
❑ Listings ❑ Design
❑ Index ❑ Page Count
❑ Price ❑ Illustrations

What do you like least about this book? Check all that apply.
❑ Content ❑ Writing Style
❑ Accuracy ❑ Examples
❑ Listings ❑ Design
❑ Index ❑ Page Count
❑ Price ❑ Illustrations

What would be a useful follow-up book to this one for you?_____

Where did you purchase this book?_____

Can you name a similar book that you like better than this one, or one that is as good? Why?_____
_____
_____

How many New Riders books do you own? _____

What are your favorite certification or general computer book titles? _____
_____

What other titles would you like to see us develop? _____
_____

Any comments for us? _____
_____

Fold here and Scotch tape to mail